A BIRDER'S GUIDE
TO
ARKANSAS

A BIRDER'S GUIDE TO ARKANSAS

by
Mel White

1995

American Birding Association, Inc.

Library of Congress Catalog Number: 95-75099
ISBN Number: 1-878788-09-4

First Edition
    1   2   3   4   5   6   7   8
Printed in the United States of America

Publisher
    American Birding Association, Inc.
    George G. Daniels, Chair, Publications Committee
Series Editor
    Paul J. Baicich
Associate Editors
    Cindy Lippincott and Bob Berman
Copy Editor
    Hugh Willoughby
Layout and Typography
    Bob Berman; using CorelVENTURA, Windows version 5.0
Maps
    Cindy Lippincott; using CorelDRAW version 5.0
Cover Photography
    front cover: Red-cockaded Woodpecker; Julia Sims
    back cover: Painted Bunting ; Rob Curtis
                Summer Tanager; Harold and Kathy Lindstrom
Illustrations
    Georges Dremeaux
    David A. Sibley
    Gail Diane Yovanovich
    Louise Zemaitis
Distributed by
    American Birding Association Sales
    PO Box 6599
    Colorado Springs, Colorado 80934-6599 USA
    phone: (800) 634-7736 or (719) 578-0607
    fax: (800) 590-2473 or (719) 578-9705
European and UK Distribution
    Subbuteo Natural History Books, Ltd.
    Treuddyn, Mold, Clwyd
    CH7 4LN UK Tel: 0352-770581; fax: 0352-771590

For my parents, with love.

ACKNOWLEDGEMENTS

This guide would not have been possible without the cooperation of birders throughout Arkansas, who shared information, suggested sites, reviewed descriptions, accompanied the writer on birding trips, and were helpful and supportive in a variety of other ways.

Special appreciation goes to Max and Helen Parker, Arkansas's perpetually peripatetic birding experts, who created the distributional bar-graphs at the end of the book; their cooperation, wide-ranging knowledge, and labor were invaluable. Max is the curator of records for the Arkansas Audubon Society, and so has access to more information about abundance and distribution of the state's avifauna than anyone else.

William M. Shepherd of the Arkansas Natural Heritage Commission offered advice, answered constant questions, shared his botanical knowledge, reviewed listings, and generally aided and abetted the book from its inception.

Among the accomplished and experienced birders who provided vital information (and in some cases wrote site descriptions that I have only edited) are Norman Lavers (Northeastern Arkansas), Charles Mills (Millwood Lake); Michael Mlodinow and Joseph C. Neal (Northwestern Arkansas); Duane Moren (Bull Shoals and Norfork area); and Don Simons (Chicot County). Others who helped in one way or another include Carl Amason, David S. Brotherton, Walter Brotherton, Kim Burnette, Carl E. Cleveland, Mark A. Clippinger, Roberta Crabtree, Neil Curry, Robert Doster, Virginia Fort, James Gracey, Barry Haas, Henry and Edith Halberg, Martha Johnson, Randy Johnson, Bill Jones, Wallace F. Keck, David F. Kimery, Sterling S. Lacy, Bill and Paula Lisowsky, Lee Lustfeldt, Ruth MacDonald, Florence Mallard, Jay S. Miller, Warren Montague, Joan E. Morris, Ellen Neaville, Kenny and LaDonna Nichols, Lance Peacock, Al Phillipy, Glenda Pryor, Frank Reuter, JoAnne Rife, Paul Rodewald, H.H. Shugart, Kimberly Smith, Keith Sutton, Vicki Trimble, M.L. "Bo" Verser, Charles West, Dennis Widner, Karen Yaich, and J. Lyndal York.

Thanks are also extended to Rob Curtis, Harold and Kathy Lindstrom, and Julia Sims, photographers of the guide's covers; and to Arkansas Department of Parks and Tourism photographers, including A.C. Haralson and Barrie Lynn Bryant. Thanks also to artists Georges Dremeaux, David A.Sibley, Gail Diane Yovanovich, and Louise Zemaitis.

I'm grateful to the American Birding Association for its inclusion of this book in the estimable *ABA Birdfinding Guide* series. I especially appreciate the efforts of the series editor, Paul J. Baicich, the associate editors, Cindy Lippincott (who worked miracles with the maps) and Bob Berman, and Hugh Willoughby, the copy editor. They played essential roles in the writing, editing, and production of this book; they were accessible, helpful, and encouraging, and they made my job easier.

Observations, comments, criticisms, corrections, and suggestions about this guide are welcome, and may be incorporated into any revisions. Please send comments to the author in care of the American Birding Association, PO Box 6599, Colorado Springs, CO 80934.

American Birding Association Code of Ethics

We, the membership of the American Birding Association, believe that all birders have an obligation at all times to protect wildlife, the natural environment, and the rights of others. We therefore pledge ourselves to provide leadership in meeting this obligation by adhering to the following general guidelines of good birding behavior.

I. Birders must always act in ways that do not endanger the welfare of birds or other wildlife.

In keeping with this principle, we will

- Observe and photograph birds without knowingly disturbing them in any significant way.

- Avoid chasing or repeatedly flushing birds.

- Only sparingly use recordings and similar methods of attracting birds and not use these methods in heavily birded areas.

- Keep an appropriate distance from nests and nesting colonies so as not to disturb them or expose them to danger.

- Refrain from handling birds or eggs unless engaged in recognized research activities.

II. Birders must always act in ways that do not harm the natural environment.

In keeping with this principle, we will

- Stay on existing roads, trails, and pathways whenever possible to avoid trampling or otherwise disturbing fragile habitat.

- Leave all habitat as we found it.

III. Birders must always respect the rights of others.

In keeping with this principle, we will

- Respect the privacy and property of others by observing "No Trespassing" signs and by asking permission to enter private or posted lands.

- Observe all laws and the rules and regulations which govern public use of birding areas.

- Practice common courtesy in our contacts with others. For example, we will limit our requests for information, and we will make them at reasonable hours of the day.

- Always behave in a manner that will enhance the image of the birding community in the eyes of the public.

IV. Birders in groups should assume special responsibilities.

As group members, we will

- Take special care to alleviate the problems and disturbances that are multiplied when more people are present.

- Act in consideration of the group's interest, as well as our own.

- Support by our actions the responsibility of the group leader(s) for the conduct of the group.

As group leaders, we will

- Assume responsibility for the conduct of the group.

- Learn and inform the group of any special rules, regulations, or conduct applicable to the area or habitat being visited.

- Limit groups to a size that does not threaten the environment or the peace and tranquility of others.

- Teach others birding ethics by our words and example.

TABLE OF CONTENTS

Magazine Mountain in the Ozarks. *Photo by A.C. Haralson,
courtesy of Arkansas Department of Parks and Tourism*

ARKANSAS: *Political and Physical Features*

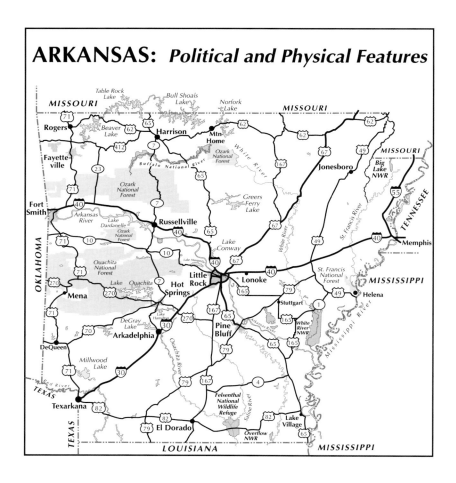

INTRODUCTION

A few years ago I was on a field trip with a group that included Edith and Henry Halberg, who have been Arkansas birding legends since the early '60s. Looking back, even squinting a little, I can't recall where we were; I do remember, at some point along the way, saying, "This would be a great place the first week of May."

Whereupon Edith laughed and, in her displaced Bostonian accent, said, "*Everyplace* in Arkansas is great the first week in May."

And she was right. At the peak of spring migration, you hardly have to work to see good birds here. Thrushes, vireos, warblers, and tanagers show up in back yards, vacant lots, and fence rows. There's no telling what you'll hear singing outside your bedroom window when the alarm clock goes off, even if you live, as I do, in the middle of the state's largest city.

Some places are better than others, though—during migration, and the rest of the year as well. This book aims to guide birders to Arkansas's best spots for finding birds: in some cases a wide variety; in others, one or more special species. I hope that it will be useful not only to visitors, but also to beginners within the state who'd like to know where they can find more and different birds.

Arkansas has never had an abundance of hard-core birders, especially considering the amount of good habitat that's out there. As a result, we undoubtedly have dozens of little ponds, marshy areas, and riverside thickets that ought to be checked regularly and aren't—in fact, that aren't even known about. This guide is by no means a complete listing of birding sites—only a selection of those that have proven to be consistently productive, reliable, and accessible. Inevitably, it is weighted toward those parts of the state where the greatest number of active birders live.

GEOGRAPHY, AND A LITTLE ORNITHOLOGY

The tourism industry likes to call Arkansas "The Natural State," and it's true that large parts of the north and west are still mountainous, rugged, and wooded. Unfortunately, the most biologically valuable and productive part of the state, the eastern lowlands, has been most affected by human activity. A lot of what's still "natural" in Arkansas is relatively

1

Natural Divisions of Arkansas

Crowley's Ridge

MISSOURI

Ozark Mountains

Arkansas River Valley

Mississippi Alluvial Plain (Delta)

Ouachita Mountains

OKLAHOMA

TENNESSEE

MISSISSIPPI

Grand Prairie

West Gulf Coastal Plain

TEXAS

North

LOUISIANA

0   Miles   60

dry, upland pine-oak-hickory forest—pretty to look at, but not really of the greatest interest to birders.

Much of eastern Arkansas was once a vast swamp so impenetrable that early explorers regretted not having language harsh enough to describe their experiences. Today it has been ditched and drained, cut over and plowed under, and retains only a small fraction of its original bottomland hardwood forest. What wetlands are left in eastern Arkansas, though, are often among our most exciting places to watch birds.

For simplicity's sake, Arkansas can be thought of as being split by a line between its northeastern and southwestern corners, with highlands in the northwest and lowlands in the southeast. Scientists have further defined six natural divisions within the state:

- **The Ozark Mountains** in the northwest, a heavily wooded "eroded plateau" with steep-sided valleys and beautiful mountain streams. The Ozark National Forest encompasses a large part of these mountains, which have some of the most spectacular scenery between the Appalachians and the Rockies. While cattle ranching, poultry operations, and lumbering are widespread, many places in the Ozarks are still wild and remote.

- **The Arkansas River Valley**, wedged between the Ozarks to the north and the Ouachita (WASH-ih-taw) Mountains to the south and combining attributes of both areas. This division, despite its name, includes land well north of the Arkansas River, stretching into northeastern Arkansas.

- **The Ouachita Mountains** in the west, where east-west ranges (unusual in North America) are a result of geological folding and faulting. Much of the area is within the Ouachita National Forest. The Ouachitas are also rugged, forested, and in many places beautiful. But there's more pine here than there is in the Ozarks, and controversial forest management has in the past included heavy clear-cutting. Nevertheless, as is the case in the Ozarks, there are places where civilization seems far away.

- **The Gulf Coastal Plain**, in the south, where gently rolling hills are covered by lowland pine forests. Large tracts are owned by timber companies, and here, too, the forest is intensively managed for high yields of lumber and pulpwood.

- **The Mississippi Alluvial Plain**, or "Delta," in the east—flat farming country that has been largely deforested. (Though not a "delta" in the classic sense, the flatlands near the Mississippi River are often referred to as "the Delta" by Southerners.) The bayous, swamps, and other wetlands that remain are among the most valuable waterfowl habitat in the world. Millions of ducks (mostly Mallards) spend at least part of the winter here. A subdivision of the Delta, the Grand Prairie once was an extensive grassland, but only a few tiny tracts of natural prairie are left; most has been lost to farming, especially of rice.

- **Crowley's Ridge** in the northeast, an anomalous raised area capped with a layer of wind-blown soil. It's often said that Crowley's Ridge has more in common with the Appalachians than with the rest of Arkansas; tall Tuliptrees (Tulip Magnolias) are among the interesting species that grow here. Some of the most attractive areas of Crowley's Ridge are found within Village Creek State Park and the St. Francis National Forest.

These natural regions don't show nearly as much diversity of birdlife as exists between, say, the mountains and deserts of southern Arizona. Arkansas is a small state with elevational extremes of 54 and 2,753 feet. Still, even lacking an ocean, and not quite far enough west to pick up many western strays, Arkansas has a list of 380 species. It's not hard to see more than 100 species in a day during spring migration (the state-record Big Day stands at 160), and several of the state's Christmas Bird Counts have broken the 100 mark.

Visitors will find some interesting differences in bird distribution across the state. House Wrens, for example, nest only in the northwestern corner, while Red-cockaded Woodpeckers and Brown-headed Nuthatches live in the pine forests of the southern half. Turkey Vultures are common in most of Arkansas, but they're scarce in the agricultural lands of the east, where row crops (and a lack of cattle ranches) mean little carrion. Wood Storks are uncommon post-breeding wanderers to Arkansas, but are rarely seen except in the extreme southern part of the state.

A FEW HISTORICAL AND ECOLOGICAL NOTES

John James Audubon visited Arkansas in the 1820s, and when we read his journals today we marvel at the abundance he found. Carolina Parakeets and Ivory-billed Woodpeckers, both of which he reported as common, are long gone. The former is extinct, while an Ivory-bill or two might still hang on in Cuba. Audubon also saw Sandhill Cranes, very rare in Arkansas today, on one of his trips down the Mississippi.

In 1822 Audubon discovered a new bird species at Arkansas Post, near the confluence of the White and Arkansas rivers in southeast Arkansas. He named it Traill's Flycatcher; we know it now as Willow Flycatcher, and it no longer breeds in the area where it was discovered. The only known nesting colony in Arkansas today is near Bentonville, in northwestern Arkansas.

Several early observers reported huge wintering flocks of Passenger Pigeons in Arkansas in the 19th century. Here, as elsewhere, they were slaughtered by the thousands for food and "sport." The last Passenger Pigeon died in the early part of this century. Bachman's Warbler once nested in the swamps of northeastern Arkansas, but disappeared as the area was cut and drained. It, too, may be extinct.

As human activity has changed the landscape in Arkansas and elsewhere in North America, some birds have suffered and others have benefited. Rice cultivation in the Grand Prairie region of eastern

Arkansas has created thousands of acres of artificial marshes, a paradise for Red-winged Blackbirds. Fish-farming in the Delta has undoubtedly increased populations of Double-crested Cormorants. On the other hand, drainage of natural swamps and marshes is one factor in the disappearance or rarity of such birds as King Rail and Purple Gallinule. Intensive management of pine forests in southern Arkansas has hurt the Red-cockaded Woodpecker, which needs large, mature pines—not easy to find in areas where trees are cut in prescribed cycles.

Both Osprey and Bald Eagle seem to be making nesting comebacks in Arkansas; the latter is more successful so far, with an increase in the number of nests reported almost every year since the 1980s. In 1993 there were at least seven Bald Eagle nests in the state, fledging 13 young; 1994 saw a few new sites. The state Game and Fish Commission has attempted to reintroduce the long-extirpated Ruffed Grouse into Arkansas in the Ozarks, and to introduce a nonmigratory race of Canada Goose in the Arkansas River Valley; the latter species seems to be doing well. Both Tree Swallow and House Finch have begun colonizing Arkansas naturally; the former is most often found in woodpecker holes in trees killed by the waters of manmade reservoirs, while the latter is now a common winter feeder bird, and even nests in façades of buildings in downtown Little Rock.

The most amazing recent bird-distribution news in Arkansas was the discovery, in 1993 and 1994, of breeding Black-throated Green and Chestnut-sided Warblers in the Ozarks, hundreds of miles from these species' nearest known nesting sites. Whether this was an anomaly or part of a long-term change remains to be seen.

Experienced Arkansas birders are convinced that more discoveries like these are possible, given thorough coverage of the state Perhaps it is fieldwork for the Arkansas Breeding Bird Atlas that will reveal such surprises. Atlas work will continue for the next few years, and help is appreciated. (Contact Kimberly Smith, Director ABBA, Department of Biological Sciences, University of Arkansas, Fayetteville, AR 72701.)

THE ARKANSAS BIRDING CALENDAR

Purple Martins start showing up in Arkansas as early as the first week of February, when Vernal Witch Hazel perfumes the streamside woods, but there'll be a lot of cold mornings (and probably a surprise snow flurry or two) before spring really arrives. The true vanguard of migrants makes its appearance in early and mid March, about the time Bloodroot, Yellow Trout Lily, and Round-lobed Hepatica bloom. For many Arkansas

birders, spring begins with the whine of the first Blue-gray Gnatcatcher—
or, some years, the *see-see, see-see, see-see* of the first Black-and-white
Warbler. Within a week or so, Yellow-throated Warblers are back in
Sycamores and Bald Cypresses beside streams, and Louisiana
Waterthrushes sing down below. Northern Parulas stutter and buzz,
usually just out of sight in the tops of trees.

From then on, spring migration builds momentum in a hurry, as most
of the summer-resident vireos, warblers, tanagers, and orioles return in a
pack (not quite literally) around the first of April. Ospreys cruise lakes
and rivers, and pairs of Broad-winged Hawks circle and call to each other
in courtship flights. Flocks of American Golden-Plovers rest and feed in
muddy fields. The cuckoos, Black-billed and Yellow-billed, and some of
the flycatchers are the stragglers, arriving just about the time we're seeing
the last of such common winter visitors as Yellow-bellied Sapsucker,
Yellow-rumped Warbler, White-throated Sparrow, and Dark-eyed Junco.

Migration peaks the first week of May, when the woods can be
dripping with songbirds—almost more than you can count, some days.
This is our chance to see such beautiful transients as Magnolia and
Blackburnian Warblers, Rose-breasted Grosbeak, Bobolink, and many
others.

By June, when the Butterfly Weed blooms, it's all over. Some of the
late warblers—Blackpoll, Mourning, Wilson's—or an Olive-sided
Flycatcher may still be around, and flocks of Cedar Waxwings still wander
aimlessly across the state, but by the second week of the month, the winter
visitors and the transients are gone. This is the time to appreciate some
of our special breeding birds: Wood Duck and Hooded Merganser, the
latter mostly confined to eastern Arkansas; Mississippi Kite, soaring over
woodlands and city parks; Red-cockaded Woodpecker, endangered in
southern and western Arkansas pinelands; Swainson's Warbler, which
inhabits dense bottomland thickets; and the flamboyant Painted Bunting,
scattered across the state but often maddeningly hard to find—especially,
it seems, when you're trying to show one to somebody who's never seen
it before.

For those with access to shorebird habitat—and in Arkansas that
usually means fish hatcheries with drained, muddy ponds—July and
August can be interesting, even exciting, months. Pectoral Sandpipers
pass through by the thousands, along with Semipalmated Plovers,
yellowlegs, "peeps," dowitchers, Wilson's Phalaropes, Black Terns, and
many other species. Here's where birders search for such rarities as
Marbled Godwit and Red-necked Phalarope. Late summer is also the

time when post-breeding wanderers from farther south sometimes show up: Tricolored Heron, Roseate Spoonbill, and Wood Stork among them.

Fall migration is a faded image of spring, with a few exceptions. Arkansas birders see flocks of dozens, or hundreds, of Broad-winged Hawks passing through in September and October. American White Pelicans fly down the Arkansas River by the hundreds, sometimes soaring around the tall buildings of downtown Little Rock as they gain altitude before continuing their migration southward. (These spectacular pelican flocks always attract attention; the newspapers and the local television news programs seem to rediscover them every year.) Ospreys and Caspian Terns also use the Arkansas River as a favorite southward migration route. Fall is the best time to find rarities like jaegers or Sabine's Gull at Millwood Lake in far southwestern Arkansas.

Late fall sees the return of Arkansas's winter visitors: the first Northern Harriers are seen quartering fields, Common Loons and Horned Grebes return to our deep water reservoirs, and Bald Eagles stand watch from tall trees at waterfowl refuges and big lakes. And the "little brown jobs" are back, too: American Pipit; Vesper, Savannah, Fox, Song, Lincoln's, and Swamp Sparrows; and Lapland Longspur—all the streaked and splotched little birds that make beginners drop their binoculars in disgust and say, "I'll *never* learn that one!" (Yes, you will.)

Winter may seem like a slow season, but the element of unpredictability makes winter birding fascinating. Unlike summer, when experienced birders can usually guess beforehand what they'll see in a certain field or patch of woods, winter always offers the potential for a northern bird that's come farther south than usual, or a migrant that's stayed around too long. Winter is the time to look for Rough-legged Hawks in northeastern Arkansas and Red-throated Loons on the reservoirs, and to listen for Western Meadowlarks. It's the season when Millwood Lake, Lake Chicot, or Beaver Lake may host Little Gull or Black-legged Kittiwake. Winter means the challenge of a Christmas Bird Count. Winter is when you're rewarded for facing the cold wind by a flock of Evening Grosbeaks in an ash tree, or a Long-eared Owl in a juniper.

And besides, it's really not that long till spring.

WEATHER AND OTHER PESTS

Arkansas is hot in the summer and cold in the winter, which is pretty much the way things are supposed to be. Of course, those are relative terms. It's not as hot as Death Valley, and it's not as cold as Minneapolis.

Summer temperatures in Arkansas are commonly above 90 degrees; add high humidity, and anything more strenuous than sitting on the porch and drinking iced tea can be unwise in the middle of the day. It can remain very hot through September. The hills of northwestern Arkansas are usually a few degrees cooler.

Winter weather often comes late to Arkansas; people wash their cars in shorts and T-shirts in December. (Again, some allowance should be made for differences between the Ozarks and the Louisiana state line.) The first really cold weather usually arrives around Christmas, and field trips to see ducks or hawks in January and February can sometimes be downright frigid, especially if the wind is blowing. On the other hand, we can have atypically balmy days anytime during the winter. While signs of spring are everywhere by March, quite chilly days occur into April.

Rainfall in Arkansas is fairly regular throughout the year, averaging seven to ten days a month of measurable precipitation—less, usually, during summer and fall. There's no pattern that's predictable enough to plan a trip around. Spring thunderstorms can be severe. At any time of year, sometimes the rain comes and goes; sometimes it comes and stays. And sometimes it doesn't rain.

Which brings up a cautionary note: rain can make unpaved roads treacherous, especially timber roads in the south and farm roads in the east. It never hurts to stop and check mudholes and wet spots before driving through them. A friendly soul in a four-wheel-drive might happen by and pull you out, but then again he could be sick that day.

You will see "no trespassing" signs often, especially in cattle and agricultural areas. This is usually because landowners have had bad experiences with hunters entering their property without permission. (Trees and fenceposts with light-purple paint mean the same thing.) If you can find the landowner, permission will often be granted to bird if you explain that you have neither guns nor dogs. (For other important standards of field behavior, pay special attention to the *ABA Code of Ethics* printed on page *viii* opposite the Table of Contents.) A new obstacle to birding in southern Arkansas is the leasing of timber-company land, once generally open to all, to hunting clubs, which install metal gates on access roads to keep everyone else out. Driving pine-woods roads to listen for American Woodcock, Prairie Warbler, and Bachman's Sparrow isn't as easy as it used to be.

Speaking of hunting, many people avoid the "deer woods" during the gun deer season in the fall, when it seems that every pickup on the road is full of guys in blaze orange caps. It might be wise to confine your birding to protected areas such as state parks at this time, usually mid-November through early December. Statistically, though, more people are accidentally shot during spring turkey season, in April, when dawn darkness and stealth lead to too many cases of mistaken identity. If you're afield then in parts of the state open to turkey hunting, take care that you can't be mistaken for a gobbler.

Since, at this writing anyway, the dreaded "killer" bees have not yet crossed our borders, there aren't too many dangerous things in the woods of Arkansas.

Snakes are usually the first critters people ask about. We have rattlesnakes (Timber, Western Pygmy, and Western Diamondback) and Copperheads in warm weather, but they're seldom seen, and most outdoorsy types know the basic rules for avoiding them: don't stick your hand into rock crevices, be careful stepping over logs or walking through tall grass, carry a flashlight (and use it) if you go out walking on warm summer nights—in general, keep an eye on your surroundings. Coral Snakes are potentially much more dangerous, but they are very, very rarely seen (they're found in southern Arkansas only) and are so small and shy that the chances of being bitten are infinitesimal. Cottonmouths, or Water Moccasins, are a different story. They are common near water, they can grow very large, and they can be aggressive when surprised or cornered. It would take a very foolish person to wade barefoot through knee-high grass at the edge of a swamp in the summertime. Again, the basic rule of watching where you step or reach will eliminate almost all danger.

The wildest parts of Arkansas have a few Black Bears, but even if you are lucky enough to see one it will almost certainly be just a glimpse of its backside as it runs away from you as fast as it can. Backpackers in the Ozarks and Ouachitas should obey bear-country rules about food storage and waste disposal when camping. Rabies is not a serious threat to birders, but never approach a skunk, Raccoon, fox, or other mammal that seems sick or acts strangely.

Ticks, chiggers, and mosquitoes are the most irritating pests in Arkansas. DEET-based repellent is the best advice here, along with tucking pants legs into socks and spraying around cuffs and necks. (We try to discourage people from wearing shorts on birding trips, but some folks won't listen.) Always check your body carefully after a trip to tick country. The longer a tick stays on you, the more likely it will give you something bad.

Watch out for fire ants, too. Their mounds, as much as 1½ feet high and 1 to 2 feet wide, are usually obvious. However, they may be hidden by logs or tall grass. Be careful where you stand while watching birds. Fire-ant stings can itch terribly and can even become infected.

Poison Ivy is ubiquitous in Arkansas, especially in parks and low, open woods where the good birds are. Learn to recognize it, and keep in mind your own level of sensitivity.

As far as nature's dangers go, that's about it. Try not to walk off any cliffs.

INFORMATION SOURCES

- For an official Arkansas state highway map, call the Arkansas Highway and Transportation Department at 501/569-2227, or write to P.O. Box 2261, Little Rock, AR 72203.
- For free general travel information about Arkansas, including a highway map, camping guides, events calendar, etc., write to Department of Parks and Tourism, One Capitol Mall, Little Rock, AR 72201, or call 800-NATURAL (800-628-8725).
- For a brochure or other information on a specific state park, call 501/682-1191.
- For information on the Ozark – St. Francis National Forest, write P.O. Box 1008, Russellville, AR 72801, or call 501/968-2354; for the Ouachita National Forest, P.O. Box 1270, Hot Springs, AR 71901, phone 501/321-5202.
- For information on U.S. Army Corps of Engineers reservoirs and campsites, write the Corps at 700 W. Capitol, Little Rock, AR 72201, or call 501/324-5551.
- For information on Arkansas Game and Fish Commission property (wildlife management areas and fishing lakes) write the Information and Education Division, 2 Natural Resources Drive, Little Rock, AR 72205, or call 501/223-6351.

The Audubon Society of Central Arkansas (in Little Rock) operates a birding "hotline" (501/753-5853) with a recorded list of good bird sightings. After the message, you can leave your name if you need more information. If you're out of the local area, you'll receive a collect return call. You can also report rare birds by leaving a message here, but see the request for documentation below.

A checklist of Arkansas birds, with notes on distribution and dates of occurrence, is available from Max Parker, Curator, Arkansas Audubon Society, 2426 S. Main, Malvern, AR 72104; copies of the checklist are 15 cents each, plus a self-addressed stamped envelope.

A vastly more comprehensive survey of the state's bird life is found in *Arkansas Birds, Their Distribution and Abundance* (1986) by Douglas A. James and Joseph C. Neal, which includes detailed accounts of all species found in Arkansas up to its publication. *A Birder's Guide to Arkansas* has relied on *Arkansas Birds* extensively for information on seasonal occurrences and ranges. For information about this excellent large-format book, write to the University of Arkansas Press, Fayetteville, AR 72701. At this writing, a revised second edition of the book is in preparation.

Birders who find unusual or out-of-season species are asked to send written documentation to Max Parker, curator of Arkansas Audubon Society bird records, at the Malvern address given at the top of this page.

PLAN OF THIS BOOK

To aid in planning birding trips, this guide divides Arkansas into five sections corresponding to geographical areas rather than to the state's official natural divisions. They are Central, Northeastern, Northwestern, Southwestern, and Southeastern. The geographical areas are divided along county lines. Each section of the book comprises an introduction describing the area and its highlights; a map with birding sites located and numbered; and the site descriptions themselves. Each site description begins with directions from a nearby city, town, or major highway junction, and some list nearby sites convenient to include in a birding trip. Details are given for birdfinding, including mileage from location to location. By looking over the section covering the area in which he/she will be traveling (and taking into consideration the season), a birder can plan a trip to see the greatest number of interesting species in the time available.

Sites Described in *A Birder's Guide to Arkansas*

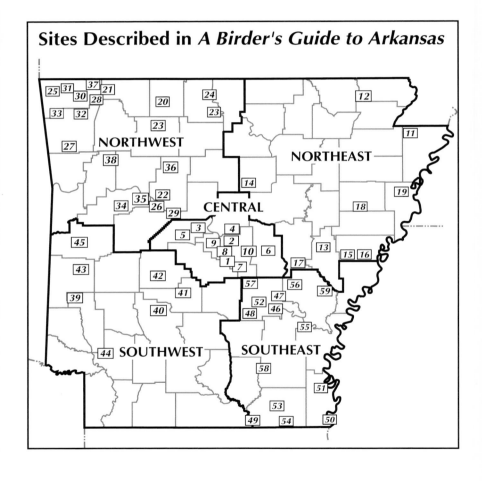

Birding Sites in Arkansas

Central Arkansas:

1 Boyle Park
2 Cook's Landing
3 Harris Brake
4 Lake Conway
5 Lake Sylvia
6 Lonoke
7 Lorance Creek Natural Area
8 Murray Park
9 Pinnacle Mtn State Park Area
10 Scott and Faulkner Lake

Northeastern Arkansas:

11 Big Lake National Wildlife Refuge
12 Black River Wildlife Mgt Area
13 Dagmar Wildlife Mgt Area
14 Greers Ferry Lake
15 Louisiana Purchase State Park
16 St. Francis National Forest
17 Stuttgart Airport
18 Village Creek State Park
19 Wapanocca Nat'l Wildlife Refuge

Northwestern Arkansas:

20 Baker Prairie Natural Area
21 Beaver Lake
22 Bona Dea Trails
23 Buffalo National River
24 Bull Shoals State Park Area
25 Centerton State Fish Hatchery
26 Dardanelle Dam
27 Devil's Den State Park
28 Hobbs State Management Area
29 Holla Bend Nat'l Wildlife Refuge

Northwestern Arkansas:

30 Lake Atalanta
31 Lake Bentonville
32 Lake Fayetteville
33 Lake Wedington
34 Magazine Mountain
35 Mount Nebo State Park
36 Page Hollow
37 Pea Ridge Nat'l Military Park
38 Redding Recreation Area

Southwestern Arkansas:

39 Cossatot River State Park Natural Area
40 DeGray Lake
41 Hulsey State Fish Hatchery
42 Lake Ouachita
43 Mena Area
44 Millwood Lake
45 Waldron Area

Southeastern Arkansas:

46 Arkansas River Levee
47 Bayou Meto Wildlife Mgt Area
48 Byrd Lake Natural Area
49 Felsenthal Nat'l Wildlife Refuge
50 Grand Lake
51 Lake Chicot State Park
52 Lake Pine Bluff
53 Levi Wilcoxon Trail
54 Overflow Nat'l Wildlife Refuge
55 Pendleton Recreation Area
56 Roth Prairie Natural Area
57 Tar Camp Recreation Area
58 Warren Prairie Natural Area
59 White River Nat'l Wildlife Refuge

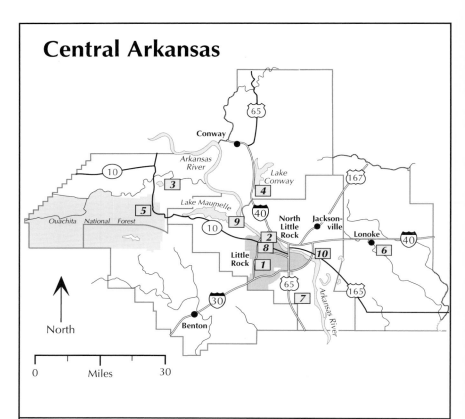

Central Arkansas

North

0   Miles   30

Birding Sites in Central Arkansas:

1	*Boyle Park*
2	*Cook's Landing*
3	*Harris Brake*
4	*Lake Conway*
5	*Lake Sylvia*
6	*Lonoke*
7	*Lorance Creek Natural Area*
8	*Murray Park*
9	*Pinnacle Mountain State Park Area*
10	*Scott and Faulkner Lake*

CENTRAL ARKANSAS

L ittle Rock is Arkansas's central city in more ways than one. It's the capital and largest city, and it sits in almost the exact geographic center of the state. More relevant to the current topic, it's located where the Ouachita Mountains, the Gulf Coastal Plain, the Delta, and the Arkansas River Valley (four of Arkansas's six natural divisions) meet, on the south bank of the Arkansas River. This is no accident. The original territorial capital was at Arkansas Post, in the Delta, but that site's tendency to flood caused officials in 1821 to move upstream to the first high ground on the Arkansas River—at the edge of the Ouachita highlands. For birders, Little Rock's location means easy access to a variety of habitats near the city.

By the way, there really is a "little rock" in Little Rock, and history buffs may wish to visit it. It served as a navigational landmark on the Arkansas River for early explorers, including the Frenchman Bénard de la Harpe, who came upriver in 1722. Today it serves as a support for a railroad bridge. It's located in Riverfront Park in downtown Little Rock; the park entrance is off La Harpe Boulevard (State Highway 10) just north of Cumberland Street.

While in downtown Little Rock, keep an eye out for Peregrine Falcons. Six young birds were hacked from a balcony of the 40-story TCBY Building in 1994; biologists hope they'll return to breed.

The best birding spots in Central Arkansas vary with the time of year. In the spring, an early-morning visit to Little Rock's Boyle Park, Murray Park sandbar, or Pinnacle Mountain State Park may turn up exciting migrants. In the breeding season, Willow Beach (see site #10, Scott and Faulkner Lake Area) has Bell's Vireo and Painted Bunting; Lake Sylvia, in the Ouachita National Forest, has nesting Ovenbird and Scarlet Tanager; Lorance Creek is an easily accessible spot for bottomland-hardwood birds. Late summer brings shorebirds to the Lonoke fish-ponds. Fall is a good time to return to Murray Park or Cook's Landing, where southbound migrants following the Arkansas River congregate. In winter, Lake Maumelle (see site #9, Pinnacle Mountain) has Common Loon, grebes, ducks, and Bald Eagle. Also in that season, the flat farmland north of Lonoke, just minutes from Interstate 40, is home to Short-eared Owl, Horned Lark, a variety of sparrows, and Lapland Longspur.

No matter what the season, travelers with time to visit only one site would do well to choose the Pinnacle Mountain area. Within a short distance here are bottomland woods, pine forests, the Arkansas River, and Lake Maumelle, which means that there's nearly always something worthwhile to see.

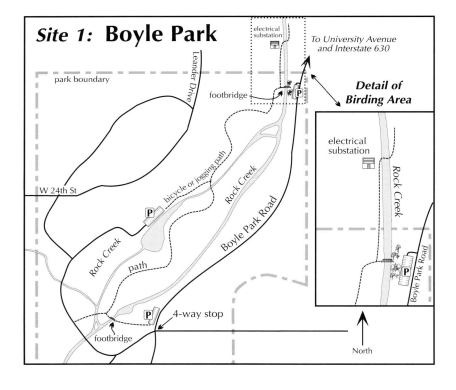

Site 1: Boyle Park

1. Boyle Park

Location: *From the intersection of Interstate 630 and University Avenue in Little Rock, go south on University Avenue 0.2 mile to 12th Street; right (west) on 12th Street 0.2 mile to Cleveland; left (south) on Cleveland 0.3 mile to a T intersection with Boyle Park Road; right on Boyle Park Road 1.0 mile to a four-way stop. Turn right here, and right again immediately into a parking lot. Look beyond the picnic shelter to a footbridge crossing Rock Creek. (See maps on pages 16 and 33.)*

Boyle Park is the best place in Little Rock to find spring migrants, especially on a species-per-acre basis. One local birder's list for the park is 113 species, including 30 kinds of warblers. Yellow-crowned Night-Heron nests here, as do Wood Duck, Mississippi Kite, Broad-winged Hawk, Barred Owl, Red-headed and Pileated Woodpeckers, Acadian Flycatcher, Wood Thrush, and Prothonotary Warbler. Boyle Park is at its best in April and May, when it seems to act as a migrant trap; it's not hard to see more than 50 species in a couple of hours during that period. Among the possibilities: Black-billed (first week of May) and Yellow-billed Cuckoos; Eastern Screech-Owl; Olive-sided Flycatcher (check bare branches at the tops of trees in May); all vireos except Bell's; Blue-winged, Golden-winged, Chestnut-sided, Magnolia, Blackburnian, Bay-breasted, Worm-eating, Swainson's (rare), Mourning, Hooded, and Canada Warblers; American Redstart; Ovenbird; Louisiana and Northern Waterthrushes; Summer and Scarlet Tanagers; Rose-breasted Grosbeak; Orchard and Northern Orioles; and many more. Boyle Park has been damaged by sewer-line construction, brush clearing, and, most recently, by the ditching and widening of a portion of Rock Creek, but despite all the abuse, it's still a productive place.

The best birding is in an area of woods and thickets along Rock Creek, which runs through the park from north to south. Rock Creek is lined with Water Tupelo and Bald Cypress, which makes Boyle Park something like a little piece of the Delta in a city residential neighborhood. The park also includes higher areas of pine woods, but these aren't as productive.

You can reach good spring and summer spots by following a paved jogging path northward, beginning at the footbridge at the parking lot. Check the trees around the bridge for Blue-gray Gnatcatcher and warblers, then cross into the woods. Turn right at the trail intersection and walk north. Gray-cheeked and Swainson's Thrushes are common here in spring. Just before you reach a small pond are tall pines where Yellow-crowned Night-Herons have nested, although they did not do so in 1993 or 1994 (the small colony tends to move around the park every few years). At the pond, listen for Belted Kingfisher and Fish Crow; scan the sky in spring and summer for Mississippi Kite, and look along the bank for Green Heron and migrant Spotted Sandpiper. The willows beside the water often have a variety of warblers.

The path continues past the pond and alongside a small creek, where you'll find breeding Wood Duck, Acadian Flycatcher, Prothonotary Warbler, and Louisiana Waterthrush. Watch for the occasional fruiting Red Mulberry tree in spring, where you're sure to find a few Gray Catbirds and possibly migrant Rose-breasted Grosbeaks. Brown Thrashers are common. Keep right after a small bridge and continue a few hundred yards to an electrical substation at the north end of the park. The bushes near the transformers may have sparrows (Lincoln's is often found in migration), Common Yellowthroat, Yellow-breasted Chat, and White-eyed Vireo. Remember to keep checking the sky occasionally for Broad-winged Hawk; Red-shouldered Hawk has been seen, too. Turn around here and return to your car

Boyle Park is good for typical winter woodland birds, including Red-breasted Nuthatch, Brown Creeper, Ruby-crowned and Golden-crowned Kinglets, and Hermit Thrush. It's a good spot to look for Solitary Vireo, which is rare in central Arkansas in winter, and Evening Grosbeak has turned up here. But spring is really the time to bird Boyle Park.

A minor cautionary note: like many city parks, Boyle Park attracts some characters who would not be described as savory. Joggers, bikers, and walkers usually provide enough company that problems are unlikely, but you wouldn't want to go into the park alone at dusk for an owl prowl.

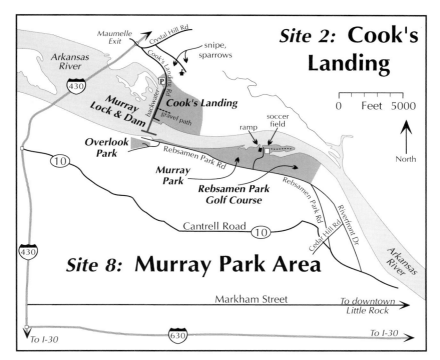

2. Cook's Landing

Location: *From the intersection of State Highway 10 and Interstate 430 in Little Rock, drive northeast on 430 for 2.3 miles to the first exit, signed "Maumelle." (Watch for nesting Cliff Swallows around the Arkansas River bridge.) Leave the interstate and go right 0.1 mile on Crystal Hill Road to Cook's Landing Road; turn right here. (Also see map on page 33.)*

Cook's Landing is a Corps of Engineers area across the Arkansas River from Murray Park (site #10), good in winter and migration for a variety of land and water birds. It's also the location of the North Little Rock city hydroelectric plant, and a popular spot for boat-launching and fishing.

As you drive toward the river on the entrance road, watch for Scissor-tailed Flycatchers perching on utility wires in breeding season and for Eastern Bluebirds and Loggerhead Shrikes year-round. The small pond on the right may have a Great Blue Heron or a few wintering

Pied-billed Grebes or ducks. A Peregrine Falcon was seen here (eating a snake!) on the 1994 Christmas Bird Count.

Continue to the parking area beyond the gates, 0.6 mile from Crystal Hill Road. Scan the river backwater in winter for Common Loon, grebes (mostly Pied-billed, but sometimes Horned and very rarely Eared), and ducks. You'll find both dabbling and diving ducks here, and possibly a small flock of Hooded Mergansers. Double-crested Cormorants sometimes roost upstream by the hundreds in winter. Ospreys often linger in the area during fall migration. Great Blue Heron and Belted Kingfisher are common permanent residents. In recent years a winter blackbird roost has formed on a peninsula just upstream from the Interstate 430 bridge. In late afternoon the birds stream by endlessly over Cook's Landing. Most are European Starlings, Red-winged Blackbirds, and Common Grackles, with lesser numbers of American Robins and Brown-headed Cowbirds. A few Rusty and Brewer's Blackbirds will probably be tagging along—but at dusk, who can tell?

Drive another 0.1 mile toward the river and watch for a gravel road on the left, closed to vehicles by a cable. Park nearby and walk in here, following one of the dirt paths along either side of a long, narrow pond. This area of mixed woods and brush is very good for woodpeckers, migrant wrens and warblers, winter sparrows, and possibly even an American Woodcock in a swampy spot. It's the kind of scruffy-looking, varied habitat where you could find just about anything. A Western Kingbird turned up here one recent May. The area has been degraded by off-road vehicles, but it's still plenty interesting.

In winter look for Sharp-shinned and Cooper's Hawks; Yellow-bellied Sapsucker; House and Winter Wrens; kinglets; Yellow-rumped Warbler (this is a good place to watch for Orange-crowned); Rufous-sided Towhee; Fox, Song, Lincoln's, Swamp, and White-throated Sparrows; and American Goldfinch. Investigate paths leading south through deeper woods toward the river. The permanent residents here are what you'd expect in such surroundings: Red-shouldered Hawk, Mourning Dove, Carolina Wren, Brown Thrasher, Northern Cardinal, and Field Sparrow. Summer residents include Yellow-billed Cuckoo, White-eyed Vireo, Common Yellowthroat, and Indigo Bunting.

Continue 0.2 mile to Murray Lock and Dam, turning left to a parking area below the spillway. In winter, watch for Bald Eagles and check the gulls below the dam. Most will be Ring-bills, but Bonaparte's and Herring are sometimes seen; Franklin's passes through quickly in October. Various informal paths and old roads lead into woods and brushy areas that are worth checking out in migration and winter.

Return to Crystal Hill Road, turn right, and then right again immediately toward an elementary school. A giant sports arena was once planned for this area, but until the area is developed the open fields here are good for winter sparrows, including Le Conte's, and the marshy places for Common Snipe.

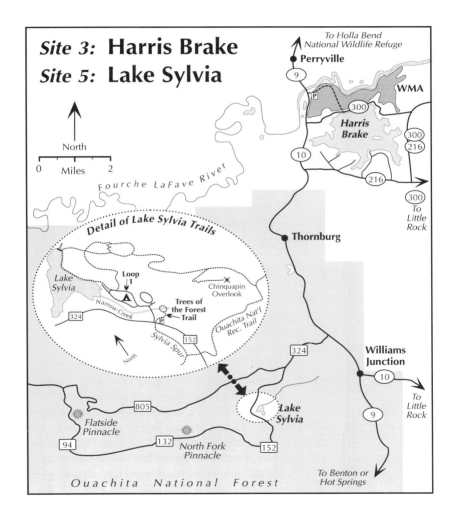

3. Harris Brake

Location: *From the intersection of State Highway 10 and Interstate 430 in Little Rock, drive west on State Highway 10 33.5 miles to the State Highway 300 turnoff on your right toward Harris Brake. Drive 1.1 miles to the lake. (See map on page 21.)*

Harris Brake is a 1,300-acre fishing lake with standing dead timber, good for a variety of waterbirds. ("Brake" is an old word for a swampy area overgrown with a particular plant, e.g., canebrake or cypress brake.) A nearby Game and Fish Commission wildlife management area can also be very productive.

There are several parking spots around Harris Brake, including one at a bait shop where State Highway 300 bends left around the lake and another at the far end of the levee. Stop wherever the light is best and scan the lake carefully. This is a great place to see Osprey during migration and Bald Eagle, Double-crested Cormorant, and ducks in winter. Tree Swallow, a scarce breeder in Arkansas, has nested here in old woodpecker holes. Red-headed Woodpeckers are common on dead snags. One April a small flock of Willets was seen perched on stumps out in the lake.

Harris Brake Wildlife Management Area encompasses a fine variety of bottomland and old-field habitats. *Photo by Mel White.*

Return to State Highway 10 and drive north 1.0 mile to the 1,200-acre Harris Brake Wildlife Management Area. There's a parking lot to the right of the highway, just before the bridge over the Fourche LaFave (slightly corrupted French for "[river] fork of the wild beast"—at least that's one interpretation). A 1.7-mile dirt road winds from here through the wildlife area to Harris Brake; it's well worth walking the whole thing in the springtime. (A shuttle from the lake back to the parking area would be nice if you're in a group with two cars.) Or you can drive it, stopping and listening here and there. Swainson's Warbler has been seen here, and in summer you'll hear Northern Parula, Black-and-white, Prothonotary, and Kentucky Warblers, and Louisiana Waterthrush. (This is assuming that you can identify anything over the constant singing of Indigo Buntings and Common Yellowthroats.) Yellow-billed Cuckoo, Acadian Flycatcher, and White-eyed Vireo are common in breeding season. You may find Great Blue Heron, Red-shouldered Hawk, Wild Turkey, Barred Owl, and Wood Duck at any time of year, and in summer Broad-winged Hawk and Green Heron.

The mixed bottomland woods, brushy areas, and fields create varied habitat for wintering finches and sparrows. This is a popular hunting area, though, so during the various game seasons you may have to pick your spots for birding. During duck season, much of the area is flooded for waterfowl habitat.

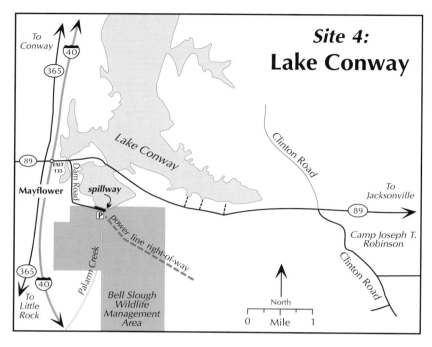

4. Lake Conway

Location: *Begin at the intersection of Interstate 40 and State Highway 89 (Exit 135) in Mayflower, about 15 miles northwest of Little Rock.*

Many of Arkansas's man-made lakes are deep-water reservoirs with steep, rocky, sterile shorelines. Lake Conway is different. Its expansive surface area was created when the state Game and Fish Commisssion dammed Palarm Creek; the lake is shallow, dotted with countless dead trees, and its shoreline is in most places wooded and swampy. Lake Conway is extremely popular with anglers, mostly of the lazy-afternoon-in-a-johnboat or cane-pole-from-the-bank variety. Representative habitats are accessible from State Highway 89 at its southern end.

From Interstate 40, drive east 0.4 mile on State Highway 89 to Dam Road and turn right. Drive 1.1 miles to a parking lot at the spillway. In winter, scan the lake for Pied-billed Grebe, Double-crested Cormorant, ducks, or Bald Eagle. In migration, watch for Osprey and swallows. Tree Swallows may well nest in dead trees out in the water.

Park and walk over the spillway. You are now in the Bell Slough Wildlife Management Area, a good place to see a variety of landbirds and an excellent place for warblers during spring migration. (In fall and winter, it's a good place to see lots of rabbit- and quail-hunters.) Several interconnecting paths branch off from the spillway, allowing visitors to range widely through woods, swampy bottomland, and fields.

Turn left and follow the edge of the lake to a slightly higher lookout point from which you can scan the water. Return to the spillway and walk downstream a few yards, more or less keeping beside Palarm Creek, to a well-used old road visible from the parking lot. Follow this about a half mile to a swampy area where Green Herons and Prothonotary Warblers breed. To reach another area of wet woods, follow the powerlines away from the creek for about a half mile, to just past the point at which they turn left (at the pole marked 29). Take the path down into the woods on your right. Here you may find Red-shouldered Hawk and Pileated Woodpecker year-round, and in breeding season you'll definitely hear Prothonotary Warbler. Some of the other breeding birds

Acadian Flycatcher
Gail Diane Yovanovich

of Bell Slough are Wood Duck; Broad-winged Hawk; Northern Bobwhite; Yellow-billed Cuckoo; Barred Owl; Eastern Wood-Pewee; Acadian and Great Crested Flycatchers; Fish Crow; Wood Thrush; Gray Catbird; Brown Thrasher; White-eyed, Yellow-throated, and Red-eyed Vireos; Northern Parula; Black-and-white and Kentucky Warblers; Common (very!) Yellowthroat; Yellow-breasted Chat; Summer Tanager; and Orchard and Northern Orioles.

Return to State Highway 89 and turn right. After 2.2 miles, a paved road on the left leads to a boat-launching area from which you can scan the lake. For the next 1.8 miles of State Highway 89, watch for dirt roads leading off to the left and running down to the lake. Explore as many as you have time for; the birds here will be much the same as those at Bell Slough. (The roads may be in bad shape; depending on your vehicle, you may want to park off the highway and walk the short distance to the water. Also, several of the parking areas have unfortunately become illegal trash-dumps.)

Four miles from Dam Road, Clinton Road leads off to the right into the huge Camp Robinson National Guard training area. You can explore it at will, except when military exercises are going on. Because the terrain is higher and drier, though, the birds probably won't be as good as those around Lake Conway.

5. Lake Sylvia

Location: *From the intersection of Interstate 430 and State Highway 10 in Little Rock, drive west on State Highway 10 for 27.0 miles to State Highway 324. Turn left and drive 3.7 miles to the entrance to Lake Sylvia. (See map on page 21.)*

After a spring birding trip in the wet woodland of Pinnacle Mountain State Park (see site #9), it can be a pleasant change to continue west to Lake Sylvia, a recreation area at the eastern edge of the huge (1.5 million-acre) Ouachita National Forest, the largest and oldest national forest in the South. Here the woods are higher and drier than those of the Pinnacle Mountain area; more pine is mixed with the oak and hickory. Instead of Prothonotary Warblers and Summer Tanagers, you're more likely to find Ovenbirds and Scarlet Tanagers.

The Lake Sylvia camping area doesn't open until late spring, but you can walk in around the gate anytime and explore nearby trails, including an interpretive wildlife trail that begins off campground Loop 1. The lake itself seldom has interesting birds. A better plan is to drive past the lake 0.3 mile to a parking lot on the left. Here a short, self-guided "Trees of the Forest" nature trail winds through a pretty woodland and bridges a rocky creek; signs along the way identify common trees. Across the road, a 0.4-mile spur trail leads to the Ouachita National Recreation Trail, which, for the extremely adventurous, runs all the way to Oklahoma—more than 180 miles west. (Better pack plenty of granola bars.) In any case, there's obviously more than enough land to roam around. In spring and early summer, Ovenbirds and Scarlet Tanagers are singing everywhere.

As is generally true for the Arkansas mountains, the birdlife here is not as rich as in the lowlands. It's worth watching for a few interesting species, though. Wild Turkey is fairly common, but seeing one is another matter. Your best bet is to walk the trails and drive the roads early in the morning and hope for good luck, or else learn to be as crafty and knowledgeable of the birds' ways as turkey hunters are. (Another good bet is to avoid the whole area during hunting season.) Broad-winged Hawks are common breeders, and you may see one flying across the road in front of you, perhaps dangling a snake from its talons. Brown-headed Nuthatches are present, though not as common as they are farther south. Red-eyed Vireo is the most abundant breeder. Rufous-sided Towhee also nests.

To see more of the Ouachita National Forest, continue past the parking lot (State Highway 324 has now become Forest Service Road 152) for 1.5 miles and turn right onto FS Road 132. Drive 4.1 miles to an intersection and continue straight ahead on FS Road 94. The land now on your left is the Flatside Wilderness Area, an officially designated primitive area within the national forest. In 2.9 miles watch for a parking area at the base of a rocky peak called Flatside Pinnacle. A steep 0.4-mile trail leads to the top and great views of 50 miles or more westward into the Arkansas River valley. Continue 0.4 mile to FS Road 805, turn right, and drive 7.9 miles back to State Highway 324, where you can turn left and return to State Highway 10.

Stop anywhere you like along this loop, concentrating on moist, shady ravines, where you'll find breeding Pileated Woodpecker, Acadian Flycatcher, Wood Thrush, Black-and-white Warbler, and Ovenbird. There are places in Arkansas with more birds, but few where you can feel so alone with the trees and the hills.

From the intersection of State Highways 10 and 324, it's only 7 miles north on Highway 10 to the Harris Brake Wildlife Management Area (see site #3).

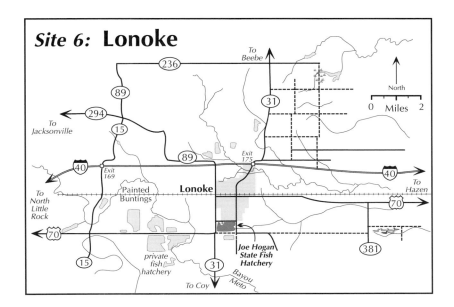

Site 6: **Lonoke**

6. Lonoke Area

Location: *Take the Lonoke exit (State Highway 31) from Interstate 40, 22 miles east of Little Rock.*

Lonoke bills itself as the "Minnow Capital of the World"; the water-retaining clay subsoil that makes Arkansas's Grand Prairie a center of rice farming also lends itself perfectly to fish farming. The flat countryside around town is dotted with hundreds of shallow rectangular ponds. When these ponds are drained to harvest fish, the mudflats that are left make the Lonoke area Arkansas's hottest spot for shorebirds—in more ways than one. Field trips here in the heat of July and August have long been a tradition for local birders. Unfortunately, a controversy over the shooting of grebes, cormorants, herons, and egrets, which supposedly cause great monetary losses to fish farmers by predation, has at this writing made the largest and most productive private farms off-limits.

The state Game and Fish Commission operates a fish hatchery here where birders are welcome. To visit it, drive south from Interstate 40 on State Highway 31 for 1.5 miles to U.S. Highway 70; turn right and drive 1.7 miles, turning left at the Joe Hogan Fish Hatchery sign; drive 0.3 mile and turn right into the hatchery. On an outside wall at the visitor center is a chart showing which ponds have been drained recently. Behind the center is a tower from which you can scan the area. Do not drive on the levees without asking permission from one of the hatchery personnel. If you walk the levees, keep an eye out for snakes.

The suitability of a pond for shorebirds can change from day to day; look for one that is nearly empty but still muddy. Shorebirds are fairly common in spring migration, but are most common from late July through September. The most likely species here are Semipalmated Plover; Greater and Lesser Yellowlegs; and Spotted, Semipalmated, Western, Least, and (especially) Pectoral Sandpipers. (Killdeer, of course, are common all year.) You may also find Black-bellied and Piping Plovers; American Golden-Plover; American Avocet; Ruddy Turnstone; Sanderling; Solitary, White-rumped, Baird's, Stilt, and Buff-breasted Sandpipers; Dunlin; Short-billed and Long-billed Dowitchers; and Wilson's Phalarope. Hudsonian Godwit is sometimes seen in spring, and Marbled Godwit is very rare in fall.

Although the species certainly isn't to be expected, Arkansas's first record of Ruff came from a dry, grassy pond here in August 1974. The Lonoke area was the site of Arkansas's first recorded nest of Black-necked Stilt, so that locally rare species is possible in summer. Ruddy Duck has also nested near Lonoke, and Pied-billed Grebe has nested at the state hatchery.

Drained ponds at Lonoke's Joe Hogan State Fish Hatchery create good shorebird habitat. *Photo by Mel White.*

Ospreys and flocks of swallows and terns (mostly Forster's and Black) stop to feed during spring and fall migration; even as unlikely a species as Royal Tern has been found at Lonoke (just one record, in 1986). Green (breeding) and Great Blue (all year) Herons are common. Snowy Egret and Little Blue Heron are seen from spring through fall, and Great Egret is often very common. July and August sometimes see large gatherings of waders on hatchery ponds. Keep an eye out for breeding Scissor-tailed Flycatcher, near the eastern edge of its range here.

Sometimes thick vegetation grows up in the shallow water along the borders of a pond; look for migrant Soras and Common Moorhens there. Least Bitterns have been seen in summer in such vegetation, although breeding has not been confirmed. Transient Yellow-headed Blackbirds have been found at the state hatchery and other local ponds.

At times in winter the ponds can be very productive for ducks, especially during hunting season, when the birds find a refuge here. American Coot can be abundant. Common Snipe and American Pipit sometimes feed in dry ponds. A few Least Sandpipers sometimes linger for the local Christmas Bird Count, along with occasional Greater Yellowlegs and Dunlin.

From fall through spring, an agricultural area east of Lonoke can be productive. To visit it, leave the hatchery and turn right along a paved road with ponds on the right and a subdivision on the left. Drive 0.5 mile to a T intersection, turn right, and drive another 0.5 mile. Turn left here, and drive east for 5.3 miles. (Continue straight ahead onto a gravel road when the paved road turns right after 1.2 miles.) Watch for Red-tailed Hawk, American Kestrel, and Loggerhead Shrike along the roadside. Turn left onto State Highway 381, then right onto another gravel road in 0.2 mile. After traveling 0.9 mile from the highway, check the fields on the right, where the landowner often keeps water standing to attract waterfowl and waders. When conditions are right, the concentration of birds here can be amazing: in winter, look for geese (Snow and Canada, with a few Greater White-fronted) and big flocks of dabbling ducks, often including Green-winged and Blue-winged Teal, Mallard, Northern Pintail, Northern Shoveler, Gadwall, and American Wigeon. At other times of year there may be numbers of herons and egrets or shorebirds. A few Black-necked Stilts, which have nested in the Lonoke area, lingered late here in 1993, although nesting was not detected at that time.

Return to State Highway 381, turn right, and drive 1.0 mile to U.S. Highway 70; turn left here and drive 5.3 miles to return to State Highway 31 in Lonoke.

The farmland north of Lonoke can be interesting in winter, when the barren fields sometimes host large flocks of Lapland Longspurs and Horned Larks. To check a representative area, drive north on State Highway 31 from its intersection with Interstate 40. After 3.5 miles, turn right onto a gravel road. Watch for American Pipit and Field, Savannah, and White-crowned Sparrows along the roadsides, and scan for flocks of longspurs and larks. Northern Harrier, Red-tailed Hawk, and American Kestrel are common; the "Harlan's" race of the Red-tail is sometimes found here in winter. Just before dark, Short-eared Owls begin quartering the fields; occasionally they're seen resting during the day, looking like clumps of dirt in the rice stubble.

Continue along this road for 2 miles to an intersection (note this spot); turn left for one mile (passing a swampy area where you can look for woodpeckers and passerines), and turn left again for 2 miles (passing fish ponds that may have ducks) back to State Highway 31. If the road through the swampy area is flooded, return to the first intersection (the spot noted above) and continue straight ahead (south) for 3 miles; turn right onto a paved road and drive 2.3 miles back to State Highway 31 near Interstate 40. This farmland route has breeding Horned Larks, Eastern Bluebirds, and Loggerhead Shrikes, but otherwise there's not much in summer— unless you'd like to see how many hundreds of Red-winged Blackbirds and Dickcissels you can count.

One spot near Lonoke has become known to local birders as a reliable place to find the often-elusive Painted Bunting. From the Hogan hatchery entrance, turn left and return to Highway 70. Turn left and drive 5.5 miles to State Highway 15. (Along the way you will pass through the mammoth Anderson fish farm, where birders are not allowed. Such birds as Roseate Spoonbill and Black Scoter have been seen from the highway recently, though.) Turn right on Highway 15 and drive 1.7 miles to a railroad crossing. (You can also reach this spot easily by taking Exit 169 from Interstate 40 and driving south along State Highway 15 for 1.3 miles.) Park well off the highway on the dirt road here; do not block drives or field entrances. Walk east (back toward Lonoke) along the seldom-used railroad track. *Do not trespass onto private land off the railroad right-of-way.* Painted Buntings are found in the trackside bushes, though you may have to walk a mile or more to find a cooperative singing male. At least five males were present along this stretch of track in the spring of 1993, and similar numbers were found in 1994.

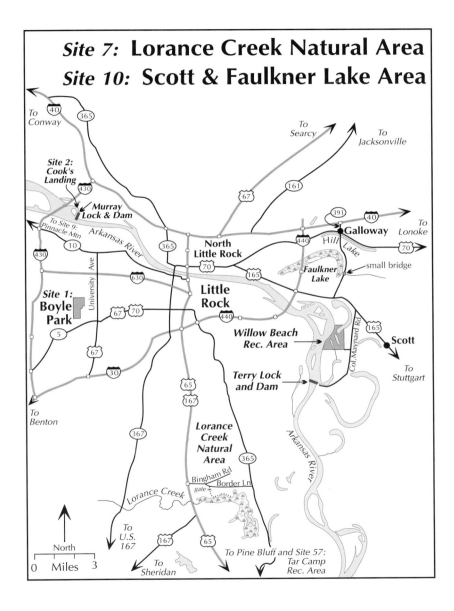

Site 7: **Lorance Creek Natural Area**
Site 10: **Scott & Faulkner Lake Area**

7. Lorance Creek Natural Area

Location: *Take the Bingham Road exit (Exit 9) from U.S. Highway 65, nine miles southeast of Little Rock. Drive east 0.7 mile on Bingham Road (which changes from pavement to gravel) to Border Lane, a gravel road that forks to the right. Turn here and drive 0.1 mile to the Lorance Creek sign and gate on the right. Park at the gate. (See map on page 33.)*

Lorance Creek, a 289-acre state natural area, is an outstanding and easily accessible tupelo swamp just minutes from Little Rock, less than a mile from the major Little Rock/Pine Bluff highway. With its combination of swampy lowland and slightly elevated woods, it's interesting to visit any time of year, though it's most productive during spring migration. For visits in spring and summer, be sure to bring a family-size bottle of bug spray to even the odds in the warfare against mosquitoes and deerflies.

After parking at the gate, walk in along the old road straight ahead. In this open area, a breeding-season visitor may hear Common Yellowthroat and Indigo Bunting. In 100 yards or so, the path bends left, slopes downward, and splits. Investigate the right-hand fork, which may end soon at high water; return to the left path, which continues alongside the swampy area. Most of the trees standing in water are Water Tupelo *(Nyssa aquatica)*, with Bald Cypresses mixed in. Look carefully, though, and you'll see a few "Swamp" Tupelos—sometimes considered a species, *N. biflora,* although sometimes classified as merely a distinctive form of the Black Tupelo *(N. sylvatica)*—a tree found in Arkansas in only four or five counties. Its leaves are narrower than those of the surrounding Water Tupelo. The trees along the path also include American Hornbeam; White, Willow, Water, and Swamp Chestnut Oaks; Sassafras; Sweetgum; Red Maple; and Flowering Dogwood. Other interesting plants found here are Virginia Water-Willow, with cherry-like flower clusters that appear in early summer, and Arrow Arum, with upright, arrowhead-shaped leaves that grow in clusters.

Birds include woodland species such as (spring through fall) Yellow-billed Cuckoo; Ruby-throated Hummingbird; Eastern Wood-Pewee; Great Crested Flycatcher; Blue-gray Gnatcatcher; Wood Thrush; Yellow-throated and Red-eyed Vireos; Black-and-white Warbler; and Summer Tanager, and, as permanent residents, Eastern Screech-Owl; Red-bellied, Downy, and Pileated Woodpeckers; Northern Flicker; Carolina Chickadee; Tufted Titmouse; White-breasted Nuthatch; and Carolina Wren.

In addition, you'll find wetland-loving birds such as (breeding) Green Heron, Acadian Flycatcher, Fish Crow, Prothonotary and Kentucky Warblers, Louisiana Waterthrush, and (all year) Wood Duck, Red-shouldered Hawk, and Barred Owl.

Orange-crowned Warbler has been found here in winter, along with such common forest birds as Yellow-bellied Sapsucker, Winter Wren, Golden-crowned and Ruby-crowned Kinglets, Hermit Thrush, Yellow-rumped Warbler, White-throated Sparrow, and Dark-eyed Junco.

Although you won't want to chase birds into the swampy part of the property, you can walk up the slope to the left to look for birds on the higher ground. Lorance Creek is just the sort of moist, rich bottomland woods that can be filled with migrant songbirds in spring, and it's well worth a visit any time of year. An interpretive trail is planned here.

Tar Camp Recreation Area (see site #57 in the Southeastern Arkansas section), with camping and picnicking sites as well as good birding, is only 11 miles south of Lorance Creek.

8. Murray Park Area

Location: *From the intersection of State Highway 10 (La Harpe Boulevard) and Markham Street in downtown Little Rock, follow State Highway 10 (soon called Cantrell Road) 2.2 miles to the stoplight at Riverfront Drive. Turn right. (See map on page 19.)*

Before getting to Murray Park, a Little Rock city park on the south bank of the Arkansas River, you pass through the Riverdale and Rebsamen Park areas. After turning off State Highway 10 and crossing a railroad track, look for an open area with tall trees (dead and alive) on your right (east). This is a good spot for woodpeckers; Red-headed, Red-bellied, and Pileated have all nested here. The Riverdale area is rapidly being developed for offices and apartments, but at this writing this small area is still intact. In the summer, you may find Eastern Kingbird, Scissor-tailed Flycatcher, and Northern Oriole here—at least until the developers cut down all the remaining trees. Western Kingbird and American Tree Sparrow have also been seen near the river levee here, but that was before the boom in businesses and condos.

Riverfront Drive soon merges with Rebsamen Park Road, and there's a turn into the Rebsamen Park golf course on your right 1.9 miles from State Highway 10. Eastern Kingbird, Scissor-tailed Flycatcher, and Northern Oriole are common nesters on the course, usually near the river, and a few Warbling Vireos nest in the trees along the shoreline. Stay out of the way of golfers if you decide to look for these birds.

One mile past the golf course is the Murray Park entrance. Drive toward the downstream boat-launching ramp and park near an open field with several soccer goals and a small but substantial grandstand. Walk around the parking area, scanning the river for Great Blue Heron, Belted Kingfisher, and anything else that happens by. It's not unusual to see Bald Eagles along here in the winter. Check the bushes upstream from the launching ramp for migrants or winter sparrows.

Return to the riverside border of the soccer field and walk downstream. A trail of sorts will lead you into an area of scrubby trees and bushes surrounding an Arkansas River backwater where Warbling Vireo nests. This area is excellent for migrant landbirds; it's probably the best place in central Arkansas in fall. For some reason (probably the abundant willows), migrating Yellow Warblers seem easier to find here than at any other place locally.

Just downstream is an extensive sandbar covered by similar habitat; cross over to it if you can. (High water sometimes makes this impossible.)

Several good birds have shown up here over the years, including Merlin, Inca Dove, Alder Flycatcher, and American Tree Sparrow. Wander around wherever a trail leads you. You may find shorebirds on the river pools. In spring and fall, constantly check for river-following migrants: American White Pelican, Double-crested Cormorant, Osprey, gulls, and terns (Caspian Tern is common in September). Grassy areas at the far end of the sandbar are good for Sedge and Marsh Wrens, and you may even flush a Sora.

Another 0.9 mile upstream along Rebsamen Park Road is a road junction. Continue straight 0.2 mile to Murray Lock and Dam, where there is a parking area and an observation deck. Gulls congregate below the dam by the hundreds in winter; nearly all will be Ring-billed, but there may be Herring and Bonaparte's. Bring a scope.

Backtrack to the junction and take the road uphill to the right. After 0.3 mile there is an overlook on your right. (The park here was closed in early 1995, but may reopen in the future. The birds listed below can also be seen, though from a lower level, from the dam parking lot.) This is a good place to set up a scope during fall migration and wait for whatever happens by. In September and early October American White Pelicans and Ospreys may fly by at eye level, and you should see a few Sharp-shinned, Cooper's, and Broad-winged Hawks. Quite often small flocks of Red-headed Woodpeckers, Northern Flickers, and Blue Jays are seen. If you hit the right day (usually the first morning after the wind has shifted to northerly), you may see hundreds of Broad-wings rising in kettles across the river and soaring over the ridge behind you.

Just across the Arkansas River is the Cook's Landing area (site #2); to reach it, you must return to State Highway 10, drive west 5.5 miles to Interstate 430, and cross the river.

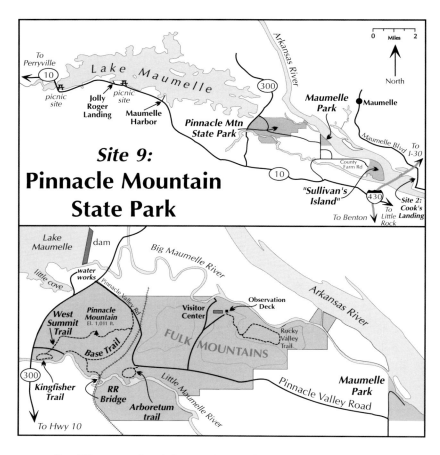

9. Pinnacle Mountain State Park Area

Location: *From the intersection of Interstate 430 and State Highway 10 in Little Rock, drive west on State Highway 10 6.4 miles to State Highway 300. Turn right and drive 2.0 miles to the Pinnacle Mountain State Park West Summit picnic area on your right.*

The area around Pinnacle Mountain State Park and Lake Maumelle was safely "out in the country" west of Little Rock not so long ago. Today it's being swallowed up as the city rapidly expands, and sometime in the not-too-distant future Pinnacle's nearly 2,000 acres will be an urban park. Trails around the picnic area offer good birding, but get here early on spring and summer weekends, ahead of the church groups, volleyballers, walkers, and fishermen. (*Note:* camping is not allowed at the state park, but is available at nearby Maumelle Park, a Corps of Engineers recreation area on the Arkansas River; see below.)

A short (1.5-mile round trip) but fairly strenuous hiking trail leads from the north side of the West Summit picnic area parking lot to the top of Pinnacle Mountain, where there's a fine view of the Arkansas River valley, from the skyscrapers of downtown Little Rock west over Lake Maumelle. This is not the park's best birding location, but it's interesting from up here to look *down* on soaring Turkey Vultures, with occasional Black Vultures and Red-tailed Hawks mixed in. Greater Roadrunner, a species that was hurt by several severe winters beginning in the late 1970s, has been seen here regularly of late; it may be found anywhere in the park, especially in rocky areas that attract the lizards on which it feeds (check around the visitor center as well). In April 1990 and again in August 1992 single Rufous-crowned Sparrows were found at the rocky summit of Pinnacle. In March and August 1993 a presumed pair was seen near the top, continuing this species' expansion eastward in Arkansas from Magazine Mountain and Mount Nebo (see sites #34 and 35). These birds were undoubtedly the easternmost of their kind in the United States. It's unlikely they'll go any farther unless they learn to like rice and soybean fields; east of Pinnacle, it's flat Delta all the way to Crowley's Ridge. At this writing it's unknown whether Rufous-crowned Sparrow might establish a breeding population on the mountain, but a singing male was back on the summit in April 1994.

By the way, the word "Maumelle," which is much in evidence around here, gives this area something in common with the Grand Tetons of Wyoming. Early French explorers thought that the prominent mountain looked like a certain prominent feature of the female anatomy. (They'd probably been cooped up with other men for a long time.) "Maumelle" is a corruption of their French term, and today we have a Maumelle lake, town, boulevard, country club, park, and two Maumelle rivers. The mountain, however, is now called Pinnacle.

Kingfisher Trail, at the opposite side of the parking lot, is a half-mile paved path that's excellent for birds, especially early on spring mornings. It winds through wet woods and alongside magnificent Bald Cypresses bordering the Little Maumelle River, where Yellow Pond-Lily blooms in summer. Barred Owls are fairly common here all year, and are seen surprisingly often in daylight, sitting in the tall trees. In the springtime you may surprise a mother Wood Duck and her fuzzy ducklings; Hooded Merganser has been seen on the river and may nest. Listen for Eastern Phoebe, which nests under the highway bridge, as well as under the pavilions in the picnic area. Yellow-throated, Prothonotary, and Kentucky Warblers breed here, as do many common woodland species including Green Heron, Ruby-throated Hummingbird, Red-bellied and Downy Woodpeckers, Acadian and Great Crested Flycatchers, Carolina Wren, White-eyed and Red-eyed Vireos, and Northern Parula. Look for Pileated Woodpecker in the tall cypresses and listen for Fish Crow. Mosquitoes can be bad here when spring rains leave standing water in low places, so bring repellent.

The Base Trail begins at a small metal bridge near the launching ramp at the east end of the picnic area. This trail circles the mountain to another parking lot 1.5 miles away, but the best area for birds is found by following the green marks for the first half-mile or so. In the spring and summer you'll probably find Broad-winged Hawk, Yellow-billed Cuckoo, three or four kinds of woodpeckers, Yellow-throated Vireo, Black-and-white and Kentucky Warblers, Louisiana Waterthrush, and Summer Tanager. By veering off the marked trail, keeping more-or-less alongside the Little Maumelle River, you'll soon reach a railroad bridge. Swainson's Warbler has been heard in the undergrowth near here in migration.

Return to State Highway 300, turn right, and drive 0.7 mile to a turnoff on your left to the Little Rock Water Works area at the Lake Maumelle dam, an excellent winter birding location. On your left just after the turnoff is a little cove where you may find Pied-billed Grebe and Hooded

Pinnacle Mountain State Park near Little Rock is home to what are almost certainly the easternmost Rufous-crowned Sparrows in the United States. Greater Roadrunners hunt lizards on the mountain's rocky slopes. *Photo by Mel White.*

Merganser in winter and Great Blue Heron and Belted Kingfisher all year. American Woodcocks have been seen in courtship flight in the open area on the left just beyond the cove. A little farther on, at the dam parking lot, scan the main body of the lake. In late fall, winter, and early spring you may see Common Loon, Horned Grebe, Lesser Scaup, Common Goldeneye, Red-breasted Merganser, and Ring-billed Gull; Bufflehead is common. Small flocks of Franklin's Gulls stop to feed in October. Scan the tall pines around the shoreline for Bald Eagles. (The state park offers eagle-watching barge tours in January.) In 1992 a pair of eagles built a nest on the lake; they've returned to it each year since, though breeding hasn't been verified. Rarities seen here have included Red-throated Loon, Western and Eared Grebes, Oldsquaw (three in early 1994), and White-winged and Black Scoters. You'll need a scope, because the ducks can be far out on the lake. Any time of year, Eastern Bluebird, Pine Warbler, and Chipping Sparrow are common around the parking lot, and Brown-headed Nuthatch is occasionally seen, as are Pine Siskins in winter. Cliff Swallows nest on the big waterworks structures between the parking lot and the dam. If you need to, you can walk out onto the earthen dam itself, or the pine-covered peninsula between the cove and the main lake, to get better views of waterbirds. Western Kingbird has been seen on the dam, and Fox Sparrows are common in the bushes below in winter. Also check the feeders in front of the waterworks manager's house.

Return to State Highway 300, turn left, drive 0.2 mile, and turn right onto Pinnacle Valley Road. Watch along this road for nesting Loggerhead Shrike. Watch on the left for a gate leading to a small pond where Wood Ducks, and possibly Hooded Mergansers, breed in nest boxes. Continue 1.1 miles to a parking lot on the right and the Arkansas Arboretum, where an easy paved trail winds through mixed woodland; Red-shouldered Hawk has nested here. Interpretive signs provide a fine introduction to Arkansas's natural divisions and identify many common trees and shrubs.

Back on Pinnacle Valley Road, it's 0.6 mile to a turnoff on your left leading uphill to the Pinnacle Mountain State Park visitor center. Here you can pick up maps of the park and its hiking trails, talk to a park naturalist, check out the feeding stations, and see interesting natural-history displays. Ruby-throated Hummingbirds keep the feeders busy in the summer and fall. During migration it's sometimes worthwhile to climb up to the observation deck overlooking the Arkansas and Big Maumelle rivers; a short trail begins at the visitor center parking lot. In spring and fall you might see American White Pelicans or Ospreys flying along the river. Double-crested Cormorants and Bald Eagles are present from fall through early spring. If you hit the right day in late September, you can catch a migrating flock of Broad-winged Hawks. Here, as elsewhere around the park, there are infrequent but regular sightings of Sharp-shinned and Cooper's Hawks from late summer through spring.

Continue east on Pinnacle Valley Road 1.9 miles and turn left into Maumelle Park, a Corps of Engineers camping area that's very busy on summer weekends. It's worth checking out the tall Cottonwoods in the campsites near the Arkansas River for Red-headed Woodpecker (year-round) and Warbling Vireo and Northern Oriole (breeding). The short, paved Nuttall Nature Trail off the parking lot at the entrance is a pleasant walk that may turn up something good in migration.

Leave Maumelle Park and drive straight south on Pinnacle Valley Road 0.8 mile to a stop sign (note this spot); turn right and drive 1.6 miles to State Highway 10. Turn left to return to Little Rock. In winter, it can be productive to turn right and check out more of Lake Maumelle. Two marinas, at 9.5 and 11.7 miles west from the Pinnacle Valley Road/Highway 10 intersection, provide lookout points for scanning the lake for ducks, loons, eagles, and gulls. In between, at 11.0 miles, is a small picnic area that makes another good observation site. There's another picnic area just before the bridge at the west end of the lake, 3.1 miles from the second marina entrance. Cliff Swallows nest under the bridge, and the woods around the parking area can be productive.

For future reference: at the stop sign noted above on Pinnacle Valley Road, turn left and drive 1.8 miles on County Farm Road; turn right to a dead end. (Don't ignore birding on the way; Sandhill Crane and Yellow-headed Blackbird have been seen along this road.) The area beyond the road's end, known as Sullivan's Island (though it's not an island but a peninsula where the Little Maumelle River meets the Arkansas River) will be the site of a Little Rock city nature park, in the planning stage at this writing. Grassland, old fields, wetlands, and woods make it an excellent birding location, good for everything from rails and ducks (a Garganey was once found here) to woodpeckers, wrens (Sedge and Marsh in winter), and sparrows (Le Conte's and Sharp-tailed have been seen). Check with local birders or the Little Rock Parks Department (371-4770) for current access to the site; it's well worth a visit.

For information on Pinnacle Mountain State Park, write 11901 Pinnacle Valley Road, Roland, AR 72135, or call 868-5806.

10. Scott and Faulkner Lake Area

Location: *From the intersection of Interstates 40 and 440 in Little Rock, drive east on I-40 1.6 miles and take the Galloway exit (State Highway 391); go south 0.7 mile to U.S. Highway 70, cross it, and continue south on State Highway 391. (See map on page 33.)*

This route, east of Little Rock in the farming country of the Delta, passes through wetlands where herons, shorebirds, and ducks are present at the right times of year. It also includes the most reliable spot near Little Rock for breeding Bell's Vireo, and a possible site for Least Bittern and Purple Gallinule.

Just south of U.S. Highway 70 on 391 is Hill Lake, a beautiful cypress-lined lake that occasionally hosts Double-crested Cormorants or Wood Ducks. One-half mile from Highway 70 you will come to a wet area in the middle of the surrounding fields that ranges seasonally from a large puddle to a good-sized pond. Check it for shorebirds, ducks, and waders; Snowy Egret, Tricolored Heron, and Black-bellied Plover have been seen here.

Drive 1.5 miles from this spot and cross a small bridge. The marshy area on your right, covered in summer with blooming Fragrant Water-Lily, has in recent years had breeding Pied-billed Grebe, Least Bittern, Purple Gallinule, and Common Moorhen. Unfortunately, human disturbance and encroaching vegetation (almost eliminating open water) seem to have discouraged these species; all have become scarce, if they're still present at all. Morning light is best; stay on the road.

Continue south on 391 to a stop sign, then drive 1.2 miles farther to U.S. Highway 165. Turn left and drive 1.2 miles to a road on your right marked Terry Lock and Dam. On the opposite side of the highway here is a small lake with dead trees where Double-crested Cormorants roost by the hundreds in spring and fall. Scan it from a road beside the bait shop opposite the turnoff.

On the road toward the dam (officially Col. Maynard Road), watch for Bobolinks in May in the ripening fields of winter wheat (this advice applies anywhere in this area, for that matter). Loggerhead Shrikes are common breeders. Some 2.0 miles from U.S. Highway 165, a road on the right leads to Willow Beach, a Corps of Engineers recreation area heavily used by anglers and picnickers. (This area may be closed in winter.) Check out the marshy areas on both sides of the entrance road for Green Heron and Prothonotary Warbler (breeding), and Wood Duck and Red-headed Woodpecker (all year). Once inside the recreation area,

Dickcissel
Louise Zemaitis

follow the road as it winds past a pond on your left; Wood Ducks are sometimes seen here, along with waders. In summer, Northern Orioles sing from the tall trees, and Scissor-tailed Flycatchers perch atop roadside shrubs. Turn left at a sign indicating the picnic area. A fishing pier on the right is a good place from which to scan for American White Pelican, Osprey, and Caspian Tern during migration.

Continue through the picnic area to a turnaround at the dead end. Park near here and investigate the brushy areas beside the road back toward the entrance. Several pairs of Bell's Vireos breed here each year; listen for their scratchy, emphatic song. By looking closely, you should be able to find a singing male perched in one of the low trees; if not, they respond quickly to pishing, popping up to take a look and then disappearing into the foliage again. Painted Bunting breeds regularly here, too, but is harder to find. If you hear one, you may have to wade through the grass to find it. (*Spray your legs, pants, and socks with insect repellent.*) Northern Bobwhite, Common Yellowthroat, Yellow-breasted Chat, Blue Grosbeak, Indigo Bunting, and Orchard Oriole are common. Male American Woodcocks perform their mating flights here at dusk in very early spring.

Return to the main road and turn right toward Terry Lock and Dam on the Arkansas River, 3.2 miles farther on. Dickcissels are abundant in breeding season, often seen on the telephone wires. It goes without saying, since we are in eastern Arkansas, that Red-winged Blackbirds are abundant, too—unless we can think of another word that implies something far beyond mere abundance.

Near the dam are wet areas where you may find herons, egrets, or ducks; the dam itself attracts cormorants and gulls in winter. An Oldsquaw showed up recently in a mixed flock of ducks that included more than 100 Canvasbacks. Cliff Swallows breed on the dam.

From here you can continue east to the Lonoke area (see site #6).

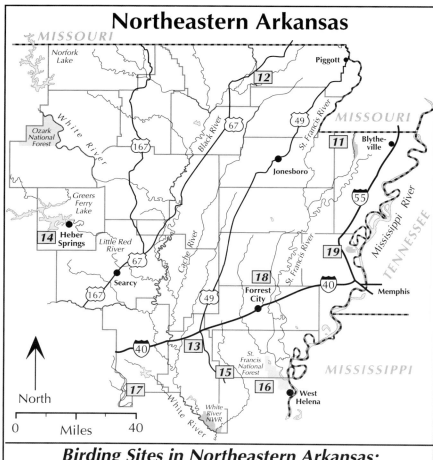

Northeastern Arkansas

MISSOURI

Norfork Lake

Piggott

12

Black River

67

49

St. Francis River

MISSOURI

Ozark National Forest

White River

167

11 Blythe-ville

Jonesboro

55

TENNESSEE

Mississippi River

Greers Ferry Lake

14 Heber Springs

Little Red River

67

Cache River

St. Francis River

19

Searcy

18 Forrest City

40

Memphis

167

49

40

13

St. Francis National Forest

MISSISSIPPI

15

16 West Helena

↑ North

17

White River NWR

0 — Miles — 40

Birding Sites in Northeastern Arkansas:

11 Big Lake National Wildlife Refuge

12 Black River Wildlife Management Area

13 Dagmar Wildlife Management Area

14 Greers Ferry Lake

15 Louisiana Purchase State Park

16 St. Francis National Forest

17 Stuttgart Airport

18 Village Creek State Park

19 Wapanocca National Wildlife Refuge

NORTHEASTERN ARKANSAS

N ortheastern Arkansas includes parts of three of the state's natural divisions: the eastern segment and foothills of the Ozark Mountains; a large part of the Mississippi Alluvial Plain; and nearly all of the unique highland called Crowley's Ridge. It's a region of rivers, too, drained by the Mississippi, the St. Francis, the L'Anguille, the White, Bayou De View, the Cache, the Black, the Spring, the Strawberry, and the Little Red, among others.

Much of the Delta in northeastern Arkansas has been drained, deforested, and given over to agriculture; in Mississippi County, for instance, only 5 percent of the original woodland still stands. Former meandering creeks and sloughs have been replaced by canals with evocative names like Ditch 28 and Ditch 81. In breeding season, Delta farmland is virtually an avian desert, supporting mostly Dickcissel and Red-winged Blackbird. In winter, though, large flocks of geese and ducks may feed in rice and soybean fields. Good bottomland forest remains along some rivers and in places such as Big Lake and Wapanocca National Wildlife Refuges and Black River Wildlife Management Area, where waterfowl winter in tremendous numbers. Here Wood Duck and Hooded Merganser nest, along with Barred Owl, Red-headed Woodpecker, and Prothonotary Warbler. Osprey and Tree Swallow also breed, although in much smaller numbers, and in recent years Big Lake has hosted successful Bald Eagle nestings. The new Cache River National Wildlife Refuge, not yet developed for visitors, will protect part of a bottomland hardwood ecosystem that has been called the most important wintering area for Mallards in the world.

Rising 200 feet above the flat Delta surrounding it, Crowley's Ridge is an Arkansas geological anomaly. It had its beginning many thousands of years ago, when the Mississippi River flowed much farther west, roughly along the path of today's Black and White Rivers. At that time, the Ohio River flowed approximately where the Mississippi does today. As the rivers slowly meandered and changed course, they swept away the deposits left by the ancient sea that once covered the area, except along a thin strip of land between them. This highland area later picked up a covering of fine, wind-blown soil called loess, which in places along the lower ridge is fifty feet deep. The effects of erosion on loess are easily seen in many spots, including the old Military Road in Village Creek State Park.

Crowley's Ridge (its name comes from that of a pioneer family in the area) today is covered by a hardwood forest that has more in common with the eastern United States than with the rest of Arkansas. It is the only place in the state where Tuliptree (also known as Tulip Poplar, Tulip Magnolia, and Yellow Poplar) grows naturally. Beech, Butternut (White Walnut), Sugar Maple, Pennywort, and Climbing Magnolia are other interesting plant species found here. Birders visiting the St. Francis National Forest may find breeding Swainson's and Worm-eating Warblers on the moist slopes of the ridge.

Part of Arkansas's Grand Prairie area also lies within this section of the state. Remnants of the once-extensive grassland can be found along an abandoned railroad right-of-way adjacent to U.S. Highway 70 between Carlisle and DeValls Bluff, as well as at Roth Prairie (site #56).

Travelers with only a short time in the region will find good wetland and bottomland birding at Wapanocca National Wildlife Refuge, just minutes from Interstate 55 north of Memphis, and Dagmar Wildlife Management Area, just south of Interstate 40 near Brinkley. Village Creek State Park, eleven miles north of Interstate 40, has good hiking trails and woodland birding.

11. Big Lake National Wildlife Refuge

Location: *Take the Burdette exit (Exit 57) from Interstate 55 six miles south of Blytheville. Go west on State Highway 148 for 5.7 miles to State Highway 181; turn right and drive 2.2 miles to State Highway 18. Turn left and drive 3.7 miles to the refuge entrance. (From the west, begin at the intersection of State Highways 77 and 18 at Manila and drive east on State Highway 18 for 1.9 miles to the entrance.) (See map on page 50.)*

Big Lake is an 11,000-acre national wildlife refuge extending for 10.5 miles from State Highway 18 north to the Missouri border. As large as it is, it is only a small remnant of the "Great Swamp" that once covered a huge area of northeast Arkansas. Beginning in the late 19th century, drainage plans turned nearly all of this wetland, once one of the most biologically productive ecosystems in the world, into cropland, and allowed the leveling of the great bottomland hardwood forest that once stretched endlessly across the Mississippi Alluvial Plain. Public concern about the disappearance of forest and wildlife moved President Woodrow Wilson to establish a refuge here in 1915, protecting an important tract of open water, cypress swamp, and seasonally flooded bottomland hardwoods.

Today, Big Lake's most important function is as a wintering area for waterfowl, with up to one million ducks and geese using it for feeding and roosting. As many as 90 per cent of these birds may be Mallards, but several other species are common at times, including Canada Goose, Green-winged Teal, Northern Pintail, Blue-winged Teal, Northern Shoveler, Gadwall, American Wigeon, Ring-necked Duck, Lesser Scaup, and Ruddy Duck. There are lesser numbers of Greater White-fronted and Snow Geese, Canvasback, Redhead, Common Goldeneye, Bufflehead, and Red-breasted Merganser, among other species.

A good place from which to see wintering waterfowl is Timm's Point, where an observation area overlooks the water. To reach it, follow the tour route from the headquarters along a levee on the west side of Big Lake 3.2 miles to a boat-launching ramp. Look out over swampy places and open water as you drive; in late summer and fall herons and egrets can be common in shallow water.

Wood Ducks breed throughout the refuge in natural tree cavities and nest boxes, with thousands of young produced each year. Hooded Mergansers also utilize nest boxes in smaller numbers, but breeding birds are usually not easy to see.

Site 11: **Big Lake National Wildlife Refuge**

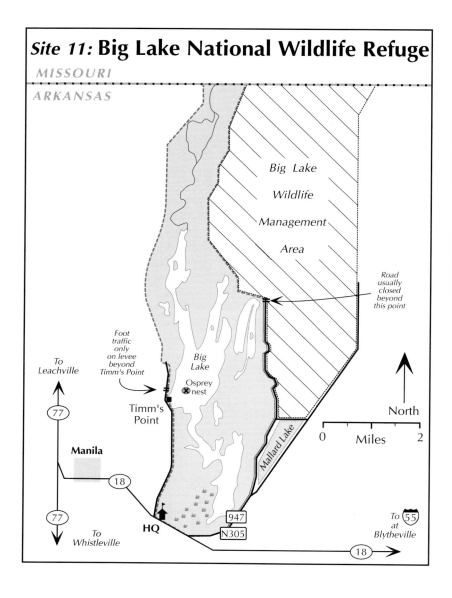

MISSOURI

ARKANSAS

Big Lake
Wildlife
Management
Area

Road
usually
closed
beyond
this point

Foot
traffic
only
on levee
beyond
Timm's Point

To
Leachville

Big
Lake

77

Osprey
nest

North

Timm's
Point

0   Miles   2

Manila

Mallard Lake

18

77

947

To 55
at
Blytheville

To
Whistleville

HQ

N305

18

Big Lake is known for recent nesting attempts by both Ospreys and Bald Eagles, neither of which had bred in Arkansas for decades before the 1980s. The first known nesting effort by Bald Eagles after that hiatus came at Big Lake in 1980; since then, there have been several other attempts here, but none was known to be successful until April 1993, when three young were hatched. The nest was visible from Timm's Point toward the east-southeast, at the far treeline. Bald Eagles are fairly common around Big Lake in winter.

Osprey nests have been found at Big Lake beginning in 1982, at first without evidence of success, later with several young fledged. In recent years, an active nest could be seen from Timm's Point on a small cypress tree about a quarter-mile out in the open water. Although Timm's Point is a popular boat-launching area and fishermen motor by many times a day, the birds nevertheless manage to go about their domestic business.

Tree Swallow, a species that has fairly recently begun breeding in small numbers in Arkansas, nests in cavities in dead trees at Big Lake. In fact, the Ospreys at Timm's Point are often harassed by Tree Swallows as they fly to and from their nest.

Like White River National Wildlife Refuge farther south, Big Lake is not easily explored without a boat. As much as 99 percent of the refuge is flooded during spring high water, so land birding is limited to the vicinity of roads. Although the west levee road is closed to vehicles beyond Timm's Point, birders are welcome to walk it. This makes access less convenient, but it eliminates the noise and dust of passing cars and trucks. Roadside birds here are much the same as those at other eastern Arkansas swamplands. Common breeders include Red-shouldered Hawk; Wild Turkey; Yellow-billed Cuckoo; Barred Owl; Belted King-fisher; Red-headed, Red-bellied, Downy, and Pileated Woodpeckers; Eastern Phoebe; Wood Thrush; White-eyed and Red-eyed Vireos; Northern Parula; Yellow-throated, Prothonotary, and Kentucky Warblers; Common Yellowthroat; Yellow-breasted Chat; Summer Tanager; and Orchard and Northern Orioles.

Another good birding road follows a levee on the east side of Big Lake, between the NWR and the adjoining state wildlife management area. Return to State Highway 18 and drive east 0.7 mile to a gravel road variously marked Mallard Lake, Game and Fish Road 947, and County Road N305. The shallow, swampy wetland just northwest of this turn can be excellent for wintering waterfowl. Stop almost immediately and park out of anyone's way; cross a small bridge on the left and walk out toward the open water (carry a scope) to see ducks and eagles.

Continue on this road past a collection of decrepit-looking fishing cabins. Just 1.9 miles from State Highway 18 you'll arrive at Mallard Lake, a Game and Fish Commission lake where Ospreys nested in 1984, marking the first successful breeding in Arkansas in at least 30 years. Hunting is prohibited on Mallard Lake, so it can have abundant waterfowl in winter. Bald Eagles are common winter residents.

Turn left here and circle the lake to a junction in 1.7 miles; turn left. (You can also get to this junction by turning right at the lake, left in 1.9 miles, and continuing 0.4 mile; turn right.) This road continues northward to a dead end in about three miles. (Cars cannot go beyond this point, but it is possible to explore on foot for some miles.) Stops along the road can be excellent for spring warblers and other migrants.

Notes about two special birds: the first nest of Bachman's Warbler ever found was located in the St. Francis River bottoms near here in 1897, and the bird was once thought to be "moderately common" in the lowlands of northeastern Arkansas (this was around the turn of the century). Several serious, but unsuccessful, attempts have been made recently to find this critically endangered (if not already extinct) bird at Big Lake. Only a tiny flicker of hope remains for the Bachman's Warbler, but—who knows?—you could be the one to rediscover it.

More recently, Big Lake was a known nesting location for King Rail, but this bird has steadily declined in Arkansas since the 1950s. Habitat destruction and (probably) pesticide contamination have played a part in the bird's virtual disappearance as a breeder in the state. It is not known to have nested at Big Lake for many years, and is seen only rarely.

For information about Big Lake, write Box 67, Manila, AR 72442, or call 564-2429.

12. Black River Wildlife Management Area

Location: *From the intersection of U.S. Highway 67 and State Highway 304 south of Pocahontas, drive east on 304 for 11.5 miles to a Black River WMA sign on the right and a gravel road on the left (County Road 101, which may not be marked as such); turn here. At 1.0 mile from the highway, continue right on 101 where the road forks. In 0.4 mile, turn left into the Lake Ashbaugh parking lot. (See map on page 54.)*

The flat farmland of northeastern Arkansas can seem endless to a traveler on one of the ruler-straight highways through the Delta; fringes of trees along streams often have *No Trespassing* signs. A good cure for this kind of birding frustration is to visit the Black River Wildlife Management Area, at nearly 22,000 acres the second-largest WMA in Arkansas (after Bayou Meto, site #47). The bottomland forest teems with typical swamp breeders in summer and ducks in winter.

The Arkansas Game and Fish Commission's wildlife management areas provide interesting, and often underutilized, birding resources. At Black River, the major complication is access. Most of the area is flooded in winter to provide habitat for tens of thousands of ducks; come spring, when birders get the urge to hit the woods, much of it is still under water.

Lake Ashbaugh, a 525-acre reservoir on the southern edge of the WMA, is accessible and worth a visit at all times. Duck hunting isn't allowed on Ashbaugh, so it can be excellent for all the regular dabblers from late fall through spring; Wood Ducks nest and are always common. Bald Eagles winter, feeding on sick and injured ducks. One local resident has seen as many as 28 eagles roosting in trees here at one time; he adds that "the colder it is, the better" for seeing concentrations of both eagles and ducks. Late afternoon is best for waterfowl; their sheer numbers usually keep the shallow lake from freezing over completely, even in extreme weather.

Ospreys stop at Ashbaugh in spring and fall, and the latter season also brings post-breeding waders such as Great and Snowy Egrets and Little Blue Heron. Great Blue Herons are always present, and Green Herons skulk around the lake edges in breeding season. Red-headed Woodpeckers love the standing dead timber. Tree Swallows gather in fall in huge numbers, and, though no one seems to have checked, they quite possibly breed here in old woodpecker holes in the snags.

Scan the lake from the parking lot, then return to County Road 101 and turn left. In 1.1 miles, turn left onto a road that may be marked 103. This road soon parallels the water's edge, providing more views of the

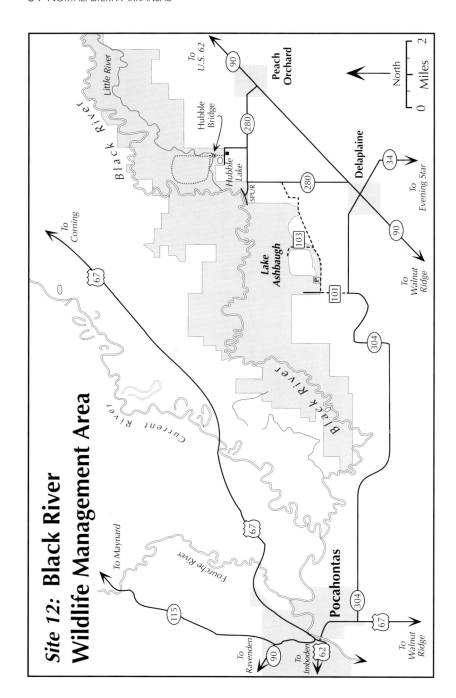

Site 12: Black River Wildlife Management Area

lake. Bell's Vireos breed in the bushes here, and Dickcissels and Field Sparrows sing nearby. There's a parking lot and boat ramp at a dead end in 0.9 mile, with access to the lake and down into the Black River bottoms.

Return to County Road 101 and turn left; in 2.4 miles you'll come to paved State Highway 280. Along the way in winter, the adjoining fields may have flocks of geese: Greater White-fronted (uncommon), Snow, and Canada. Turn left onto State Highway 280; turn right in 1.1 miles where Spur 280 joins from the left. In 1.0 mile, turn left onto a paved road where a sign marks another entrance to the WMA. In 1.0 mile you'll reach the area; the manager's house, on the left, may have dozens of Ruby-throated Hummingbirds around its feeders in late summer. (People who've worked in the Black River bottoms say they've seen more hummers here than anyplace else they've ever been.)

The wooden Hubble Bridge here provides access to the interior of the WMA during summer and fall; in winter and spring, the bottomland beyond is flooded. The water usually recedes enough to allow auto traffic in May, though it varies from year to year. In late spring, muddy foot travel is sometimes possible even when the road is still perilous for cars. If you do enter this swampy forest in breeding season, you'll find all the expected birds, including Green Heron; Wood Duck; Red-shouldered Hawk; Barred Owl (very common); Eastern Wood-Pewee; Acadian Flycatcher; White-breasted Nuthatch; White-eyed, Yellow-throated, and Red-eyed Vireos; Prothonotary Warbler; and Indigo Bunting. Yellow-billed Cuckoo and Red-headed Woodpecker are present in truly astounding numbers. Wild Turkey is uncommon and elusive. Mosquitoes are abundant and impossible to ignore.

Some 0.2 mile after crossing the bridge, you'll come to a T junction. Turn left here and you can make a four-mile loop drive on a slightly raised levee. (If you turn right to start the loop, stay left where the road splits in 0.5 mile.) The dirt road is usually dry and passable in summer, but watch for bad spots; it could be a long trudge back to phone for a tow. You'll be in excellent bottomland-hardwood forest all the way, constantly alongside streams and sloughs.

A road to the left between the manager's house and Hubble Bridge runs 0.2 mile to diminutive Hubble Lake, an area often accessible even when the road beyond the bridge is flooded. The lake and the marshy area to the left of the road are worth checking for ducks and waders.

In winter and spring, the fields north and east of Black River can have enormous flocks of geese. To investigate, return to State Highway 280 and turn left toward Peach Orchard, two miles away. There, turn left on Highway 90 and watch for geese in the roadside cropland.

13. Dagmar Wildlife Management Area

Location: *Coming from the west, leave Interstate 40 at State Highway 33, just east of the White River. Drive south 1.9 miles to U.S. Highway 70, then east 7 miles to the entrance road. Coming from the east, leave Interstate 40 at U.S. Highway 49 (Brinkley). Drive south 1.4 miles to U.S. Highway 70, then west 7.4 miles to the entrance road.*

Dagmar is an 8,000-acre hunting and fishing area owned by the state Game and Fish Commission. Its proximity to Interstate 40 provides an excellent opportunity for travelers, even those who don't have much time, to experience a real east Arkansas bottomland forest. Dagmar is very wet nearly all year; much of it may be flooded in winter for ducks, and high water in spring may close roads in the area as well. The extent of flooding varies from year to year.

The 1.3-mile road from U.S. Highway 70 to the gate passes through wet woods where Red-headed Woodpeckers, Great Crested Flycatchers, and Prothonotary Warblers are common. Stop anywhere along here to look and listen. Just before you reach the WMA gate, a large field opens up on your right. This is often flooded in the spring and can attract shorebirds and ducks; the uncommon American Black Duck has been seen here, and a   Tricolored Heron showed up during one recent

Dagmar Wildlife Management Area. *Photo by A.C. Haralson, courtesy of Arkansas Department of Parks and Tourism.*

September. Most shorebirds will be common species like yellowlegs and Pectoral and Spotted Sandpipers, but other interesting types could appear. Scan the trees around the perimeter for Red-tailed and Red-shouldered Hawks.

The entrance gate is just past an abandoned railroad track. Even if the wildlife area is closed because of flooding, you can walk along the raised rail-bed in either direction and see (in breeding season) Green Heron, Yellow-billed Cuckoo, Northern Parula, Prothonotary and Kentucky Warblers, Common Yellowthroat, Yellow-breasted Chat, Summer Tanager, and Indigo Bunting.

Once in the wildlife area and past the administration buildings, stop at a fork in the road and walk to the right for a hundred yards or so. Return to your car, take the left road, and continue north under elevated Interstate 40. This is a dead-end road that passes for several miles through swampy woods and past bayous and lakes. Stop anywhere that looks good. Dagmar is great for migrant vireos and warblers. In spring and summer, you'll almost never be out of earshot of singing Wood Thrushes, Prothonotary Warblers, and Orchard Orioles. Other common birds include (all year) Wood Duck, Barred Owl, Red-bellied and Pileated Woodpeckers, Fish Crow, Carolina Chickadee, Tufted Titmouse, and Carolina Wren, and (breeding) Ruby-throated Hummingbird, Eastern Wood-Pewee, Acadian Flycatcher, Eastern Phoebe, Blue-gray Gnatcatcher, White-eyed and Red-eyed Vireos, and Northern Oriole.

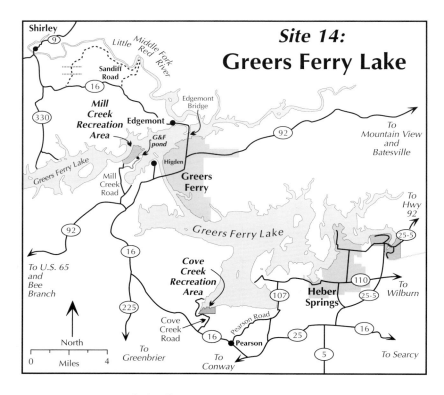

Site 14:
Greers Ferry Lake

14. Greers Ferry Lake

Location: *Begin at the junction of State Highways 25-5 and 110 just east of the town of Heber Springs.*

Greers Ferry Lake is a sprawling, 40,000-acre reservoir in the foothills of the Ozark Mountains of north-central Arkansas, just north of the tourist town of Heber Springs. The cold tailwaters of the Little Red River below the dam attract fishermen from all over the country in search of monsters like the 40-pound (!) Brown Trout that was caught here in May 1992. Above the dam, bass, and walleye are favorite game fish; summer brings hordes of water-skiers.

For birders, the attractions at Greers Ferry are the same as those at most of the big Corps of Engineers lakes in Arkansas: winter loons, grebes, ducks, and Bald Eagles. Get a Corps map (Resident Engineer, P.O. Box 1088, Heber Springs, AR 72543; 362-2416), head for one of the shoreline recreation areas, and scope the lake. The most-seen species will be

Common Loon, Pied-billed and Horned Grebes, Lesser Scaup, and Bufflehead, but with this much open water the possibilities are endless. The following route will serve as an introduction to local birding in all seasons, including some interesting breeding warblers.

From the intersection of State Highways 25-5 and 110, drive south on State Highway 25 0.7 mile and turn left toward the Heber Springs sewer ponds. Park on the old road above the ponds to scan for winter ducks and gulls. Lesser Scaup, Common Goldeneye, and Ring-billed Gull are common; Common Merganser has been seen.

Return to the highway junction and turn right (east). Drive 3.8 miles, turn left onto a dirt road (Hays Road) opposite the Sovereign Grace Baptist Church, and continue 0.5 mile to a sharp left turn. The small lake here has hosted both Trumpeter and Tundra Swans in recent winters (eight Trumpeters were present in December 1994). The Trumpeters, probably from stock introduced in attempts to reestablish breeding populations at midwestern wildlife refuges, sometimes even vocalize. Assorted ducks, including Common Goldeneye and Hooded Merganser, winter here as well. Bald Eagle and Wild Turkey have been seen. This is private property; do not cross the fence to view the lake.

Return to the 25-5/110 junction and turn right (north) on State Highway 25-5. Drive 1.9 miles to the Corps of Engineers visitor center on the right. Stop here and pick up a lake map. The Mossy Bluff Trail is a pleasant walk with good views down into the steep Little Red River valley. Pine Warblers are permanent residents. If you don't care to walk it (1.7 miles to the end and back), drive 0.8 mile to the observation point at the end of the road, where you can see hundreds of vultures (mostly Turkey, with a few Blacks) coming to roost at dusk in winter.

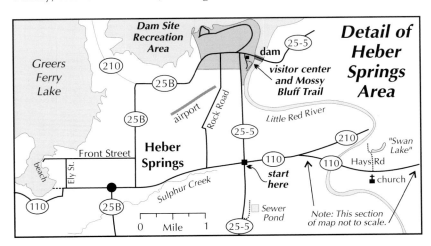

Greers Ferry Lake. *Photo courtesy of Arkansas Department of Parks and Tourism.*

Go back to State Highway 25-5, turn left, and in 0.1 mile turn right onto State Highway 25B. After 0.5 mile, turn right into the Dam Site recreation area, drive 0.4 mile, and turn left toward a camping area with a good view of the lake. Scan here for winter waterbirds and eagles.

Back on State Highway 25B, turn right toward Heber Springs and drive 2.5 miles to Front Street. Turn right and drive 1.5 miles to a small beach area that is a particularly good place for wintering Common Loon and Horned Grebe (sometimes 30 or more at one time). Return to State Highway 25B , turn right, and drive 0.5 mile to State Highway 110; turn right and follow it through town 1.2 miles to a road that continues straight to the lake, where State Highway 110 turns left. Check the lake again from here and return to State Highway 110.

Turn right and drive 2.5 miles to State Highway 107; turn left, drive 2.4 miles to Pearson Road, and turn right. Follow it 2.7 miles to State Highway 16. Turn right, drive 1.8 miles to Cove Creek Road, turn right again, and drive 1.7 miles to the Cove Creek recreation area, a fine all-around birding spot.

The view of the lake is particularly wide here; bear right toward the turnaround at camping Area C for a good lookout post. Migrant Osprey and terns (Caspian and Forster's are most common) are seen regularly, and southbound hawks follow the ridgeline to the left in late September and October. The shrubby broomsedge fields near Area C are good for winter sparrows, and the wooded hillsides can be full of warblers in the spring.

Go back to State Highway 16, turn right, and drive 8.9 miles to State Highway 92. Turn left, drive 0.4 mile, and turn right onto Mill Creek Road. Follow it 2.3 miles to a dirt road where the paved road makes a left turn. Drive down the dirt road 1.0 mile to a Game and Fish Commission nursery pond on the left. A very lost Pacific Loon showed up here in 1991; while the odds of this happening again are admittedly low, some good ducks usually winter here, and Sedge Wren has been found in nearby vegetation. Hooded Merganser nests, and Yellow Warbler is suspected of doing so.

Return to Mill Creek Road. If you haven't had enough of scanning the lake by now, turn right and drive down to the Mill Creek recreation area. Otherwise, go back to State Highway 16.

In spring and summer, turn left here and follow State Highway 16 5.7 miles to the Edgemont Bridge, where Cliff Swallows nest. Continue over the bridge 5.0 miles to Sandiff Road on the right, just past a cemetery on the left. This dirt road is narrow, crooked, steep, and rutted, but it leads to a productive area for breeding warblers. Follow it down 2.4 miles to the Little Red River, and another 1.8 miles to a creek crossing. (It may be impassable in some conditions.) Cerulean Warbler, an elusive species in Arkansas, breeds in the riverside trees; you can see it by walking along the road and listening for its song, which sounds much like that of a Northern Parula. Continue past the bridge; the next stretch of road passes through woods with nesting Hooded Warblers and Ovenbirds. Just 0.7 mile past the bridge are old fields where Blue-winged and Prairie Warblers have nested, although recent clearing has hurt their habitat. This is quite an assemblage of good warblers, well worth the trouble to explore the area. American Woodcock also nests here, beginning its breeding displays long before spring. The road circles back uphill to State Highway 16, some 4.7 miles past the creek crossing. Ignore all crossing roads on the way.

15. Louisiana Purchase State Park

Location: *From Interstate 40 at Brinkley, take U.S. Highway 49 south for 21.1 miles to State Highway 362. Turn left (east) for 1.7 miles to a parking lot.*

This small state park and natural area has both historical and biological significance. In 1815, the original surveyors of the Louisiana Purchase established a zero point here from which townships and ranges of much of this vast new area of the United States were subsequently numbered. Over a century later, the original "witness trees" of the survey party were found, and the area was later set aside to commemorate this milestone in America's Manifest Destiny.

As it happens, the Louisiana Purchase park also preserves an example of an unusual "headwater" swamp. Unlike a typical low-country wetland, a headwater swamp keeps a fairly constant water level for most of the year. Because such areas are easy to drain and clear, few of them remain in Arkansas.

On the way to the park from U.S. Highway 49, check the marshy areas alongside State Highway 362. Such waders as Great Blue and Little Blue Herons and Great and Snowy Egrets are often seen here from spring through fall. Shorebirds are sometimes seen in migration. In 1993, a pair of Black-necked Stilts, a species that seems to be colonizing Arkansas, lingered here well into June.

A 950-foot boardwalk winds from the parking lot to a small stone monument, passing through a stand of Bald Cypress, Water Tupelo, Red Maple, and Swamp Cottonwood, the last an uncommon tree in Arkansas. As you walk here, imagine this kind of terrain stretching for miles in all directions; it's easy to see why eastern Arkansas was so disheartening to early travelers and settlers, and why it took so long to build a railroad from Memphis to Little Rock.

Perhaps because the park receives few visitors, or because the flooded woods provide some protection from predators, the birds here seem absurdly tame. Prothonotary Warblers are extremely common in spring and summer, nesting in holes in trees beside the boardwalk. They often seem to fly close to investigate walkers. In the still of the swamp, their *sweet-sweet-sweet-sweet* rings out like a trumpet call. Other common birds include (breeding) Yellow-billed Cuckoo, Acadian Flycatcher, Great Crested Flycatcher, Blue-gray Gnatcatcher, Northern Parula, and (all year) Red-bellied and Pileated Woodpeckers, Carolina Chickadee, Tufted Titmouse, and Carolina Wren. Listen, too, in spring

Louisiana Purchase State Park. *Photo by A.C. Haralson, courtesy of Arkansas Department of Parks and Tourism.*

for the rapid whistle of the uncommon Bird-voiced Treefrog (*Hyla avivoca*), which sounds like someone whistling for a dog.

Louisiana Purchase Monument is a good place to look for migrant passerines in spring and fall. The only drawback is that visitors are confined to the boardwalk; you can't leave the trail to chase after something interesting.

From Louisiana Purchase Monument it's a short drive to the northern section of the White River National Wildlife Refuge or the St. Francis National Forest (see sites #59 and #16).

Site 16: St. Francis National Forest

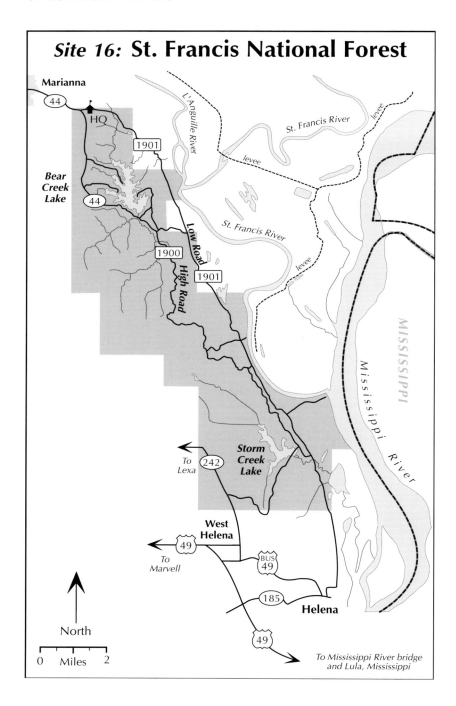

16. St. Francis National Forest

Location: *From Interstate 40 at Forrest City, drive south 19 miles on State Highway 1 to Marianna and take State Highway 1B. From the intersection of State Highways 1B and 44, drive east on 44 2.7 miles to the district ranger office.*

St. Francis is a midget compared with the state's other two national forests, Ouachita and Ozark, but it's like a little bit of woodland heaven in the midst of the denuded agricultural expanses of eastern Arkansas. The 21,000-acre national forest stretches for about 16 miles between the cities of Marianna and Helena along the southern end of Crowley's Ridge, the anomalous strip of high ground that runs from the Mississippi River up into Missouri. (See the introduction to the Northeastern Arkansas section for information about Crowley's Ridge.)

Stop at the ranger office for a map of the area and information on road conditions. Then continue southeast on State Highway 44 for 4.4 miles to Bear Creek Lake, where there's a short hiking trail good for a variety of birds. As you reach the dam, turn right down a dirt road marked "Overflow Camping" and park at its end, near an abandoned cabin. Walk straight ahead into the woods to a pair of wooden footbridges. Turn right and follow the trail, a loop of a little less than a mile. (The trail is also accessible from the main campground.) As you walk through the shady hollows of this dense hardwood forest, past tall oaks, hickories, American Beeches, and Tuliptrees, you'll find it hard to believe that just minutes earlier you were in the flat, deforested lowlands of the Mississippi Delta.

St. Francis has a good population of Wild Turkey, and in early summer you may surprise a hen and her young. Other breeding birds include Red-shouldered and Broad-winged Hawks, Yellow-billed Cuckoo, Eastern Wood-Pewee, Acadian and Great Crested Flycatchers, Eastern Phoebe, Wood Thrush, White-eyed and Red-eyed Vireos, Northern Parula, Louisiana Waterthrush, Kentucky Warbler, Summer Tanager, and Northern Oriole. Swainson's Warbler is not common, but listen for it in low areas with heavy undergrowth, especially where there are stands of cane. Cerulean and Worm-eating Warblers are also present as breeders, and are also uncommon.

Return to the highway, cross the dam, turn right, and follow the gravel road (Forest Service 1900, the "high road" through the forest) 11.8 miles to Storm Creek Lake. Stop anywhere you like to bird, concentrating on the low, swampy places. Side roads may be gated, but you can walk in

St. Francis National Forest. *Photo by Barrie Lynn Bryant, courtesy of Arkansas Department of Parks and Tourism.*

to explore areas away from the main route. (Note that the road sometimes passes through private property.) Red-headed Woodpecker is common throughout the forest, and if you're lucky you may scare up a Wild Turkey from the roadside. Because this is near the eastern boundary of Arkansas, certain migrant species are more likely here than elsewhere in the state, among them Veery and Palm and Blackpoll Warblers. Your chances are better here, too, of seeing such extreme rarities as Cape May, Black-throated Blue, and Connecticut Warblers.

As you reach the paved road at Storm Creek Lake, turn left down a dirt road to a T intersection with Forest Service Road 1901. This is the "low road" through the bottomland of the St. Francis and Mississippi Rivers, and it may occasionally be impassibly muddy in spring; use caution. Turn left or right and bird along the roadside; you may find different species here from those which you saw on the high road. The low road passes by wetlands areas where waders sometimes congregate in summer and fall; this is a possible spot for Anhinga. If you like, you can follow this road to the right (south) 5.0 miles into the historic old Mississippi River town of Helena. Or retrace your route back to Storm Creek Lake and turn left to West Helena or right back to Marianna.

For information on the St. Francis National Forest, write St. Francis Ranger District, Marianna, AR 72360, or call 295-5278.

Swainson's Warbler
David A. Sibley

17. Stuttgart Airport

Location: *From Interstate 40 at Hazen (Exit 193), take State Highway 11 south 2.6 miles to State Highway 70; drive east 0.9 mile and then south on State Highway 11 for 12.8 miles to the airport entrance on the west side of the highway. Alternatively, from U.S. Highways 165 and 79 in Stuttgart, take U.S. Highway 165, then State Highway 11 north 6.0 miles to the entrance.*

During World War II, a sprawling air base was built here in the isolated heart of Arkansas's Grand Prairie. Little of that operation is left today, except for the long, wide concrete runways. They're used mostly by small planes, although during the fall it's not unusual to see several private jets parked on the apron. Stuttgart bills itself as the "Duck Hunting Capital of the World," and high-rollers fly in from all directions to take Mallards in the nearby swamps and rice fields.

Birders visit the Stuttgart airport for winter grassland birds, especially longspurs, sparrows, and Short-eared Owls. One small area here is Arkansas's most reliable spot for Smith's Longspur, and the owls are common at times.

Note: birders have occasionally not been allowed near the runways. Recently a set of guidelines was agreed on to permit access. Before you bird the airport, check in at the small brick terminal building for permission, get a copy of the guidelines, read them, and obey them. Most importantly, stay out of the way of planes landing and taking off. Move away from the runway, and turn your back to it, to let the pilot know that you're not going to walk out in front of the airplane. Plane/pedestrian conflicts might terminate access to this productive area.

Check along the edges of the runways for Horned Larks and Savannah Sparrows, both common. Although not seen for many years, Sprague's Pipit has been found here in the past, and birders should always be alert to the possible presence of this very rare visitor.

By wading out through the taller grass between the runways, you may flush up a Short-eared Owl; quite possibly, you'll flush up a half-dozen or more. Most will fly around for a while and then drop back into the grass, but occasionally one will land in a bare area and allow a longer look. *Please don't chase the owls, or repeatedly flush the same bird.* Much more difficult to see well are Le Conte's Sparrows, which also flush in front of walkers but inevitably disappear into thick grass and run away. If one perches on a grass stalk, look quick: it may be the only chance you get. Also watch, and listen, for Sedge Wren in the tall grass.

Scan the fields surrounding the runways for longspurs; Lapland is the common species, but if you have the patience to sort through hundreds of birds, maybe you'll be the one who discovers a Chestnut-collared or a McCown's.

Smith's Longspur has regularly been found in a very small patch of *Aristida*, a three-awned grass, at the south terminus of the main north-south (0-36) runway. Look for this short, light-colored grass past the lights marking the end of the runway. Walk across the area slowly; it's sometimes hard to see the birds before they fly, but if you retreat quickly to the edge of the area and keep still, they may return. Often, though, they circle for a minute or so and then head off for parts unknown. Look for the males' prominent white wing patch and overall buffy color, and listen for the call note, like a Lapland Longspur's but with a subtly sharper and more metallic quality.

In early 1994, Smith's Longspurs were also found in a similar patch of grass at the far north end of the same runway. Check there if the birds aren't at the south end. Some birders suspect that the species may move farther south with extreme cold weather in midwinter.

Keep alert for other rarities here. Rough-legged Hawk is a rare but fairly regular winter visitor to this part of the state, and one winter a Burrowing Owl set up housekeeping in a hole in a disused runway. Other good birds seen here have included Say's Phoebe and Henslow's Sparrow.

Barn Owl has nested in various structures around the airport grounds, most recently in the last hangar south of the office, where a nest box has been set up.

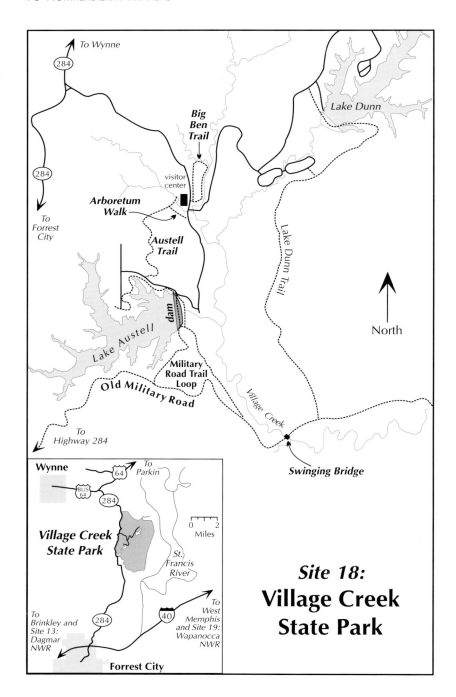

To Wynne

284

284

To Forrest City

Big Ben Trail

Lake Dunn

visitor center

Arboretum Walk

Austell Trail

Lake Dunn Trail

↑ North

dam

Lake Austell

Military Road Trail Loop

Old Military Road

Village Creek

To Highway 284

Swinging Bridge

Wynne

64

To Parkin

BUS 64

284

0   2
Miles

Village Creek State Park

St. Francis River

To Brinkley and Site 13: Dagmar NWR

284

40

To West Memphis and Site 19: Wapanocca NWR

Forrest City

Site 18:
Village Creek State Park

18. Village Creek State Park

Location: *From Interstate 40, take the State Highway 284 exit (Exit 242) just east of Forrest City and drive north 11.1 miles to the park entrance. Turn right and drive 1.0 mile to the visitor center.*

Village Creek is an excellent example of the beauty and unusual flora of Crowley's Ridge (see the introduction to the Northeastern Arkansas section). This 7,000-acre park, established in 1976, has good campsites, several housekeeping cabins, and hiking trails. Birds found here are mostly woodland species, although the park's lakes attract a few wintering ducks and an occasional migrant Osprey. Both Chuck-will's-widow and Whip-poor-will breed in this area of Crowley's Ridge.

Stop at the visitor center to pick up maps, a bird list, and a trail guide, and to examine displays interpreting the natural and cultural history of Crowley's Ridge. Just across the road is the start of the short (half-mile) Big Ben nature trail, an interesting walk beside the bank of Village Creek. As you begin, note how deeply erosion has cut into the fine wind-blown soil, called loess, that covers the ridge. Alas, Big Ben itself, a huge beech tree named for early settler Benjamin Crowley, was toppled by a storm some years ago, leaving a gaping hole in the forest canopy. Eastern Wood-Pewees whistle their thin little songs here, and Northern Parulas buzz from the treetops. The Arboretum Trail, an even shorter walk near the visitor center, identifies some of the park's trees and shrubs. Watch for Red-headed Woodpeckers on the telephone poles at the parking lot.

There's good birding along the Military Road trail, a 2.1-mile loop named for the first improved road between Memphis and Little Rock. From the visitor center, drive 0.8 mile to the parking lot at the Lake Austell boat-launching ramp, where the trail begins. When you reach the Lake Austell dam, take the lower path running below the embankment. (This section of the trail may be weedy and marshy, but persevere.) Indigo Bunting, Northern Oriole, and American Goldfinch breed near this open space. At the far end of the dam you'll enter a swampy area; look for Pileated Woodpecker, Wood Thrush, White-eyed Vireo, Prothonotary and Kentucky Warblers, and Louisiana Waterthrush. Most interesting, Swainson's Warbler has been found singing here and may breed. It has also been seen on the fitness trail near Lake Dunn.

If time is short, explore the next 200 yards of this trail and then return. Otherwise, walk to the intersection with the old Military Road. If you're lucky, you may find Wild Turkey; in any case, you'll see magnificent

Fine loess soil on Crowley's Ridge is highly susceptible to erosion, as here along the old Military Road at Village Creek State Park. *Photo by Mel White.*

American Beeches and Tuliptrees on the hogback ridges and, in season, a variety of wildflowers. Turn left and walk a short distance to the swinging bridge over Village Creek, then backtrack and return to the dam on Military Road. Over the years, erosion has sunk the pathway here several feet below the loess banks on both sides.

For information about Village Creek State Park, write Route 3, Box 49B, Wynne, AR 72396, or call 238-9406.

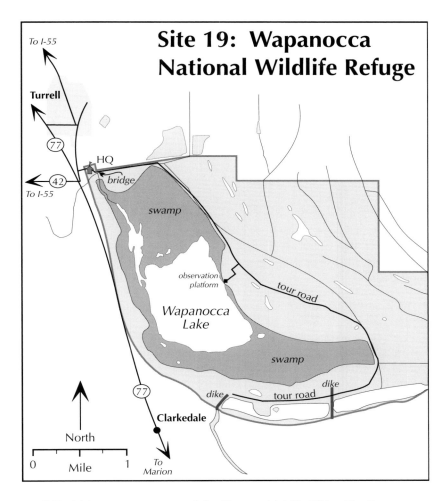

Site 19: Wapanocca National Wildlife Refuge

To I-55

Turrell

To I-55

77

42

HQ

bridge

swamp

observation platform

Wapanocca Lake

swamp

tour road

dike

tour road

dike

77

Clarkedale

North

0   Mile   1

To Marion

19. Wapanocca National Wildlife Refuge

Location: From Interstate 55, 14 miles north of West Memphis, take the Turrell (State Highway 42) exit. Drive east on State Highway 42 for 1.5 miles, across State Highway 77 and under a railroad bridge, to the refuge entrance.

Wapanocca National Wildlife Refuge is a convenient place (just two minutes from Interstate 55) for travelers to see breeding bottomland forest birds and wintering waterfowl. It was once a prestigious hunting club, and thus protected from the land clearing that has made it a 5,485-acre island of forest and wetlands surrounded by endless fields of rice, soybeans, and wheat. Today it's about one-third lake and other water, one-third forest (much of which is often flooded), and one-third farmland. Part of the crops grown here are left in the fields to feed Wapanocca's impressive winter populations of ducks and geese.

Stop at the visitor center for a bird list and road information, then pass through the gate onto the six-mile auto tour route. The area just past the bridge here can be excellent for spring migrants. Much of the drive is over levees with swamp on both sides of the road; watch in winter for dabbling ducks and year-round for Wild Turkey (listen for gobbling in early morning and late afternoon), Barred Owl, and Red-headed and Pileated Woodpeckers. Breeding birds include Acadian and Great Crested Flycatchers; Eastern Phoebe; Blue-gray Gnatcatcher; Wood Thrush; White-eyed and Red-eyed Vireos; Northern Parula; Yellow-throated, Prothonotary, and Kentucky Warblers; Summer Tanager; and Orchard and Northern Orioles. Wood Duck is a common breeder at Wapanocca. Smaller numbers of Hooded Mergansers are also present, using Wood Duck boxes as nesting cavities; they're hard to find in summer, easier the rest of the year.

During spring migration, look for such uncommon to rare (in Arkansas) species as Cape May, Black-throated Blue, Palm, and Blackpoll Warblers; all are more common in Arkansas the farther east you go, and Wapanocca is only about five miles from the Mississippi River. A Glaucous Gull appeared here in February 1995, and birders who visited

Bald Cypresses along the shoreline of Wapanocca Lake. *Photo by Mel White.*

Wapanocca looking for it found a flock of a dozen or more Palm Warblers.

When the road passes into cropland, look for breeding Horned Lark and wintering flocks of geese—mostly Canada, with smaller numbers of Snow (both morphs) and Greater White-fronted. Arkansas's first documented Brant was seen near Wapanocca in the company of grazing Canadas, so check flocks carefully. Dickcissel is common in grassy areas in summer, and Common Yellowthroat and Yellow-breasted Chat breed in scrubby spots. You may see Mississippi Kites sailing over the trees. Late summer brings numbers of waders to roadside wetlands, including Great Blue Heron (present year-round); Great, Snowy, and Cattle Egrets; and Little Blue and Green Herons. (In the early 1980s, a few Tricolored Herons bred at a heronry 35 miles north of here, but the species is not to be expected.) In winter, Northern Harrier, Red-tailed Hawk, and American Kestrel are common in open areas.

Except in summer, take the turnoff to 600-acre Wapanocca Lake to look for ducks, which can be abundant. Most will be Mallards, but the refuge bird list includes 20 other species; Ruddy Ducks are often very common. Canada Geese roost at the lake after feeding in nearby cropland by day. Look for wintering Bald Eagles in the big Bald Cypress trees around the lake, or on the ice when the lake freezes. Eagles once built a nest on the far side of the lake, but did not fledge young. According to local birder and butterfly enthusiast Norman Lavers, Arkansas's only known colony of Broad-winged Skippers is found near the observation platform here.

If you have time, go all the way to the end of the auto tour road, where a picturesque cypress-filled lake may have ducks and waders. From the parking pull-off, there is a poorly marked loop trail through the woods of about a mile following a line of Wood Duck nest sites. The road out to the end, however, is not a loop; turn around at the finish to return to the refuge entrance.

For information on Wapanocca, write Box 279, Turrell, AR 72384, or call 343-2595.

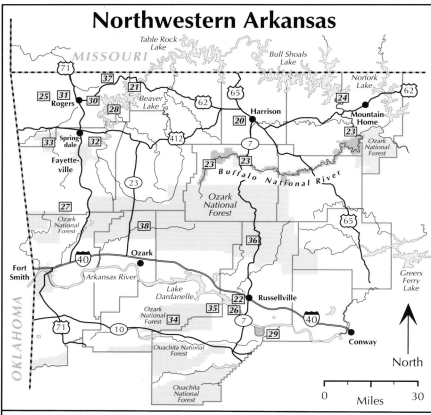

Northwestern Arkansas

Birding Sites in Northwestern Arkansas:

20	Baker Prairie Natural Area	30	Lake Atalanta
21	Beaver Lake	31	Lake Bentonville
22	Bona Dea Trails	32	Lake Fayetteville
23	Buffalo National River	33	Lake Wedington
24	Bull Shoals State Park Area	34	Magazine Mountain
25	Centerton State Fish Hatchery	35	Mount Nebo State Park
26	Dardanelle Dam	36	Page Hollow
27	Devil's Den State Park	37	Pea Ridge Nat'l Military Park
28	Hobbs State Management Area	38	Redding Recreation Area
29	Holla Bend Nat'l Wildlife Refuge		

NORTHWESTERN
ARKANSAS

To many people, northwestern Arkansas is synonymous with the Ozark Mountains, a rugged area of rounded hills and deep "hollers". The Ozarks, in geological terms an eroded plateau, are indeed the dominant physical feature of the region, but the birding sites listed here also include Arkansas River bottomland, America's first National River, sprawling man-made reservoirs, and even (surprisingly enough in this upland area) a local hotspot for migrant shorebirds.

As you might expect, there are differences in bird distribution between the northern Arkansas mountains and the flatlands of the south and east. House Wren (a common recent colonizer) and Blue-winged and Yellow Warblers (both uncommon) nest in the northwest, while some waders are much less often seen than in the southern part of the state. Great-tailed Grackle is invading the region from the west. Arkansas's only known breeding site for Willow Flycatcher is near Bentonville. Such western visitors as Swainson's Hawk, Prairie Falcon, Harris's Sparrow, Western Meadowlark, and Yellow-headed Blackbird, while uncommon to rare, are more likely to show up in the northwest, as is the case with more-northerly winter birds such as American Tree Sparrow (fairly common) and Common Redpoll (very rare).

Birders traveling along Interstate 40 can take State Highway 7 at Russellville to visit the Bona Dea trails, less than a mile from the freeway, for typical woodland birds and an interesting wetland area. Those with a little more time can drive twenty minutes or so to Holla Bend, one of Arkansas's best overall birding locations (especially in winter), or Mount Nebo, where Rufous-crowned Sparrow breeds.

A new metropolitan area is rapidly developing in the corner of Arkansas bordered by Missouri and Oklahoma. The cities of Fayetteville, Springdale, Rogers, and Bentonville are growing together along U.S. Highway 71 into one nearly continuous strip. Growth is relative, though, and even in this booming area it's easy to get away to fine birding spots. The Centerton State Fish Hatchery, operated by the Arkansas Game and Fish Commission, consistently produces good shorebirds on drained, muddy ponds in spring and fall. Beaver Lake offers an interesting variety of birds, both water and land species; and Devil's Den State Park is a beautiful location productive for spring migrants. Worm-eating Warbler can be found on moist hillsides in the Ozarks—and, as was proven recently, there are discoveries still to be made....

Arkansas birders were stunned in 1993 when a University of Arkansas graduate student found evidence of breeding by Black-throated Green Warblers in northern Pope County (see the Page Hollow listing, site #36), several hundred miles from the nearest known locations in the southern Appalachians. At least 15 adults and three sets of young indicated that this was not simply a one-year anomaly brought about, for instance, when a cool, wet spring lasted longer than the birds' urge to migrate. The species returned to breed in 1994, when observers also confirmed that Chestnut-sided Warblers were nesting nearby. In Arkansas, as elsewhere, the mysteries of bird distribution are far from being solved.

A directional note: a new, four-lane limited-access Highway 71 is under construction at this writing, to run from Alma on Interstate 40 to the Missouri line; the bypass around Fayetteville and Springdale is already open. Directions to some sites, including Devil's Den State Park, will change when the new 71 is finished, which may not be until close to the year 2000.

A revised edition of *Birding in the Western Arkansas Ozarks*, written by Michael A. Mlodinow and Joseph C. Neal and published in 1988, is in preparation; it will contain detailed information about additional sites in this part of the state.

20. Baker Prairie Natural Area

Location: *From the northwestern intersection of U.S. Highways 65 and 65B (U.S. Highway 65 and Main Street) in Harrison, drive west 1.0 mile on Industrial Park Road; turn left (south) onto Goblin Drive and drive 0.5 mile to the first parking lot on the left. (See map on page 86.)*

B aker Prairie is one of the jewels of the Arkansas natural areas system: the most important remaining example of the tallgrass prairie that once was more common in this part of the state. In spring and summer, the rolling landscape (including many of the low mounds called "prairie pimples," the geologic origin of which is still debated) sparkles with the colors of White Trout-Lily, Virginia Spring Beauty, Indian Paintbrush, Shooting Star, Bastard Toadflax, Prairie Buttercup, Orange Puccoon, Wild Hyacinth, Wood Betony, Long-bracted Wild Indigo, Wild Blue Larkspur, Ox-eye Daisy, Deptford Pink, and Pale-purple Coneflower, as well as three rare wildflower species, Royal Catchfly, Prairie Violet, and Ozark Trillium. Later in the year, tall grasses—Little Bluestem, Big Bluestem, and Indian Grass—wave in the wind.

The prairie was degraded some years ago by construction of a new high school and access road, but it's still well worth a visit. Thanks to tireless efforts by local and state conservationists, 71 very expensive acres are now being preserved and protected. The main attraction for birders at Baker Prairie is its breeding population of Grasshopper Sparrows, an uncommon species found only locally in Arkansas. Late April is a good time to see the prairie; the sparrows return in the middle of the month, and many of the most interesting flowers are at the peak of bloom then, also.

The prairie is found on both sides of Goblin Drive (named for the high-school mascot) north of the school parking lot. The large section is west of the road. From the parking lot, cross the road, walk north a short distance, and head west across the prairie, crossing the rise. (Check fencerows around the borders for migrants in spring and fall; Merlin has been found here.) Painted Bunting has been seen and heard in scrubby areas along the prairie borders, and may breed; Bell's Vireo almost certainly nests here.

Once on the prairie, listen for the bell-like tinkling of Horned Larks, which nest in early spring on sections that have been burned or closely mowed. Grasshopper Sparrows prefer areas with taller grass; their song may be a simple insect-like buzz or a buzz mixed with varied, jangly notes ("like a hearing-aid going haywire," as one birder describes it).

They're often reluctant to perch high enough to provide a good look. Scissor-tailed Flycatchers (spring through fall) are more cooperative, perching on small trees around the prairie as if to show off their exaggerated tail feathers.

Eastern Meadowlarks are of course common all year, and Bobolinks stop over in migration when the grass is tall enough to attract them in late April and early May. Upland Sandpiper is another occasional migrant. Eastern Bluebirds are often seen on roadside telephone wires. Rufous-sided Towhee and Field Sparrow are permanent residents, while other sparrows—Savannah, Le Conte's, Fox, Song, Lincoln's, and Swamp—may visit in winter, depending on how tall or short the grass is and how wet or dry the ground. Other species found here from spring through fall include Eastern Kingbird, White-eyed Vireo, Common Yellowthroat, and Indigo Bunting. Permanent residents include Red-tailed Hawk, American Kestrel, Killdeer, and Brown-headed Cowbird.

As you walk the prairie, watch for turtles; both the Eastern Box Turtle and the strikingly patterned Ornate Box Turtle (rare in Arkansas, and decreasing) have been found here, although some observers fear the latter may have been wiped out by collecting. You may also come upon an active Coyote den.

Scissor-tailed Flycatcher
Gail Diane Yovanovich

21. Beaver Lake

Location: *From the intersection of U.S. Highways 62 and 62B (2nd Street) in Rogers, follow U.S. Highway 62 for 24.2 miles east to State Highway 187 and turn right (south). (See map on page 82.)*

From Eureka Springs, begin where State Highway 23 goes north from U.S. Highway 62. Follow 62 west for 8.5 miles to State Highway 187; note that you do not turn the first time you see Highway 187, which makes a loop to the Beaver Lake dam. Continue to the second intersection.

B eaver Lake is another of the big, deep, artificial reservoirs with which the U.S. Army Corps of Engineers has so blessed Arkansas. As is the case with most of them, in summer its waters usually support nothing but anglers and water-skiers, but in winter almost anything can show up. Among the most expected species are Common Loon, Pied-billed and Horned (250 in a recent February) Grebes, Common Goldeneye, Bufflehead, and Bald Eagle. A list of Beaver's rarities includes Pacific and Yellow-billed (the first state record) Loons, Western Grebe, Tundra and Trumpeter Swans, Oldsquaw, Surf Scoter, Marbled Godwit, and Black-legged Kittiwake. Greater Scaup and all three mergansers have been found on the lake, and Bonaparte's Gull is a fairly common winter visitor.

Campgrounds, picnic areas, and launching ramps ring the lake. Pick up a map from a Corps office or local outdoor shop and scan the water from as many lookout points as you have time to visit. Unless someone has staked something out, your odds of finding a rarity are probably as good at one place as another. The following directions will take you to the dam area, which not only is fine for scoping waterbirds but also has some interesting breeding species.

From U.S. Highway 62 and the western end of State Highway 187, drive toward the dam 2.0 miles. In spring or summer, turn left here, then left again in 0.6 mile to follow a road along the north side of the White River below the dam. This road passes two campgrounds and then dead-ends about a mile from the last turn. Park here and listen for Swainson's Warbler, which has occasionally nested in the vicinity of a canebrake a short distance back up the road. Back a little farther is a brushy area where Blue-winged Warblers, an uncommon breeder in Arkansas, have nested. Yellow-throated Warbler sings from sycamores along the river. Look around for Tree Swallow (which is suspected of

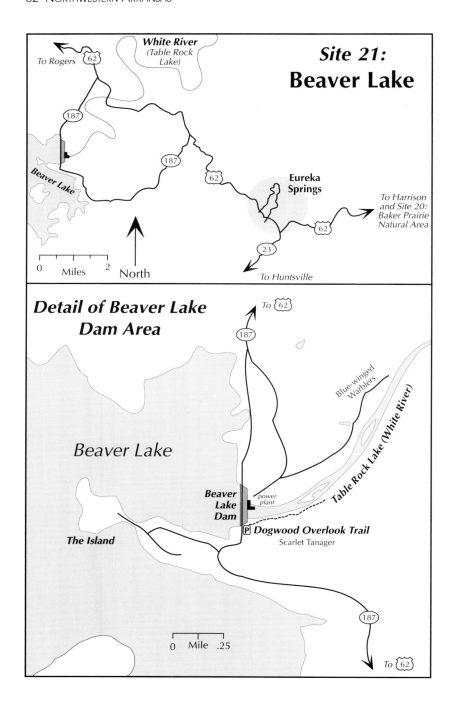

Site 21:
Beaver Lake

White River
(Table Rock Lake)

To Rogers 62

187

187

62

Beaver Lake

Eureka Springs

To Harrison and Site 20: Baker Prairie Natural Area

62

23

0 Miles 2   North

To Huntsville

Detail of Beaver Lake Dam Area

To 62

187

Blue-winged Warblers

Beaver Lake

Table Rock Lake (White River)

Beaver Lake Dam

power plant

The Island

P **Dogwood Overlook Trail**
Scarlet Tanager

187

0 Mile .25

To 62

breeding locally in bluebird boxes), Cliff Swallow, and Scissor-tailed Flycatcher. Camp Area A also has nesting Blue-winged Warblers.

Return to State Highway 187, turn left, and drive 1.0 mile over the dam; turn left and drive 0.2 mile to a parking lot. The Dogwood Overlook Trail, which climbs steeply across the road from the restrooms, has breeding Scarlet Tanagers.   Also look for Worm-eating Warblers, Yellow-throated Warblers (in the pines), Wood Thrushes, and Acadian Flycatchers.

In winter, you'll want to skip all the above. Instead, drive across the dam and turn right to a campground on a peninsula of land stretching out into the lake (known to birders as "the island"). Find a convenient lookout point here (perhaps a picnic table), set up your scope, and hope that the birdwatching gods are smiling on you. Scan carefully; the state's next Yellow-billed Loon may be out there, popping up only occasionally. As local birder Mike Mlodinow says, "Patience is definitely a virtue here."

When you leave this area and return to State Highway 187, you can turn either left or right to go back to U.S. Highway 62, depending on whether you want to go to Rogers or Eureka Springs. Pea Ridge National Military Park (site #37) is about 20 miles to the west on U.S. Highway 62.

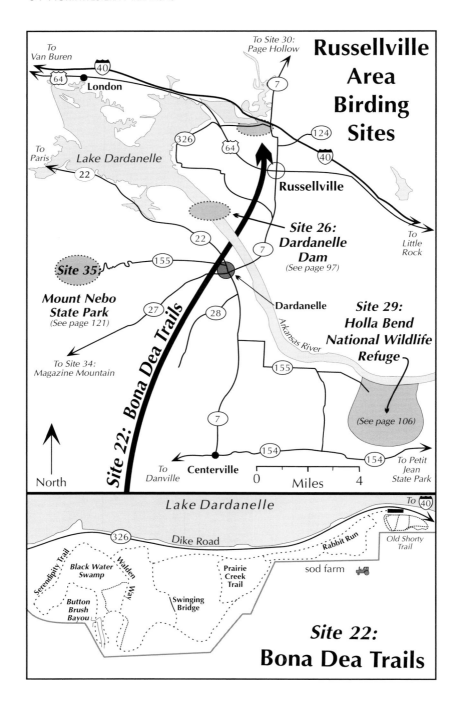

To
Van Buren

64

London

To Site 30:
Page Hollow

Russellville Area Birding Sites

7

326

64

124

40

To
Paris

Lake Dardanelle

22

Russellville

Site 26:
Dardanelle
Dam
(See page 97)

22

155

7

Site 35:

To
Little
Rock

Mount Nebo
State Park
(See page 121)

27

28

Dardanelle

Arkansas River

Site 29:
Holla Bend
National Wildlife
Refuge

155

To Site 34:
Magazine Mountain

Site 22: Bona Dea Trails

7

(See page 106)

North

154

To
Danville

Centerville

0   Miles   4

154

To Petit
Jean
State Park

Lake Dardanelle

To 40

326

Dike Road

Rabbit Run

Old Shorty
Trail

Serendipity Trail

Black Water
Swamp

Walden Way

Prairie
Creek
Trail

sod farm

Button
Brush
Bayou

Swinging
Bridge

Site 22:
Bona Dea Trails

22. Bona Dea Trails

Location: *From Interstate 40 at Russellville, take Exit 81 and drive south on State Highway 7 for 0.1 mile (watch for a sign on Dike Road—also signed for Lake Dardanelle State Park); turn right for 0.4 mile to the parking lot on your left.*

The Bona Dea trail system, developed by the Army Corps of Engineers near an arm of Lake Dardanelle, is an excellent birding spot easily accessible to travelers on Interstate 40. Paved paths with names like Walden Way and Rabbit Run loop through 186 acres of old fields, scrub, wet woods, and swamps, and past several good-sized ponds. This variety of habitat makes Bona Dea a productive area for a diversity of birds. By choosing different routes (there are maps at the parking lot and at most trail intersections), you can make round trips of from 1.0 to 3.5 miles. The trails are mostly broad and flat, making Bona Dea especially appropriate for birders with physical disabilities.

Keep left on Rabbit Run at the trailhead near the parking lot; you'll soon arrive at a fenceline with views of an adjoining sod farm. Scan this area for migrant shorebirds and swallows. Scissor-tailed Flycatchers are common breeders. The Canada Geese here, and elsewhere in this area, are birds of a nonmigratory "giant" race introduced by the state Game and Fish Commission. The population seems to be thriving; the population in all of northwestern Arkansas was estimated at about 5,000 birds in early 1994.

Bona Dea's major attraction is its variety of wetland areas. The longest loop, Serendipity Trail, passes through Black Water Swamp as well as other swampy and marshy spots. Be sure to take the path across the swinging bridge, which provides access to a small creek. Look for Great Blue Heron, Wood Duck, and Red-shouldered Hawk (all year), and Green Heron, Eastern Wood-Pewee, Acadian Flycatcher, Northern Parula, Prothonotary and Kentucky Warblers, Yellow-breasted Chat, Painted Bunting, and Orchard Oriole (summer). Flooding has left a great number of standing dead trees, good for all Arkansas woodpeckers except, of course, Red-cockaded. In winter, watch for ducks and Swamp and White-crowned Sparrows; this would be a likely place to find Harris's Sparrow among the flocks of White-crowneds.

Bona Dea is heavily used by local walkers and joggers, so early morning is an even better time than usual to visit. Parts of some trails may be inundated during periods of high water.

For information, write the Lake Dardanelle Project Office, P.O. Box 1087, Russellville, AR 72801, or call 968-5008.

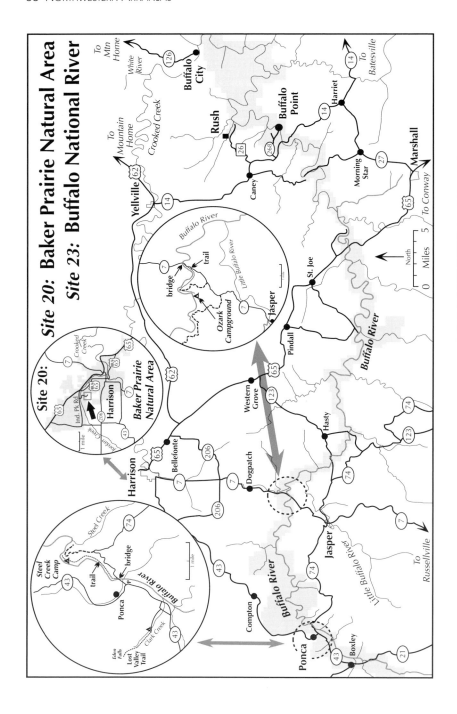

Site 20: Baker Prairie Natural Area
Site 23: Buffalo National River

23. Buffalo National River

Location: *The Buffalo River flows for more than 130 miles across northwestern and north-central Arkansas. Park headquarters are in Harrison, 13 miles north of the river; there are information stations at Pruitt, 5 miles north of Jasper on State Highway 7; at Silver Hill, off U.S. Highway 65 nine miles north of Marshall; and on State Highway 268 at Buffalo Point, off State Highway 14, 14 miles south of Yellville.*

The Buffalo is one of Arkansas's treasures: a wild, free-flowing river in a region where too many once-pristine streams have been lost to dams and development. It was protected as America's first National River in 1972, after a long and difficult fight by conservationists to save it. (Administered by the National Park Service, a national river is essentially a long, skinny national recreation area.) The Buffalo is a legendary canoeing stream, with exciting spring whitewater in the upper reaches around Ponca, but it's also a great place to camp, swim, fish, and enjoy mountain scenery, wildflowers, and birds.

Compared with a bottomland forest in the Delta, the Ozark Mountains do not have a rich avifauna. The total number of species found on the Buffalo River Christmas Bird Count, for instance, is usually among the lowest in Arkansas. But the interesting species that are here, combined with the grandeur of the wilderness setting, make for a wonderful birding experience. This is especially true for people from places not blessed with such a profligacy of natural beauty—e.g., just about everybody who doesn't live near the Buffalo.

Green Heron; Red-shouldered and Broad-winged Hawks; Yellow-billed Cuckoo; Chuck-will's-widow; Whip-poor-will; Pileated Woodpecker; Eastern Wood-Pewee; Acadian Flycatcher; Eastern Phoebe; Wood Thrush; White-eyed, Yellow-throated, and Red-eyed Vireos; Yellow-throated, Black-and-white, Worm-eating, Kentucky, and Hooded Warblers; Northern Parula; American Redstart; Ovenbird; Louisiana Waterthrush; Common Yellowthroat; Yellow-breasted Chat; Scarlet Tanager; Rufous-sided Towhee; and Indigo Bunting are among the common breeding birds of the Buffalo. Cerulean Warbler, a riverside specialty, is also present, but hard to find because it stays high in trees and because its song can sound so much like that of the more-common Northern Parula. This also is among the state's best sites for nesting Yellow Warbler, a very uncommon breeder in Arkansas.

A good place to find many of these birds in spring and early summer is along a beautiful and seldom-used path that runs from Ponca to the

Steel Creek camping area. Park in a gravel lot (marked "river access") off State Highway 43, just south of where State Highways 43 and 74 divide at Ponca. You can reach this spot by driving north from Clarksville for 47 miles on Highway 21 to Boxley, then continuing north 5 miles on Highway 43. (Watch for Greater Roadrunner along the way.)

Cross to the east side of the river on the old low-water bridge, then follow the trail under the new Highway 74 bridge. It's 2.3 miles to Steel Creek, but if you're feeling lazy you can turn around when the trail begins to descend the bluff and avoid having to climb back up. You may be more likely to find Cerulean Warbler, though, if you continue to Steel Creek and check the riverside sycamores. Bewick's Wren, a scarce bird in Arkansas, has nested in the riverside vegetation near the campground here. (Some maps show that you can cross the river at Steel Creek and return to Ponca on the other bank, but that trail is sometimes poorly maintained and may not be worth the trouble—although it is flat.)

You can also reach Steel Creek by car by driving east toward Jasper on State Highway 74; watch for a sign, 1.5 miles from the bridge, marking the left turn toward the river access. From there, it's a steep, twisting 1.1 miles down to the water.

Do not be shocked if, in walking near Steel Creek, you come upon a very large brown mammal calmly grazing in a field. Some years ago the state Game and Fish Commission began importing Elk into the Buffalo area in an attempt to re-establish this species into a habitat where it once

High limestone bluffs along the Buffalo River. *Photo by Mel White.*

was native. The Buffalo-area Elk herd has done fairly well and now numbers 300-400 or more; Steel Creek is one of the best places to see them, especially in the early morning.

The Game and Fish Commission also has reintroduced Ruffed Grouse, extirpated from Arkansas before 1900, in the Ponca area; the odds of seeing one are slim, but you might hear a male "drumming" in spring.

Many of the birds mentioned earlier can also be found along the very pretty Lost Valley trail, which begins at a campground 0.9 mile south of the Ponca low-water bridge off State Highway 43, about four miles north of Highway 21. The one-way trail follows Clark Creek up a narrow valley to Eden Falls. Eastern Phoebes nest under cliff overhangs along the creek.

Another good trail begins at the picnic area near the State Highway 7 bridge over the Buffalo, 13 miles south of Harrison (or 5 miles north of Jasper), and follows the south bank of the river 2.5 miles upstream to the Ozark campground. Local birders have found this area particularly good for migrant warblers. There's an old record from near here for nesting Cedar Waxwing, so it wouldn't hurt to keep an eye out for this erratic wanderer. This spot is also terrific for spring wildflowers, including Fire Pink, Jack-in-the-pulpit, Green Dragon, Bloodroot, Shooting Star, Trillium, Hepatica, Bellwort, Columbine, and many others.

At the eastern end of the river, the ghost town of Rush is an interesting place to visit. This abandoned zinc-mining community, which may have had a population of 2,000 in the boom days of the late 19th century, is reached by turning east off State Highway 14 2.0 miles north of State Highway 268 at Buffalo Point. Not only are the old buildings and mine structures fascinating, but also Swainson's Warbler has been found nearby. Listen for its *teer, teer, teer, see the teer* song in underbrush near the river.

Even if you aren't an experienced canoeist, consider taking a short float trip in the calm water around Buffalo Point; outfitters, of which there are many, can set up a trip of just a few hours, dropping you off at one launching area and picking you up downstream. As you float silently down the river (no law says that you have to paddle like an Olympic kayaker), you'll get close-up views of birds that you wouldn't be able to approach on foot. You may pass within a few feet of a Louisiana Waterthrush or a migrant Spotted Sandpiper teetering on a rock, or a Great Blue Heron or Green Heron fishing along the shore. You'll get a feel for the river in a way that you simply can't appreciate from the trails.

For information about the Buffalo, write the Superintendent, P.O. Box 1173, Harrison, AR 72602, or call 741-5443.

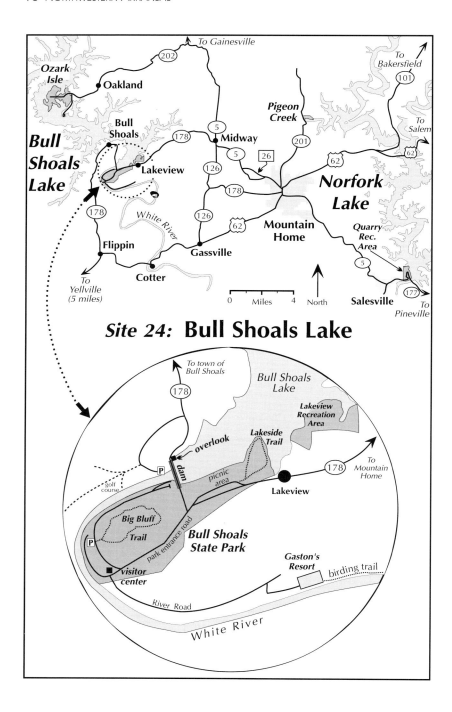

Site 24: **Bull Shoals Lake**

24. Bull Shoals State Park Area

Location: *From Mountain Home, drive northwest six miles on State Highway 5 to State Highway 178, then west on 178 7.3 miles to the park entrance road, just before the Bull Shoals Lake dam. Follow signs 1.1 miles to the park visitor center.*

Bull Shoals and Norfork are two large lakes on the Missouri boundary of north-central Arkansas formed by the damming of, respectively, the White and the North Fork Rivers. Water discharged into the rivers, coming from the bottom of these deep lakes, is so cold that native fishes have disappeared for several miles downstream; as mitigation, the federal government stocks hatchery-raised trout, a policy that has created an important sport fishery. Mountain Home, located between the lakes, is something of a tourist and retirement boomtown, hosting thousands of visitors yearly in all manner of motels, resorts, and fishing camps.

Bull Shoals State Park includes a stretch of the White River just downstream from the dam, as well as a small area on the lakeshore along State Highway 178. Stop at the visitor center for advice and directions and to pick up a bird list. Continue to the camping area along the river, where Great Blue Herons fish along the banks. Red-headed Woodpeckers nest in the park, and Eastern Bluebirds are common; in breeding season look for Warbling Vireo in riverside trees. You'll hear Northern Parula, Prothonotary Warbler, and Louisiana Waterthrush in this area in spring and summer. Chipping Sparrows are common except in winter.

Gaston's White River Resort, located 2.5 miles down River Road from the state park visitor center, is a popular fishing resort with a fine restaurant perched on stilts over the river. (If you can't manage to catch and cook your own trout, they'll fix one here any way you want it.) Birders may be most interested, though, in the resort's nature trail, located at the end of the long row of riverside cottages. For its entire 1.5-mile length the trail borders the White River, and offers some of the most diverse habitat in the area, passing through woods of Cottonwood, Sycamore, Box Elder, Bitternut Hickory, and occasional Black Walnut and Pecan. The trail passes a slough-like creek where water backs up during releases from the dam, as well as open fields over which vultures and hawks soar. Among the more than 150 species recorded on this trail are breeding Great Blue Heron (rookery across the river), Wood Duck, Eastern Kingbird, Tree Swallow (nests in bluebird boxes), Loggerhead Shrike, Prothonotary Warbler, Louisiana Waterthrush, and Blue

Grosbeak. Among the shorebirds seen along the river in fall: Greater and Lesser Yellowlegs; Solitary, Spotted, Semipalmated, Western, Least, and Pectoral Sandpipers; and Sanderling.

Return to the intersection east of the turn to the park visitor center. Make a sharp left turn toward the dam and power station. In 0.5 mile you'll find a parking area on your left and the beginning of the Big Bluff Trail, a 1.5-mile walk good for woodland birds and migrants. Bell's Vireo has been seen in the brushy woods near the road. There's a great view of the river and the dam from the top of the bluff.

Continue along this road 0.6 mile to the power station gate. Take an unpaved road that follows the fence to the left. This leads to a good view of the river just below the dam. In winter you may find numbers of Lesser Scaup, Common Goldeneye, Bufflehead, and Hooded Merganser here, as well as Ring-billed Gulls and, often, Bonaparte's Gulls, which can be seen regularly in migration. In spring and fall watch for Ospreys migrating along the river, and in winter look for Bald Eagles flying over the dam from the lake to the river and back.

Return to State Highway 178; just east of the park entrance turnoff, on the opposite side of the highway, is the Lakeside picnic area. The tall trees here are excellent for migrant warblers in spring.

Cross the dam and immediately turn right into a parking area at a lake overlook. Cliff Swallows nest in large numbers on the dam; look for them in spring and summer. Bull Shoals is a typical Corps of Engineers lake:

Bull Shoals Dam from the fire tower. *Photo courtesy of Arkansas Department of Parks and Tourism.*

American White Pelicans
David A. Sibley

deep and sprawling, with a steep, often sterile, shoreline. Almost no interesting birds are found on the lake itself in summer, but the rest of the year is a different story. Ospreys stop to fish in spring and fall, as do American White Pelicans (uncommon in spring, fairly common in fall). A Brown Pelican showed up one September. Bald Eagles reside here in excellent numbers in winter; 84 were counted on the lake in one recent midwinter survey. You may see several from this overlook, as well as Common Loon, Pied-billed and Horned Grebes, and gulls and other waterbirds. A scope is usually needed.

Bull Shoals and Norfork are big lakes, and birds move around. Check out the view from as many of the recreation areas on both lakes as you have time for. (Maps of the lakes are available at the state park or the Corps office at 324 West 7th in Mountain Home, or write Resident Engineer, P.O. Box 369, Mountain Home, AR 72653.) Ask at the state park office for a schedule of naturalist-led barge tours; you'll see many more birds from a boat than from shore.

Continue along State Highway 178 for 0.4 mile to a turnoff on your left to the Rivercliff Golf Club; drive 0.8 mile to the bottom of the hill. By turning left here you can drive 0.2 mile to a parking area that overlooks the river just below the dam, where you may find ducks and gulls in winter. If you turn right, you will arrive in 0.2 mile at the golf course entrance. Turn left here and immediately right onto an unpaved road.

Drive this road and stop to bird likely-looking spots. It passes through a variety of habitats and can be very productive for migrant and resident passerines. The road ends after 0.5 mile; turn around wherever you like and return to State Highway 178 and the Bull Shoals dam.

Drive east on State Highway 178 toward Mountain Home. Less than 2 miles from the dam you will pass through the town of Lakeview, where (in winter) you should turn left to check out the view of Bull Shoals from the Lakeview recreation area. Continue along State Highway 178 to State Highway 5, 7.6 miles from the dam.

To visit another interesting area on Bulls Shoals Lake, drive north on State Highway 5 for 8.1 miles to State Highway 202 and turn left; drive 9.6 miles to the entrance to the Oakland and Ozark Isle recreation areas. Turn left toward Ozark Isle. In less than a mile you'll come to a causeway. The shallow, sheltered bays on both sides of the road attract wintering ducks; Common Merganser has been seen here, and Common Loon is found often. Ozark Isle itself is crisscrossed by several roads to campsites, picnic areas, and boat-launching ramps. It contains a good variety of habitat from fields to woods, and can be productive for landbirds year-round. Painted Bunting is sometimes found breeding in lakeside shrubs around the shorelines of the big north Arkansas reservoirs.

Retrace your route to the intersection of State Highways 5 and 178. Continue south on State Highway 5 for 2.6 miles to County Road 26 on your left. Drive 0.9 mile to a small pond on your left where dabbling ducks sometimes gather in good numbers in winter; this spot can also be good for shorebirds in migration. Keep going on this road 1.2 miles to return to State Highway 5, where you can make a left turn toward Mountain Home. In 1.1 miles State Highway 5 intersects with Highway 201.

Norfork Lake is located east of Mountain Home; it hosts many of the same winter waterbird species as Bull Shoals. To look over a nearby area of the lake, drive north on Highway 201 for 5.4 miles and make a right turn into the Pigeon Creek recreation area. Watch here for loons, grebes, and ducks, as well as breeding Tree Swallows. To visit the Norfork dam, drive south on State Highway 5 from its intersection with State Highway 201 for 10.9 miles to Salesville; turn left onto State Highway 177 and drive 2 miles to the dam and the Quarry recreation area, where Tree Swallows also nest.

For information about Bull Shoals State Park write P.O. Box 205, Bull Shoals, AR 72619, or call 431-5521.

25. Centerton State Fish Hatchery

Location: *From the intersection of State Highways 71B and 102 in Bentonville, drive west on 102 for 4.0 miles to Centerton Road. Turn left and drive 0.5 mile to a road on your right. Turn here; the hatchery entrances will be on your left.*

Centerton State Fish Hatchery is a collection of 17 ponds of varying sizes operated by the Arkansas Game and Fish Commission. It's also northwest Arkansas's most productive place to look for shorebirds, rarities, and western strays. It's easily accessible and heavily birded (for Arkansas, that is), so the list of interesting species recorded here grows every year.

Some of the good birds that have turned up recently are Eared Grebe, American White Pelican, American and Least Bitterns, Black-crowned Night-Heron, White-faced Ibis, Tundra Swan, Oldsquaw, Peregrine and Prairie Falcons, King and Virginia Rails, Sora, Wilson's and Piping Plovers, American Avocet, Whimbrel (the three found here on May 14, 1994, are the highest number of this locally rare species seen at one time in Arkansas), Marbled Godwit, Sanderling, Ruff, Red-necked and Red Phalaropes, Least Tern (rare in northwestern Arkansas), Alder Flycatcher, Palm Warbler, and American Tree, Clay-colored, and Sharp-tailed Sparrows. Because Centerton is less than 20 miles from Oklahoma, it's a good place to look for western wanderers like Cinnamon Teal, Swainson's Hawk, Harris's Sparrow, Great-tailed Grackle, and Yellow-headed Blackbird. A few Ross's Geese have been seen here in the company of spring migrant Snows. In 1993, Blue-winged Teal bred at the hatchery, the first known nesting in northwestern Arkansas.

The hatchery is worth a visit any time of year, although the short break between the end of spring migration and the beginning of the fall shorebird flight is unlikely to turn up much. There are two access-points along the road just north of the ponds (Highway 904, in part) where you can enter. (*Signs say not to drive on the levees, but birders have been doing it for years, and no one objects. Still, if you see a Game and Fish worker around, it wouldn't hurt to ask.*) Your strategy then will depend on the time of year and what you're looking for.

For ducks, drive carefully, trying not to flush birds on the ponds before you have a chance to check them out. For shorebirds, look for a recently drained pond with a muddy bottom. By walking near grassy pond edges and drainage ditches, you may scare up a bittern, rail (Soras are most common; others, rare), or Sedge or Marsh Wren. Fencerows and the woodlot at the southwest corner are places to look for migrant flycatchers and warblers. Warbling Vireo nests in the fencerows. Some informal, often overgrown trails wind through the woodlot.

A valuable study conducted by Kimberly G. Smith, Joseph C. Neal, and Michael A. Mlodinow has indicated the best times to see Centerton's shorebirds. A very brief summary:

Killdeer is common all year. Least Sandpiper and Common Snipe are common from fall through spring. Semipalmated Plover, Greater and Lesser Yellowlegs, and Solitary, Spotted, Semipalmated, Pectoral, and Stilt Sandpipers all are common at times in both spring and fall (peaks around the first of May and late August).

Best times to see other species: Black-bellied Plover, rare, mid-April through May; American Golden-Plover, common first half of April, rare in fall; American Avocet, uncommon to rare, best chance early May; Willet, uncommon, best chance late April; Hudsonian Godwit, uncommon in early May; Ruddy Turnstone, uncommon, best chance late May; Western Sandpiper, uncommon in spring, common in fall; White-rumped Sandpiper, common late May and first week of June; Baird's Sandpiper, fairly common in spring and uncommon in fall; Dunlin, uncommon in May, common mid-October through early November; Buff-breasted Sandpiper, uncommon first half of September; Short-billed Dowitcher, rare in spring, uncommon late July through early October; Long-billed Dowitcher, uncommon in spring and fall, becoming common early October; and Wilson's Phalarope, common in early May, rare in fall.

Shorebird occurrence at these ponds depends on when the ponds are drained and when the birds are moving. These events don't always happen at the same time. Despite movement being greatest in August, habitat is generally poor then. Recently, July has been good, as has late September to November.

American Golden-Plover, Upland Sandpiper, Horned Lark, and Yellow-headed Blackbird are seen in the surrounding pastures, while Great-tailed Grackle is usually seen near the ponds or flying over. *Remember that most land around the hatchery is private.*

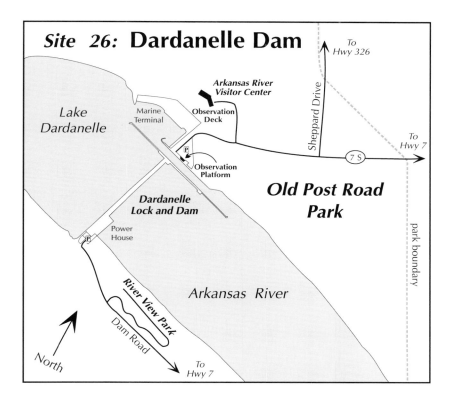

Site 26: **Dardanelle Dam**

To Hwy 326

Arkansas River Visitor Center

Sheppard Drive

Lake Dardanelle

Marine Terminal

Observation Deck

To Hwy 7

7 S

P

Observation Platform

Dardanelle Lock and Dam

Old Post Road Park

park boundary

Power House

P

River View Park

Dam Road

Arkansas River

North

To Hwy 7

26. Dardanelle Dam

Location: *From the State Highway 7 exit (Exit 81) on Interstate 40 at Russellville, drive south on Highway 7 4.3 miles to Highway 7S. Turn right and drive straight 1.7 miles to Old Post Road Park. (Also see map on page 84.)*

Corps of Engineers dams on the Arkansas River are good places to look for gulls in winter, and the river itself attracts increasing numbers of wintering Bald Eagles. Although something unusual is as likely to show up in one place as another, the Lake Dardanelle Dam is described here because it's easy to get to, and because it's close to other good birding spots (Bona Dea trails, Mount Nebo State Park, and Holla Bend National Wildlife Refuge sites—#22, #35, and #29 respectively).

Once you've arrived at Old Post Road Park, follow the road left below the dam to find spots from which to scan the river in winter. Although one hesitates ever to describe Bald Eagles as common, there are almost always a few perched in riverside trees here, or soaring overhead, from November into March. (Holla Bend NWR, where wintering eagles are also easily found, is just nine river miles downstream.) The Canada Geese that you may see walking through the park are of the nonmigratory "giant" race, introduced by the state Game and Fish Commission; Canadas are now quite common in places along the Arkansas River Valley.

Drive back to the lock house and climb the viewing platform above the lock to sort through the gulls just below the dam. Nearly all wintering gulls in Arkansas are Ring-bills, but you may find a few Herring or Bonaparte's—or if you're lucky, something better. The road to the right will let you scan the lake above the dam for ducks.

Stop at the Arkansas River visitor center to pick up a Lake Dardanelle map, which also shows several nearby parks. The Caudle Overlook to the right is not very productive for looking over the river (too far away), but the road passes near grassy areas where you may find winter sparrows.

The best summering birds at the park are probably Greater Roadrunner, Scissor-tailed Flycatcher, and Chipping Sparrow.

It may be more convenient to scan the river from the other side. To do so, return to State Highway 7, turn right, and drive 2.2 miles (crossing the river) to Second Street in Dardanelle. Turn right, drive 0.7 mile to Dam Road, turn right again, and drive 1.1 miles to River View Park. (Watch for Greater Roadrunner along the way.) Here various shelters and side roads provide lookouts. Drive down to the powerhouse parking lot and walk up to the dam to look over the lake upstream.

By the way, if you don't find any good birds, there's some fine consolation nearby: Catfish 'N, which you pass along Dam Road, is one of the better catfish houses in Arkansas, with great hushpuppies.

27. Devil's Den State Park

Location: From the intersection of U.S. Highway 71 and State Highway 74 at Winslow, drive west on State Highway 74 for 12.8 miles to the park visitor center. (Note: a new four-lane replacement for State Highway 71 is under construction at this writing; these directions are from the old road.) (See map on page 100.)

Devil's Den is one of the prettiest state parks in Arkansas, and certainly one of the most pleasant in which to watch birds. Bisected by Lee Creek, the 2,000-acre park lies in a steep-sided Ozark Mountain valley covered by a hardwood forest. The park's annual spring birding weekend regularly records more than 100 species, even lacking habitat for most shorebirds, waterfowl, and waders. Spring is the best time to visit Devil's Den, but interesting breeding species make a summer visit worthwhile, too.

As you drive along the ridgetop approaching the park, watch for Eastern Bluebird on the telephone wires and Greater Roadrunner along the roadside any time of year. (Roadrunners are not found in the valley, but are regularly seen on the hills above.) As the highway snakes its way down to Devil's Den, you may occasionally wonder whether Lucifer himself designed the tortuous route; those driving campers and trailers need to be especially careful. Stop at the visitor center for a bird list and park map; the park naturalists are happy to answer questions.

Return to the main road, turn left, and drive a short distance to a T intersection near a store, restaurant, and swimming pool. To see a large roost of Turkey and Black Vultures at dusk, turn left here and drive 0.2 mile to a parking area near the suspension bridge over Lee Creek. As many as 100 vultures regularly roost in large trees to the left.

Return to the T intersection and continue straight 0.1 mile toward the highway bridge over Lee Creek. On the right just before the bridge is the trailhead for the Devil's Den Trail, one of the best spring and summer birding walks in the park. Keep left at trail junctions as it runs alongside the creek toward Twin Falls; watch and listen for Yellow-throated and Red-eyed Vireos; Northern Parula; Yellow-throated, Cerulean (rare), Black-and-white, Worm-eating, Kentucky, and Hooded (rare) Warblers; American Redstart; Ovenbird; and Louisiana Waterthrush. All are either confirmed or suspected nesters in the park. Walk the entire 1.5-mile trail if you have time; otherwise, concentrate on the area near Lee Creek.

Drive across the bridge and immediately turn right toward camping area A. After 0.2 mile, stop at a small gravel parking area on the right. If

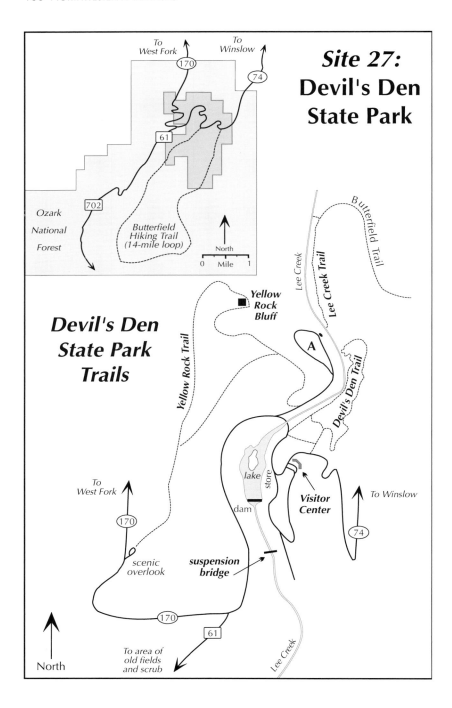

Site 27:
Devil's Den
State Park

To
West Fork

To
Winslow

170

74

61

702

Ozark
National
Forest

Butterfield
Hiking Trail
(14-mile loop)

North

0   Mile   1

Butterfield Trail

Yellow
Rock
Bluff

Lee Creek

Lee Creek Trail

Devil's Den
State Park
Trails

Yellow Rock Trail

A

Devil's Den Trail

lake

store

Visitor
Center

To Winslow

74

To
West Fork

170

dam

scenic
overlook

suspension
bridge

170

61

North

To area of
old fields
and scrub

Lee Creek

you have only a short time at Devil's Den, simply walking this road beside Lee Creek and into the camping area can be productive, especially for migrant warblers. Cape May Warbler was added to the park list from this site in 1992; more-common migrant warblers include Tennessee, Chestnut-sided, and Wilson's. In summer, Broad-winged Hawks whistle overhead and Yellow-throated Warblers sing from the sycamores. Be sure to go back toward the highway to the Yellow Rock trailhead. Walk at least the first couple of hundred yards of this trail for migrants and woodland breeders. Climb higher for a mile or so to reach Yellow Rock Bluff, where modest hawk flights can be seen on fall days with northerly winds. Migrating American White Pelicans (hardly a typical Ozark mountain bird) can be seen from this vantage, and even Swainson's Hawk has been found among the more-common Sharp-shinned, Cooper's, and Broad-winged.

Continue to the loop drive at campground A and park at the trailhead for the Butterfield and Lee Creek trails. Chipping Sparrows are common around this and other campgrounds except in winter. The mile-long Lee Creek Trail has many of the same birds as the Devil's Den Trail, as well as open areas for variety. The trail crosses the creek and passes through mixed woods, eventually winding back to the creek; here you can either retrace your path or make like a Rockhopper Penguin and return along the creekbed itself. If you take the latter route, spend a few minutes examining the limestone under your feet. If you know what to look for, you can find exposed coal veins and fossilized corals, bryozoa, and crinoids. *Still, be careful; the rocks can be slippery and the water high.*

Return to the main road and turn right. Follow State Highway 170 for 0.7 mile to County Road 61 on the left. Drive down this road 1.1 miles to an area of old fields and scrub, good for American Kestrel (mostly in fall), Rufous-sided Towhee, and Eastern Meadowlark (mostly in fall), and from spring through fall for Scissor-tailed Flycatcher and Blue-winged Warbler. From October to early December this is an excellent area for sparrows.

Return to State Highway 170, turn left, and drive 0.8 mile to the scenic overlook on the right (good for watching for soaring hawks), where a trailhead leads down another route to Yellow Rock Bluff. Greater Roadrunner is possible along the highway near the overlook, or anywhere along the next 15.7 miles to U.S. Highway 71 at West Fork. (This is an alternative route into the park for those approaching from the north.)

Devil's Den's permanent residents include Red-shouldered and Red-tailed Hawks; Wild Turkey; Eastern Screech-, Great Horned, and Barred Owls; Belted Kingfisher; Red-bellied, Downy, Hairy, and Pileated

Woodpeckers; American Crow; Field Sparrow; and American Goldfinch. Migrant breeders include Green Heron, Wood Duck, Yellow-billed Cuckoo, Chuck-will's-widow, Whip-poor-will, Ruby-throated Hummingbird, Eastern Wood-Pewee, Acadian and Great Crested Flycatchers, Eastern Phoebe, Eastern Kingbird, Northern Rough-winged Swallow, Fish Crow, Wood Thrush, White-eyed Vireo (Warbling might also nest), Prairie (formerly at field edges among young trees) and Blue-winged (in brushy fields) Warblers, Yellow-breasted Chat, Summer and Scarlet (less common, usually up on the ridges) Tanagers, Blue Grosbeak (uncommon), Indigo Bunting, and Orchard Oriole.

The state park has thirteen housekeeping cabins, but they're often booked weeks or months in advance on weekends; the campgrounds are very nice. For information, write Devil's Den State Park, 11333 West Highway 74, West Fork, AR 72774, or call 761-3325.

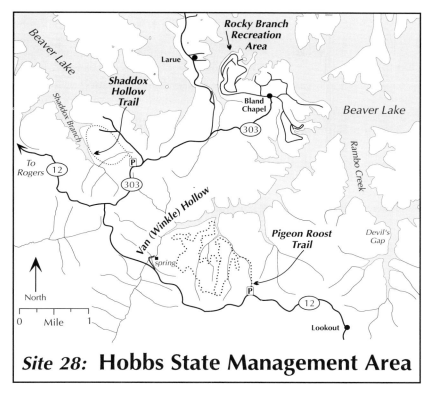

Site 28: **Hobbs State Management Area**

28. Hobbs State Management Area

Location: *From the intersection of U.S. Highway 71B and State Highway 12 in Rogers, drive east on State Highway 12 for 11.0 miles to Highway 303.*

Hobbs State Management Area comprises 11,646 acres on the southeastern shore of Beaver Lake (see site #21), managed jointly by the state Game and Fish, Forestry, and Natural Heritage commissions. Contained within the SMA is also the new Beaver Lake State Park. Because the area was acquired by the state relatively recently, few facilities are available at this writing. Nonetheless, birders have begun to explore the possibilities of this vast tract of public lands.

From State Highway 12, drive north 1.5 miles on State Highway 303; turn left into the parking area for the Shaddox Hollow Trail. This 1.5-mile loop follows a ridgeline before dropping down into the hollow (or "holler," as many Ozarkians say), with views of Beaver Lake. Pine

Warblers, not nearly so common in northwest Arkansas as farther south, are summer residents in pines on the ridges; Louisiana Waterthrushes breed in lower, wetter areas. The trail passes through a mixed woodland of White Oak, hickory, Flowering Dogwood, Blackgum (Black Tupelo), Ozark Chinquapin (affected by chestnut blight and sprouting in clumps), and Shortleaf Pine, where some of the migratory breeding birds include Green Heron (near the lake), Broad-winged Hawk, Yellow-billed Cuckoo, Eastern Wood-Pewee, Acadian and Great Crested Flycatchers, Red-eyed Vireo, Black-and-white Warbler, and Scarlet Tanager. Permanent residents include Great Blue Heron (near the lake), Barred Owl, Downy and Pileated Woodpeckers, White-breasted Nuthatch, and Rufous-sided Towhee.

In winter, continue north on State Highway 303 for 3.1 miles to the Rocky Branch recreation area, where you can scan the lake for loons, grebes, Bald Eagles (fairly common in large trees along the shoreline), and ducks.

Return to State Highway 12, turn left, and drive for 1.3 miles to a low area called Van Winkle Hollow (shown on most maps as Van Hollow), an excellent spot for migratory and permanent-resident breeding birds. Watch for a dirt pulloff on the right. Park here well off the highway and explore the woods to the south (right, or upstream); look for an old road, now deteriorated into a path, and follow it away from the highway, more-or-less alongside the stream.

Just 0.2 mile farther along State Highway 12, turn onto a dirt road leading left into the lower part of the hollow. Park along this road and walk the short distance down to the lake for woodland birds. Among the permanent residents in the hollow, north or south of State Highway 12, are Turkey Vulture (nests under limestone ledges), Red-shouldered Hawk, American Woodcock, and American Goldfinch. Present in breeding season only are Chuck-will's-widow; Eastern Phoebe (nests under the highway bridge and along the bluffs); Blue-winged, Yellow-throated, Black-and-white, Prothonotary, Kentucky, and Hooded Warblers; Northern Parula; American Redstart; Ovenbird; and Louisiana Waterthrush. Swainson's Warbler has been seen here, though breeding hasn't been confirmed.

Continue east on State Highway 12 for 1.9 miles and turn left into the parking area for the Pigeon Roost Trail. The Dry Creek Loop is a hike of 4.1 miles; adding the Huckleberry Loop brings the distance to more than 8 miles. The Pigeon Roost Trail offers a good diversity of habitat, with much the same birds as Shaddox Hollow. Worm-eating and Kentucky Warblers breed here, though you will have to search for the former. This

Chuck-will's-widow
Georges Dremeaux

is also a great spot for Ovenbirds. If you don't feel up to a long walk, make a right turn where the Huckleberry Loop divides and walk to the trail's northernmost point near the lake. Turn around here and return, for a hike of about 2.3 miles.

Little printed information is available yet on Hobbs SMA, but its outlines are shown on the Beaver Lake map published by the Corps of Engineers. Direct questions to Route 5, Box 900, Rogers, AR 72756, or call 789-2380. At Hobbs, it is especially appropriate for visiting birders to report notable sightings to help this new park compile its bird checklist.

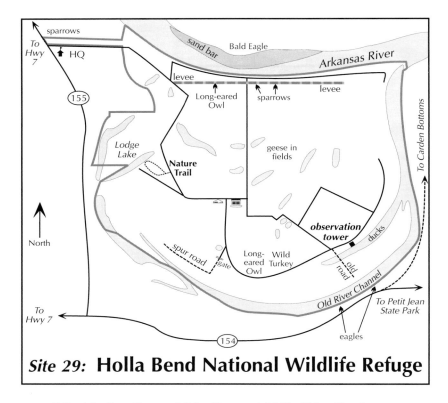

Site 29: **Holla Bend National Wildlife Refuge**

29. Holla Bend National Wildlife Refuge

Location: *From Interstate 40 at Russellville, take Exit 81 and drive south on State Highway 7 for 9.7 miles to State Highway 155; turn left and drive 4.2 miles to the refuge entrance. (Also see map on page 84.)*

Holla Bend, a 6,486-acre national wildlife refuge located within a former curve of the Arkansas River (now cut off by channel straightening), is one of Arkansas's most popular birding locations; it ought to be near the top of any visitor's list of destinations. The refuge is known primarily for its winter birds, especially large flocks of geese (mostly Canada and Snow, with occasional Greater White-fronted and rare Ross's) and good numbers of Bald Eagles. Up to 30,000 geese may winter on the refuge, along with an equal number of ducks.

But Holla Bend isn't just a winter birding destination. Varied habitats of cultivated fields, ponds, scrub, and   bottomland forest make it good

During periods of high water, the Arkansas River backs up to border the entrance road into Holla Bend National Wildlife Refuge. *Photo by Mel White.*

any time of year. Raptors, Wild Turkey, Greater Roadrunner, and migrant landbirds are among its attractions, as well as White-tailed Deer, Bobcat, Armadillo, and Coyote. Holla Bend's breeding species include Red-tailed, Red-shouldered, and Broad-winged Hawks; Northern Bobwhite; Eastern Screech-, Great Horned, and Barred Owls; Scissor-tailed Flycatcher (abundant); Fish Crow; Wood Thrush; Loggerhead Shrike; Bell's and Warbling Vireos; Painted Bunting; and Lark and Field Sparrows.

A list of the rarities seen at Holla Bend in recent years includes Tundra Swan, Swainson's Hawk, Golden Eagle, Peregrine and Prairie Falcons, Sandhill Crane, Hudsonian Godwit, and Yellow-headed Blackbird. This is the most likely place in Arkansas to find Ross's Goose; a careful search around the edges of a flock of Snows will often turn up a few.

Check the bushes on either side of the road at the refuge entrance; Harris's Sparrow has been seen here with some regularity in winter, associating with White-crowneds. Stop at the entrance stand, near the new headquarters, to pay a small fee. Some 1.1 miles farther on, there's a map display on the right; opposite this, a road turns left down to the river. Where this road turns right at the river, 0.3 mile from the map display, an old road runs left upstream along the bank. Walk this and check the brush for sparrows and other land birds; you may also scare up a Great Blue Heron or a small flock of ducks. Bald Eagles are sometimes seen in trees on the opposite bank from November through March. On one occasion, 19 eagles were seen at once in a large oak

Geese lifting off from Holla Bend National Wildlife Refuge. *Photo by A.C. Harlason, courtesy of Arkansas Department of Parks and Tourism.*

here. Eagles may also be seen loafing on the sandy riverbank. During migration, you may find American White Pelican, Osprey, or terns (this is true of any place along the Arkansas River). Double-crested Cormorant is common from fall through spring.

Follow the gravel road along the river; listen for the flowing song of Warbling Vireo in small trees. Just after another display board, 1.2 miles from the first one, turn right toward the levee crossing. The brush-covered levee is a good place to look for winter sparrows; American Tree Sparrow has been seen here, although it is rare, and Le Conte's is a possibility. Long-eared Owls have been found in this vicinity with some regularity in recent years, wintering in thick stands of junipers. Brush clearing has hurt this habitat, though, and there may now be an equally good chance of finding the owls elsewhere on the refuge (see below).

Look out over the fields as you continue. Northern Harriers are common in winter; ducks may be resting on ponds in low places; flocks of geese may be anywhere in the cropland. In April and May, Bobolinks are sometimes found in the fields. Lark Sparrows nest in open areas with sandy soil. Check the sky often for soaring eagles and other raptors. Wintering Short-eared Owls rest in grassy areas, and it was near here that a Burrowing Owl took up residence one winter.

Bell's Vireo and Painted Bunting, birds that are sometimes hard to find, both breed at Holla Bend. Listen for their songs in brushy areas with scattered small trees.

At a junction 1.2 miles from the levee, continue straight ahead, then follow the auto tour route 2.3 miles to a viewing platform near the old river channel at the eastern edge of the refuge. This is an excellent place to find eagles; they perch in large trees on the far bank. Ducks and geese that feed in the refuge fields return to rest on the slough at night. At the edge of the woods, 0.3 mile farther on, walk down a track to the left (often muddy, and flooded at periods of high water) toward the channel to check the cormorants, geese, ducks, and gulls there. Le Conte's Sparrow has been found in the grassy field between the road and the oxbow lake in winter.

The road continues through mixed woodland good for such typical breeding birds as Yellow-billed Cuckoo, Ruby-throated Hummingbird, Eastern Wood-Pewee, Acadian and Great Crested Flycatchers, Wood Thrush, Red-eyed Vireo, and Summer Tanager. Kentucky Warbler is especially common. With luck you may see a few Wild Turkeys; in summer, flocks of a dozen or more young birds congregate along the road. In winter, check thick stands of junipers for roosting Long-eared Owls; one was found here on the 1994 Christmas count.

Where the road leaves the woods, look for a spur leading left. Park and walk this old road into tall bottomland forest. Barred Owl is common here all year. Rusty Blackbird is sometimes found in wet woods in winter.

The tour route returns you to the old headquarters, through fields where Scissor-tailed Flycatchers display and Dickcissels are abundant in breeding season; turn left to leave the refuge. If you have time, check Lodge Lake for ducks on your way out; the turn is 0.4 mile from the headquarters. Anywhere you see Wood Duck boxes, scan the entry holes; Eastern Screech-Owls are sometimes seen sunning themselves during daylight hours.

For another chance at woodland birds, look for an obscure turnoff to the left 0.5 mile after the Lodge Lake road. This leads to a nature trail that can be especially good for migrant passerines. Another wildlife trail follows the levee 0.8 mile beyond this one.

For information on Holla Bend, write Box 1043, Russellville, AR 72801, or call 968-2800.

30. Lake Atalanta

Location: *From 8th and Walnut Streets in Rogers (where U.S. Highway 71B makes a 90-degree turn), drive east on Walnut Street. Do not follow State Highway 12 where it turns left, but continue on Walnut Street as it curves downhill 1.2 miles to the park entrance on left.*

Lake Atalanta is a small spring-fed recreational reservoir in a Rogers city park. A narrow road circles the lake, allowing car-window birding, but it can be hard to find a place to pull over if there's much traffic. On warm weekends the lake attracts too many people to be an ideal birding spot, but on weekdays, and especially during a heavy migration, the area can be good. In winter, a visitor may find the lake area almost deserted.

Winter waterbirds expected here include Pied-billed Grebe, Gadwall, Lesser Scaup, Common Goldeneye, and Bufflehead, with the possibility of Canada Goose, Ring-necked Duck, Canvasback, and Redhead. The uncommon Common Merganser has been found, as well as the rare Oldsquaw. The most notable duck often present, though, is Greater Scaup, a species that is infrequently reported across the state. Fayetteville birder Mike Mlodinow has found the "big bluebill" on more than three-quarters of his winter trips to Lake Atalanta. He reports that a close comparison can often be made here between Greater and Lesser.

Although it appears that the lake is easily covered, it's bigger than it looks at first glance, so take time to make sure that you've searched the little coves. Look for sparrows and other brushy-habitat species around the levee at the north end, and check dead trees for Red-headed Woodpecker, which is fairly common (especially on the road to the residential area branching off the eastern side of the lake road). An occasional Bald Eagle is seen perched on a lakeside tree in winter. A Yellow-bellied Flycatcher turned up here in May 1994.

With enough time for exploring, try the bluff trail which begins on the east side near Walnut Street and ends about 2.5 miles to the north where the paved road becomes gravel.

For spring migration birding, check the eastern arm of the lake, where warblers can be common and Veery has been seen. Also watch for Spotted Sandpiper along the stream below the spillway and migrant Osprey diving for fish at the north end of the lake.

Lake Atalanta is better for transients than Devil's Den State Park (site #27), despite its small size and the greater likelihood of traffic.

31. Lake Bentonville

Location: *From the intersection of U.S. Highway 71B and State Highway 102 in Bentonville, drive west on 102 for 0.5 mile to a road on your left, which may be signed SW 1 Street. Turn left (south) and drive 0.3 mile to the lake entrance on your left. Turn here and follow the road around the lake a short entrance to a dead end.*

Lake Bentonville is a tiny public fishing lake at the north end of the Bentonville airport. Birders visit it because it is Arkansas's only known breeding site for Willow Flycatcher. John James Audubon discovered this bird (formerly called Traill's Flycatcher) in 1822 near Arkansas Post. It once nested in the Grand Prairie region, but has not been found breeding there for many years.

From the dead-end lake road, notice the small area of trees to your right (south), along the east side of the lake. It is here that Willow Flycatchers nest. Although the area is not fenced and birders visit with no problem, it wouldn't hurt to call Billy Moore (273-5745), who owns the land, for permission. The grassy field around the trees is often quite marshy, so boots are recommended. *Remember: this species is barely hanging on in Arkansas; disturb the birds as little as possible.*

Bell's Vireo, Blue Grosbeak, and Painted Bunting have nested here in the past, along with such common species as Yellow-billed Cuckoo, Common Yellowthroat, Yellow-breasted Chat, Indigo Bunting, and Dickcissel. During breeding season the lake may have a Great Blue or Green Heron.

Local birder Joe Neal points out that the area around Lake Bentonville comprises several "prairie pimples," the small mounds of much-debated origin found in prairie habitats in Arkansas and elsewhere.

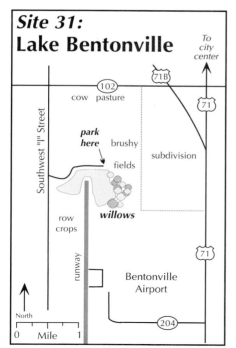

Site 31: Lake Bentonville

There are also remnants, now much disturbed, of prairie flora. He suspects that the prairie affinities of this area account for the presence of Willow Flycatcher and Bell's Vireo. Unfortunately, the housing subdivision to the east may be expanding, leaving even less habitat for these birds.

If you come here in the fall or winter, birding along the edge of the lake, by the airport, and at the field margins can be productive. Western Meadowlarks have been found here, and Harris's and Tree Sparrows seem to occur here with some regularity.

You can continue west on State Highway 102 from here to the Centerton State Fish Hatchery (site #25).

Yellow-breasted Chat
Georges Dremeaux

32. Lake Fayetteville

Location: *Begin at the intersection of Zion Road and U.S. Highway 71B (North College Street) in Fayetteville (near the Northwest Arkansas Mall).*

Lake Fayetteville is a 194-acre oasis of nature in the middle of one of the fastest-growing areas of Arkansas—literally a minute or two from a busy highway, shopping centers, and housing developments. Nonetheless, it is one of the best places in northwest Arkansas for transient landbirds. Diligent local birders have found Common Loon, Eared Grebe, Cinnamon Teal, Greater Scaup, Oldsquaw, Surf Scoter, and Hooded and Common Mergansers among the lake's wintering waterfowl, and Bald Eagle is possible in mid-winter.

From Zion Road and U.S. Highway 71B, drive north 0.5 mile and turn right toward the lake. Follow the road left and right for 0.3 mile to the dam and boat dock. Find a convenient lookout here (walk out onto the dam) and scan for whatever is on the lake. Waterfowl migration can be excellent, especially in bad weather, which keeps boats off the lake and brings birds down to rest. Bufflehead, Ruddy Duck, and American Coot are likely among mixed rafts of ducks that may number in the hundreds.

The brushy areas below the levee are worth checking for fall migrant warblers (Orange-crowned, Yellow, Chestnut-sided, Magnolia, Yellow-throated, Prairie, Mourning, and Wilson's have been found) and winter sparrows (Song, Swamp, and White-throated are likely). Lincoln's Sparrow is possible in spring and fall and has even been found in winter.

Return to U.S. Highway 71B, turn right, and drive 0.25 mile to Lakeview Drive. Turn right and drive 1.0 mile to a spot where the road makes a left turn. Look for a metal gate on the right. If it is open, drive the short distance to the parking lot of the Springdale-Fayetteville Center for the Study of Aquatic Resources. If it is closed, park off the road and walk in.

Follow the paved path on the right of the center to the lake, where there is a deck built over shallow water. Set up your scope here to look for waterbirds. In winter there may a flock of ducks to check out. Great Blue (all year) and Green (breeding) Herons perch along the shore. Noteworthy birds seen nearby have included Black-crowned Night-Heron; Swainson's Hawk; Olive-sided, Yellow-bellied, and Alder Flycatchers; Western Kingbird; Veery; and Cape May and Palm Warblers.

Trails and paths lead into good deciduous woods and old fields around the center; explore as many as you have time for. One that follows the shoreline east of the center building passes through a marshy area where Northern Waterthrush can be found in spring migration and Green Heron, Wood Duck, and Prothonotary Warbler breed. In old-field areas, American Goldfinches twitter in their bouncy song flight in late summer. Grassy areas can be good for migrant and wintering sparrows; Clay-colored has been found in spring, and both Le Conte's and Henslow's have turned up near the lake in winter or early spring. You may also flush a Northern Bobwhite any time of year; you're almost sure to at least hear one. The variety of habitats make this an excellent all-around birding spot in any season.

One Lake Fayetteville specialty is the spring display flight of the American Woodcock, visible from the center's parking lot from mid-February through early April. Watch (and listen) for it at dusk and dawn, even on snowy days.

Hooded Merganser
Georges Dremeaux

33. Lake Wedington

Location: *Begin at the intersection of U.S. Highway 71 (the new 71) and State Highway 16 in Fayetteville, driving west on State Highway 16. (See maps on page 116.)*

Lake Wedington is a U.S. Forest Service recreation area located in a non-contiguous part of the Ozark National Forest. The lake itself is not particularly productive for waterbirds, although it has wintering Pied-billed Grebe and may host an occasional Common Loon, a few Common Goldeneyes, or some Buffleheads from fall through spring. The mixed forest around the lake can be good in migration, though, and includes stands of mature pine—something not common in this part of the state. The pines can be good for winter birds.

Where State Highway 16 bends right, 10.5 miles from U.S. Highway 71, look for a dirt road on the left. Park and walk in past the gate toward the water-treatment facility and the dam. The grown-up old fields here have breeding Blue-winged Warbler, as well as the usual Common Yellowthroat, Yellow-breasted Chat, Indigo Bunting, and Field Sparrow. The creek to the south of the old-field area has nesting Northern Parula, Louisiana Waterthrush, and Kentucky Warbler. By walking around the south side of the sewage lagoon you can follow a trail to the dam levee, where you can scan the lake. You may find a Bald Eagle in mid-winter.

Follow a trail to the right (north) along the lakeshore to the pine woods, where winter birding can be productive. Red-breasted Nuthatch, Winter Wren, Ruby-crowned Kinglet, Hermit Thrush, Lincoln's Sparrow (along the levee), Purple Finch, Pine Siskin, and Evening Grosbeak have been found in varying degrees of abundance or rarity. This area can be good in migration, as well: 21 kinds of warblers were seen here on May 11 one year, and 15 on one September 6. Breeding birds in the pine woods include Yellow-throated Warbler and Chipping Sparrow.

Go back to State Highway 16 and continue 1.2 miles to the campground entrance on the left. Turn in here to scan the lake or bird the woodland around the campsites. This woodland attracts many of the same pine-forest birds as the dam area. In another 0.1 mile, on the right, is the trailhead for a seven-mile hiking trail through the national forest, for those feeling energetic. Drive another 0.1 mile and make a left turn toward the swimming area, cabins, and Forest Service office.

Cedar Waxwings have been found recently in mid-summer in large pines near the swimming beach; no one would be too surprised if these unpredictable birds are found to be breeding nearby. (Waxwings were

Site 33: Lake Wedington

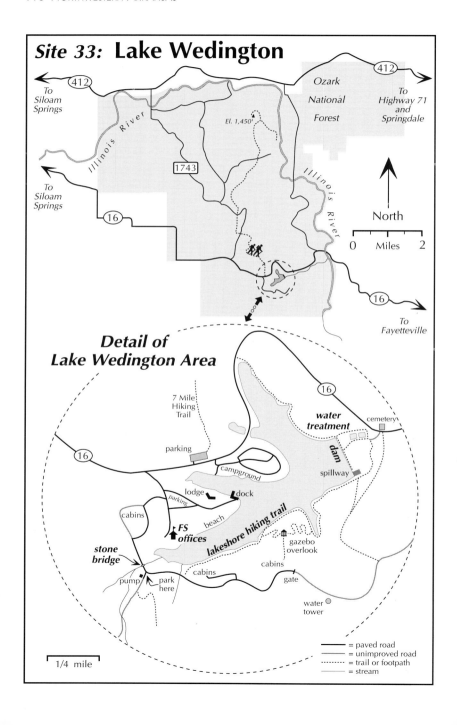

To
Siloam
Springs

Illinois River

El. 1,450'

Ozark

National

Forest

To
Highway 71
and
Springdale

1743

Illinois River

To
Siloam
Springs

16

North

0   Miles   2

16

To
Fayetteville

Detail of
Lake Wedington Area

7 Mile
Hiking
Trail

16

water
treatment

cemetery

parking

16

dam

campground

spillway

lodge

dock

parking

cabins

beach

FS
offices

lakeshore hiking trail

gazebo
overlook

stone
bridge

cabins

cabins

gate

pump

park
here

water
tower

1/4 mile

= paved road
= unimproved road
= trail or footpath
= stream

discovered nesting in a couple of places in northwestern Arkansas in 1993.) During office hours, drive straight through a gate to the ranger office for a map of the area. Return to the large parking area, turn left opposite it, and follow the road as it winds past cabins for 0.3 mile; park on the right just beyond a small stone bridge, near the pump-house. The abandoned and gated road on the right can be good for migrants and woodland breeders such as Yellow-billed Cuckoo, Great Crested Flycatcher, Wood Thrush, Black-and-white Warbler, and Scarlet Tanager. Walk along the main road another 0.2 mile to the start of the Lakeshore Hiking Trail on the left. (There's no place to park along the road at this trailhead.) This path follows the lake edge all the way back to the dam, if you'd like to walk that far.

To explore more of this section of the Ozark National Forest, return to State Highway 16, turn left (west), and drive 1.1 miles to Forest Service Road 1743 on the right. Turn here and follow it north, stopping where things look interesting. (*Do not do this during fall deer-hunting season; check locally for dates. Take care, also, about the condition of the road in bad weather.*) This road runs seven miles north to U.S. Highway 412, where you can turn right toward U.S. Highway 71 and Springdale, or you can turn around wherever you like and return to State Highway 16. The birds here will be much the same as those around Lake Wedington. It's worthwhile to drive slowly in breeding season and listen, depending on the habitat, for Broad-winged Hawk; Acadian Flycatcher; Wood Thrush; White-eyed and Red-eyed Vireos; Blue-winged, Yellow-throated, Pine, and Worm-eating Warblers; Ovenbird; Yellow-breasted Chat; Summer and Scarlet Tanagers; Blue Grosbeak; Rufous-sided Towhee; and Chipping and Field Sparrows. FS Road 1743 crosses Illinois Bayou just before joining Highway 412; the wet woodland here can be excellent in migration, and has breeding Fish Crow and Prothonotary Warbler.

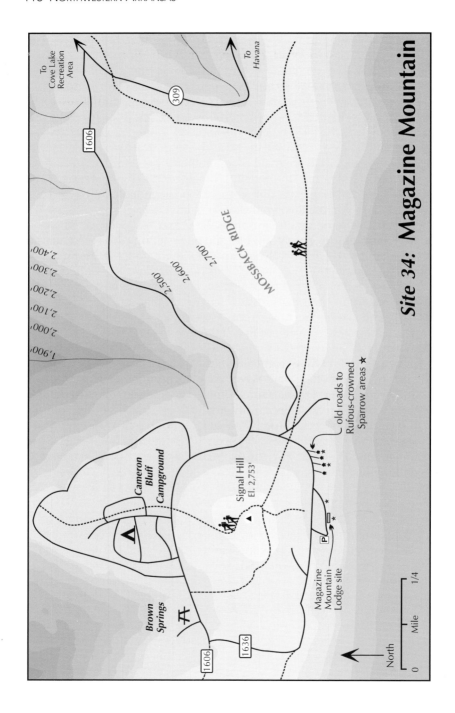

Site 34: Magazine Mountain

34. Magazine Mountain

Location: *From Exit 81 on Interstate 40 at Russellville, take State Highway 7 south 7.0 miles to State Highway 27; follow it southwest 18.5 miles to State Highway 10. Then turn right and drive west 8.4 miles to State Highway 309. Turn right and drive 10.3 miles to Forest Service Road 1606 on top of the mountain. (See photo on page xi.)*

Magazine Mountain is one of Arkansas's most ecologically distinctive areas. At 2,753 feet, its summit is the highest point in the state, and its steep, wooded slopes shelter a number of rare (and, in some cases endemic) plants and animals. Magazine, which is something of an isolated island of slightly cooler climate looming above the Arkansas River valley, is so biologically fascinating that it was once the subject of an article in *Natural History* magazine. Among the special plants here are two ferns, Hay-scented Fern and Rocky Mountain Woodsia, found in moist woods, and Small-headed Pipewort, found at seeps. The mountain's birds are not as notable as its overall ecology, but it's a pleasant place to look for spring migrants, and its bluffs offer lookout points from which to watch for fall raptors.

Magazine, like Mount Nebo 25 miles east, was once a resort, back in the pre-air-conditioning days when people looked to mountaintops for relief from summer heat and mosquitoes. A lodge and cabins operated for many years on the summit, but fire and time have left little but the foundations. The Forest Service operates a campground here today. At this writing a new state park, complete with lodge, restaurant, swimming pool, campsites, and other amenities, is planned for Magazine. There is, of course, considerable concern among biologists over just what this will do to the ecology of the mountain. Environmentalists are watching carefully as development proceeds to try to protect as much critical habitat as possible. It may all be moot for the near future, though, since the state seems to have no money to proceed with actual construction.

The rocky summit of Magazine was the first, and at one time the only, place where Rufous-crowned Sparrows were known to be present in Arkansas. Mount Nebo (see next site listing, #35) may now be a more reliable spot for the bird, but Rufous-crowneds are still seen on Magazine. To look for them, drive west from State Highway 309 for 1.4 miles to a fork in the road. Turn left, and watch on your left for the (now mostly overgrown) entrances to the old cabin sites on the edge of the summit. Park and walk the short distance to the bluff edge at any or all of them. Sparrows have been seen at these sites, especially the first and third from the road fork. Continuing down the main road 0.4 mile, you'll come to a large parking lot at the old lodge site. Sparrows are sometimes seen in rocky areas down the slope from here. (A herpetological note: Magazine is also noted for its healthy population of Western Diamond-backed Rattlesnakes. Watch where you put your hands and feet.) In 1993, the Forest Service instituted a program of fire and mechanical clearing to try to restore conditions favorable for Rufous-crowneds; if it's successful, Magazine may once again host good numbers of the species.

Continue on this road 0.7 mile to a dirt road on the left marked "Electronic Site". If it's not too muddy, drive down this road and investigate the woods on both sides. Two species found only locally in much of Arkansas are common breeders atop Magazine: look for both Ovenbird and Scarlet Tanager here and elsewhere.

Turn around, return to the paved road, and turn left. Immediately on the left is the Brown Spring picnic area. The "Maple-leaved Oak," a tree of some controversy, is found here on the cliff edge to the right of the spring. There is a debate over whether this is a true species or simply a sport or mutation of the Shumard Oak. At any rate, Magazine is one of the few places in the world where it is found. In the spring itself is *Stygobromus elatus*, a tiny amphipod endemic to Magazine.

Return to the main road and turn left. In 0.4 mile you'll come to the Cameron Bluff campground, where you can walk the roads to see Ovenbird, Scarlet Tanager, and other woodland birds. Ruffed Grouse have been reintroduced on the north slopes nearby, so there's a slight chance of hearing the males' "drumming" in spring.

The Signal Hill Trail begins just opposite the campground entrance. If you'd like to say that you've stood on the highest spot in Arkansas, it's only a short trudge up to Magazine's summit. A female Black-throated Green Warbler was found along this path in July 1994; see Page Hollow (site #36) for more information about this species in the Ozarks.

Turn left from the campground to return to State Highway 309. (Magazine can also be reached by taking Exit 35 from Interstate 40 at Ozark and following State Highways 23 and 309 40 miles to the summit.)

35. Mount Nebo State Park

Location: *From Exit 81 on Interstate 40 at Russellville, take State Highway 7 south 7.0 miles to State Highway 22; turn right 0.3 mile to State Highway 155. Take this road to a T intersection at the top of the mountain, 6.1 miles from State Highway 22. (See maps on pages 84 and 122.)*

Mount Nebo is an agreeable place to camp or picnic; the state park has cabins for rent, and 14 miles of hiking trails through mixed woods circle the mountaintop. Its birdlife is typical for the Ozark region except for one species: in recent years it has been the most accessible and reliable place to find Rufous-crowned Sparrow in Arkansas, and, until the birds began showing up at Pinnacle Mountain State Park (see site #9), probably the easternmost such spot in the United States. A fire in 1980 created the grassy, rocky habitat which the species needs; the forest has been recovering steadily since then, but the park plans to implement a management program for the sparrows.

The road to the top of Mount Nebo is one of the most tortuous you'll ever drive; it follows an old wagon road dating from the turn of the century, when resort hotels on the mountain provided a cool retreat for summer vacationers. Look for Greater Roadrunner on the way up. Once you get to the summit, you'll come to a T intersection and a stop sign.

Rufous-crowned Sparrow habitat at Mount Nebo State Park. *Photo by Mel White.*

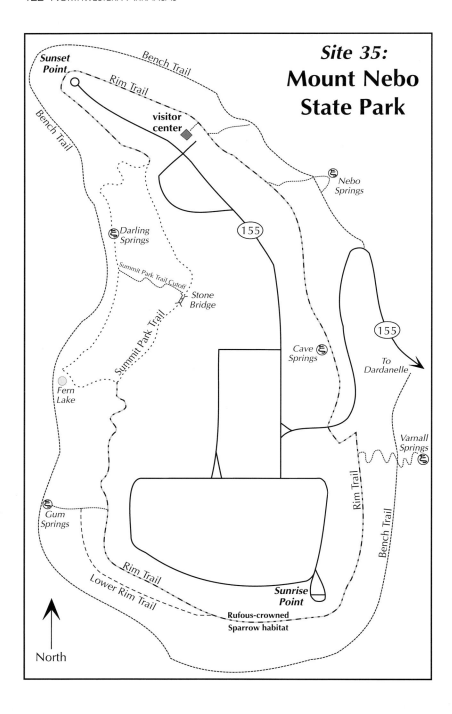

Site 35:
Mount Nebo State Park

Sunset Point

Bench Trail

Rim Trail

Bench Trail

visitor center

Nebo Springs

Darling Springs

155

Summit Park Trail Cutoff

Stone Bridge

Summit Park Trail

Cave Springs

155

To Dardanelle

Fern Lake

Varnall Springs

Rim Trail

Gum Springs

Bench Trail

Rim Trail

Lower Rim Trail

Sunrise Point

Rufous-crowned Sparrow habitat

North

Turn right and drive 0.7 mile to visit the park headquarters and pick up a map. Turn left, and left again at the next intersection, to get to Sunrise Point, where the sparrows are found.

There's a small parking area at the point, with a path leading down to a trail that follows the rim of the mountaintop. Once you're on the trail, you're in Rufous-crowned Sparrow habitat, although they're usually found a little farther to the right (south); you may have to walk as much as a quarter-mile to find them. The birds are occasionally seen at the parking area, on top of the rock bench. Watch for them near the ground in rocky areas. By the way, a Townsend's Solitaire showed up one February (for only the second Arkansas record) and stayed for several weeks, so it pays to lift your eyes every now and then. Rock Wren, another western rarity, has also been found here.

For information about Mount Nebo State Park, write Route 3, Box 374, Dardanelle, AR 72834, or call 229-3655.

36. Page Hollow

Location: *From Exit 81 off Interstate 40 at Russellville, drive north on State Highway 7 for 25.0 miles to Forest Service Road 1810 (Page Hollow Road) on the left.*

Within its more than one million acres, the Ozark National Forest contains rugged hills and bluffs, deep valleys, clear mountain streams—and, even after decades of exploration, a few surprises.

It has long been known that moist coves and north-facing slopes in the Ozarks are good places to find warblers, but nobody knew how good until University of Arkansas graduate student Paul Rodewald made an astonishing discovery in the summer of 1993. While researching the effects of various logging practices on bird populations, he found a small group of breeding Black-throated Green Warblers hundreds of miles from the known nesting range, which approaches Arkansas most closely in central Tennessee and northeastern Alabama. Rodewald also found four singing male Chestnut-sided Warblers nearby, well past their normal migration period and well out of their normal range, although without proof of breeding. In 1994, nesting was confirmed for this species; the BTGs returned as well.

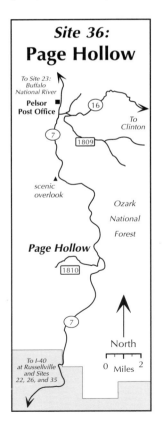

Immediately, the name Page Hollow entered the vocabulary of Arkansas birders. While, at this writing, no one knows the significance of the find—is it a temporary aberration, or part of a long-term trend? Have the birds been overlooked for years?—this area, with or without the BTGs and Chestnut-sideds, is a good place for interesting warblers and typical Ozark birds.

From State Highway 7, drive west on Forest Service Road 1810 (Page Hollow Road); you may find small yellow-and-black warning signs at culverts 2.0, 2.2, and 2.8 miles from the highway. BTGs were most often seen between the second and third of these sets of signs. Three family groups were found along Page Hollow Road in June 1993 and more than 15 adult birds were seen altogether, here and at nearby areas. Although there are a few pines on this steep hillside, the BTGs were found in deciduous trees only.

The next-most-special bird in Page Hollow is the Worm-eating Warbler, a species seldom seen in much of the state but fairly common in the Ozarks. Its reeling, mechanical chipping notes are much faster than those of Pine Warbler, found here in patches of pines. It responds well to pishing, as do the beautiful Hooded Warblers that nest in similar habitat. Other breeding birds of Page Hollow include Red-shouldered Hawk; Yellow-billed Cuckoo; Ruby-throated Hummingbird; Red-bellied, Downy, Hairy, and Pileated Woodpeckers; Acadian Flycatcher; White-breasted Nuthatch; Wood Thrush; Yellow-throated and Red-eyed (abundant, and incessantly vocal) Vireos; Black-and-white and Kentucky Warblers; Ovenbird; and Scarlet Tanager.

Three other birds to keep in mind while visiting these parts: Ruffed Grouse, a bird extirpated from the state before the turn of the century, has been reintroduced nearby; you may hear its "drumming" in springtime. Cedar Waxwing, that notoriously erratic wanderer, was discovered nesting not far from here in 1993. And Sharp-shinned Hawk, another new breeding species for Arkansas, was observed carrying food in June 1994. (Two additional pairs were seen elsewhere in the Ozark National Forest in the same month.)

Forest Service Road 1810 dead-ends shortly, having run fairly consistently downhill its entire length. A good strategy for exploring it is to park at various wide spots and walk uphill along the road, thus making your return to the car easier. Any place along this road can be good in migration; during the breeding season, birding is best beyond the first sharp bend in the road. You'll probably have to leave the road and kick around in the woods a little to get a look at a Worm-eating Warbler.

Return to State Highway 7 and turn left (north). In 6.8 miles, a scenic overlook on the left provides a long-distance view of the mountains, showing the flat-topped form of the "eroded plateau" that is the Ozarks' geological origin. Continue to the intersection of State Highways 7 and 16, 10.7 miles from Forest Service Road 1810. (A single Black-throated Green was seen in nesting season near the tiny Pelsor post office here.) Turn right onto State Highway 16; the stretch of this road between 0.4 and 0.7 mile from State Highway 7 is excellent for Cerulean Warbler. (Three males were territorial in 1993 and 1994.) In 0.7 mile turn right onto Forest Service Road 1809, which may be marked "Piney Creeks

Wildlife Management Area." The area near the junction of this road and State Highway 7 can be very productive during migration.

A short 0.4 mile from State Highway 16, you'll pass through a cut-over area with scrubby pines on the right. A Black-throated Green was seen here in July 1993, and others were found in this general area in 1994. Look also for Eastern Wood-Pewee, White-breasted Nuthatch, Blue-gray Gnatcatcher, Pine and Black-and-white Warblers, Scarlet Tanager, Blue Grosbeak, Indigo Bunting, and Rufous-sided Towhee.

Another 0.6 mile along is a clear-cut on the right; here is where three singing male Chestnut-sided Warblers were seen in 1993 and where the species was confirmed breeding in 1994 (a pair was seen feeding young on June 30). Chestnut-sideds seem to prefer overgrown clearcut areas with hardwoods between 10 and 15 feet tall. Other common nesting birds include Blue-gray Gnatcatcher; Wood Thrush; White-eyed and Red-eyed Vireos; Blue-winged, Worm-eating, Kentucky, and Hooded Warblers; Ovenbird; Yellow-breasted Chat; Scarlet Tanager; and Indigo Bunting. Hooded Warblers sing, among other variants, *a-weet, a-weet, a-weet, weet-whee-oh!* (with an insistent wolf whistle on the end), and *weet-weet-weet-weet sweet-sweet* (ending with two quick upslurred whistles).

Three or more Cerulean Warbler pairs have their territories across the road from the clearcut. The edge effect, where clearcut and forest meet, makes this a productive place in migration as well as during breeding season. Veery is a species noted here; several were present in May 1993 and 1994. A Cape May Warbler was found in May 1994.

Botanists should note that Moore's Delphinium (*Delphinium newtonianum*), an Arkansas endemic known from only four counties, is found in this area. The two-foot-high plant, with flowers in shades of blue or, rarely, white, blooms in June and July. It grows commonly along the road edge and inside the forest.

Some 0.3 mile beyond the clearcut you will enter mature woodland, excellent for forest birds. More Cerulean Warblers sing their song, *buzz-buzz-buzz-buzz-byeeez*, with a rising final note, in the canopy here. Road 1809 continues for several miles, connecting with other Forest Service routes. Exploring these roads can be a productive (and often extremely solitary) undertaking; you should equip yourself with one of the Forest Service's large-scale maps, showing the maze of interconnecting logging roads, before you begin. A compass would be a good idea, too.

From the intersection of State Highways 7 and 16, it's less than 35 miles north on 7 to the Buffalo River (see site #23). State Highway 7 from

Russellville to Harrison often makes lists of "America's ten most scenic roads," and it certainly has its high points; some of us, though, believe that Highways 21 and 23 (see Buffalo National River, site #23, and Redding Recreation Area, site #38), to the west, surpass it in beauty—and certainly in solitude.

37. Pea Ridge National Military Park

Location: *From the intersection of U.S. Highways 62 and 62B (Second Street) in Rogers, drive northeast 8.3 miles on U.S. Highway 62 to the park entrance.*

Pea Ridge National Military Park preserves the site of one of the most important Civil War clashes west of the Mississippi River. The Battle of Pea Ridge (also known as the Battle of Elkhorn Tavern) is often called "the battle that saved Missouri for the Union." A seven-mile auto tour route takes visitors across the battlefield where, after a fight that began May 7, 1862, and lasted a day and a half, Confederate forces withdrew when they ran low on ammunition.

Birders visit Pea Ridge primarily to find nesting Blue-winged Warbler, an uncommon and local breeder in Arkansas. Listen for the bird's raspy, two-note song in scrubby areas and old fields with small trees around the park from mid-April through June. The Leetown Battlefield stop on the tour route may be the best location.

Other breeding birds of Pea Ridge include Broad-winged Hawk; Northern Bobwhite; Acadian and Scissor-tailed Flycatchers; Blue-gray Gnatcatcher; Yellow-throated Vireo; Prairie, Kentucky, and Black-and-white Warblers; Yellow-breasted Chat; Summer Tanager; Dickcissel; Blue Grosbeak; Rufous-sided Towhee; and Field Sparrow. Grasshopper Sparrow, an uncommon and local breeder in Arkansas, has been found in fields near the headquarters. Bobolinks sometimes visit the park in spring migration, and Western Kingbird has been seen here in mid-May.

Pea Ridge National Military Park. *Photo by A.C. Haralson, courtesy of Arkansas Department of Parks and Tourism.*

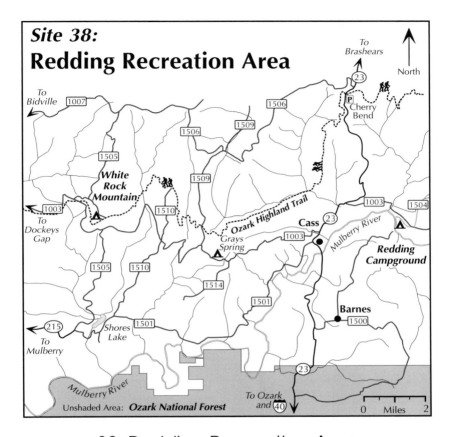

Site 38:
Redding Recreation Area

38. Redding Recreation Area

Location: *From Exit 35 on Interstate 40 at Ozark, take State Highway 23 north 14 miles to Forest Service Road 1003 (may also be marked as County Road 83; look for the Redding Campground sign). Turn right and drive 2.8 miles to another sign at a road on the right. Turn here and drive 0.7 mile to the campground.*

People from flat parts of the world may be ready for a rest after traveling to the Redding Recreation Area. State Highway 23, one of the hilliest, curviest roads you'll ever see, has been semi-affectionately known to Arkansas drivers for decades as "the pig trail;" today, the U.S. Forest Service has officially designated it as the Pig Trail Scenic Byway. Don't let that name dissuade you from driving it. It's not dangerous; just keep your eyes on the road and don't plan on doing a lot of birding from behind the wheel.

The Redding Recreation Area is operated by the Ozark National Forest. Located on the pretty Mulberry River, one of the state's top canoe streams, it's an excellent place to find a good variety of Ozark Mountain birds. If you camp here in spring or summer, you'll awake to the drumming of Pileated Woodpecker and the songs and calls of Yellow-billed Cuckoo; Acadian and Great Crested Flycatchers; Carolina Chickadee; Tufted Titmouse; White-breasted Nuthatch; Blue-gray Gnatcatcher; Wood Thrush; Yellow-throated and Red-eyed (the most abundant breeder) Vireos; Northern Parula; Black-and-white, Worm-eating, Kentucky, and Hooded Warblers; Ovenbird; and Scarlet Tanager. When it's time to turn in, you may hear lullabies from Eastern Screech- and Barred Owls. There may be Cerulean Warblers in the tall trees; perhaps you will find a Swainson's Warbler near the campsites.

The road into the camping area from State Highway 23 passes through private property with many *No Trespassing* signs, but once you're in the national forest, check clear-cuts and old-field habitat for Blue-winged and Prairie Warblers. Cedar Waxwing, a rare and irregular breeder in Arkansas, has been found nesting near here recently. This is also one of the sites chosen by the state Game and Fish Commission for restocking Ruffed Grouse.

If the campground itself is too crowded for good birding, walk or drive back along the entrance road to Road 1003 and bird anywhere you like along the roadsides or hillsides. Hiking trails begin in the campground, as well. Or drive back to State Highway 23, turn right (north), and drive 5.0 miles to a parking area on the right that provides access to the Ozark Highlands Trail. This 140-mile route runs from Lake Fort Smith State Park all the way across the national forest. The trail crosses State Highway 23 at a dependable birding spot called Cherry Bend, where the same birds listed for Redding can usually be found. The trailhead is across the highway from the parking area; from here, the trail runs both east and west. This is an excellent location for Cerulean Warblers, and most of the birds of the area can be picked up without much hiking or walking around.

Other highways and Forest Service roads provide access to the Ozark Highlands Trail for short (or long) hikes. If you're going very far from a road, get a trail map from Ozark National Forest headquarters (see address in the Introduction). You'll also need a good national forest map to explore some of the recreation and logging roads that crisscross it from one end to the other (see the Page Hollow listing, site #36).

A good place to investigate is the area around White Rock Mountain; one access route is Forest Service Road 1003, heading west from State Highway 23 1.4 miles south of the Redding campground road. There are countless hollows and hillsides for birding, and the effort to drive to the top of White Rock will be rewarded with some of the most fabulous panoramic vistas in Arkansas. Wandering around and stopping wherever the habitat looks productive is a good plan—but get a map first.

Barred Owl
Louise Zemaitis

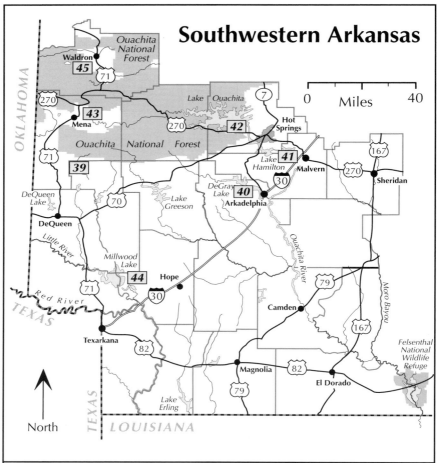

Southwestern Arkansas

0 Miles 40

North

Birding Sites in Southwestern Arkansas:

39	*Cossatot River State Park Natural Area*
40	*DeGray Lake*
41	*Hulsey State Fish Hatchery*
42	*Lake Ouachita*
43	*Mena Area*
44	*Millwood Lake*
45	*Waldron Area*

SOUTHWESTERN ARKANSAS

S outhwestern Arkansas, as delineated in this book, includes much of the Ouachita Mountains and Coastal Plain natural divisions. The Ouachitas are rugged ridges, running east and west, pushed up by geologic forces from the south; the Ouachita National Forest covers a vast area of west-central Arkansas, comprising mostly upland pine woods. The Coastal Plain is a land of rolling hills, with intensive exploitation of its lowland pine forest by timber companies. Areas of bottomland hardwoods exist along rivers; several large reservoirs, including Millwood, Ouachita, DeGray, and Greeson, have been formed by damming mountain streams.

Birding in southwestern Arkansas is dominated by Millwood Lake, among the state's hottest hotspots. Most of the credit for this ranking goes to Charles Mills of nearby Wilton, who consistently and conscientiously scours the lake and its environs for rarities, especially waders, shorebirds, and gulls—some of which have been seen nowhere else in Arkansas. The famed Millwood dam area is probably the most productive, but the Okay Dike is also well worth a visit; Max and Helen Parker found Arkansas's first Northern Wheatear there in 1990. It goes without saying that Millwood, located less than half an hour from Interstate 30, is a must stop for traveling birders.

The endangered Red-cockaded Woodpecker is found at scattered locations throughout the region; because this bird needs areas of mature pine trees, it has been hurt by modern timber practices, which involve fire suppression and cutting of large tracts at relatively short intervals. The Brown-headed Nuthatch is common in southern Arkansas pines, and Bachman's Sparrow sings its sweet song in clear-cuts, where Prairie Warbler also finds a home. Unfortunately for those who'd like to cruise timber-company land to search for the last-named species, much of it is now leased to hunting clubs, which put up massive locked gates to keep out non-members.

A note on Hot Springs National Park: Curious travelers may be misled by the name of this federal reservation, which in truth is more like a national monument or historic site. You will find no truly wild areas here, only historical displays and a few short nature trails through mature pines,

133

which may have Brown-headed Nuthatches. Most birders in the area would rather visit the Hulsey State Fish Hatchery south of Lake Hamilton to look for migrant shorebirds and wintering ducks.

Cossatot River State Park. *Photo by A.C. Haralson, courtesy of Arkansas Department of Parks and Tourism.*

39. Cossatot River State Park Natural Area

Location: *From the intersection of U.S. Highway 71 and State Highway 246, about 18 miles south of Mena, drive east on State Highway 246 for 9.1 miles to the Cossatot River bridge. (See map on page 136.)*

This relatively new (established in 1988) state park protects a narrow strip of land bordering 11 miles of the Cossatot (CAHSS-uh-tot) River, a nationally designated Wild and Scenic River. The Cossatot's main appeal is for kayakers and canoeists who challenge its exciting, but treacherous, whitewater. "Cossatot" comes from the French *casse-tête*, or tomahawk—literally, "head-breaker" or "skull-crusher." Especially during periods of high water, the Class III-V rapids are not for the casual paddler. Birders will find a ruggedly beautiful stream corridor with typical breeding birds of the Ouachita Mountains. Cerulean and Hooded Warblers are probably the best birds here, the former quite rare in tall trees near the river and the latter in moist, wooded coves.

Stop at the Brushy Creek Access Area at the State Highway 246 bridge, where you'll find picnic sites (on the east bank) and a swimming hole great for cooling off on a hot day. At this writing, the park, which is intended to remain a primitive area, has no visitor center, and a bulletin board on the west bank may be the only locally available source of information. (Before visiting the park, write or call the office, listed below, for a brochure.) There's a short nature trail on the east bank where you may find Pileated Woodpecker and Pine Warbler all year, and breeding Broad-winged Hawk and Summer and Scarlet Tanagers.

Return to State Highway 246 and continue east 2.6 miles to a dirt road on the right. Access to downstream areas of the Cossatot is by way of a tangled maze of Weyerhaeuser logging roads, and first-time visitors would do well to arm themselves with the company's Southwest Arkansas Recreation Map, available free by calling Weyerhaeuser's Hot Springs office at 624-8000, or by writing to Weyerhaeuser, P.O. Box 1060, Hot Springs, AR 71902. This road is number 52200, and it should also be signed "CRSPNA River Access." Similar signs should be located at major intersections. *If you visit on a workday, watch for heavy log trucks on the narrow roads.*

You will pass through areas that could only be (1) nuclear test sites or (2) timber-company clearcuts. The beautiful, and now-protected, river is surrounded by a giant, intensively worked pine-tree farm, and denuded land is everywhere. It wouldn't be safe to drive these roads with your eyes closed, so try to distract yourself by thinking of ways to promote

Site 39: Cossatot River State Park Natural Area

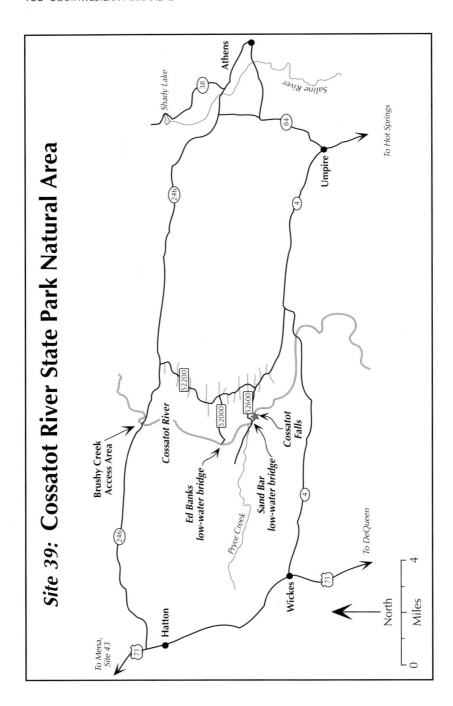

waste-paper recycling. (Remember, too, that Weyerhaeuser's cooperation made a significant contribution to the river's preservation.) During spring and summer listen for White-eyed Vireo, Prairie Warbler, Common Yellowthroat, and Indigo Bunting. At any time of year, a roadside Wild Turkey or Greater Roadrunner may reward those who have been living right.

At an intersection 3.3 miles from the highway, turn right on a road that may or may not be marked 52000. (A park access sign points in the other direction, to the Falls, which you'll visit later.) At crossings, stay on what seems the main route. After 1.5 miles you will arrive at the park boundary, and 0.6 mile farther, at the Ed Banks low-water bridge. Park near here and take a moment to enjoy the rushing, rocky river. Although there is no formal trail, you can walk along the road in either direction, or pick your way along the river, to bird. The sound of the water may make it hard to hear at streamside. Watch for (permanent residents) Great Blue Heron, Red-shouldered Hawk, Northern Bobwhite, Belted Kingfisher, Greater Roadrunner, Barred Owl, Field Sparrow, and American Goldfinch, and (breeding) Green Heron; Yellow-billed Cuckoo; Acadian and Great Crested Flycatchers; Wood Thrush; Yellow-throated and Red-eyed Vireos; Northern Parula; Cerulean, Black-and-white, Kentucky, and Hooded Warblers; Ovenbird; Louisiana Waterthrush; and Yellow-breasted Chat. Both Chuck-will's-widow and Whip-poor-will breed in the area.

Return to road 52200, turn right, and drive 2.1 miles to a T intersection at road 52600. Turn right again. In 0.8 mile, a short spur on the left leads to the beautiful Cossatot Falls, where tilted rock ledges testify to the tectonic forces that folded, fractured, and pushed up the Ouachita Mountains. You can bird along the river, but this site is sometimes crowded with swimmers and campers. (Primitive camping is allowed here; there are few facilities, and the road in is much too rough for trailers.) Two very rare plants, Waterfalls Sedge and Ouachita Mountain Twistflower, grow nearby; the latter displays a long spike of purple flowers in May and June. Another extreme rarity, the highly threatened Leopard Darter, is found in Arkansas only in the Cossatot.

Return to 52600 turn left, and drive 0.8 mile to the Sand Bar bridge, or 0.2 mile farther to another bridge on Pryor Creek. Again, walk along the river or along the roads. You'll find the same birds here as at the Falls, and the area is likely to have fewer people.

The Cossatot isn't a birding hotspot like Millwood Lake to the south, but it is a good spot for warblers and other woodland birds, and a place at which to experience one of Arkansas's finest wild rivers. Developed campsites are located in the Ouachita National Forest east of the park, at the Shady Lake Recreation Area. Return to State Highway 246 and drive east approximately 13 miles to Forest Service Road 38; turn left (north) and drive five miles to the recreation area.

For information on Cossatot River State Park Natural Area, write P.O. Box 170-A, Wickes, AR 71937, or call 385-2201.

Cerulean Warbler
Gail Diane Yovanovich

40. DeGray Lake

Location: *Take the State Highway 7 exit (Exit 78) on Interstate 30 north of Arkadelphia. (See map on page 140.)*

DeGray is a 13,800-acre Corps of Engineers reservoir located only a few miles from Interstate 30. Several recreation areas ring the lake, comprising scores of camping and picnicking sites. In addition, DeGray State Park, on the north shore of the reservoir, offers visitors a lodge, a restaurant, camping, swimming, a golf course, a marina, nature trails, and seasonal naturalist-led boat tours.

DeGray's breeding birds are interesting, although they may not be the area's main attraction. Bachman's Sparrow and Prairie Warbler breed near the dam, where there's a chance of seeing a Greater Roadrunner. Scissor-tailed Flycatchers can be found on the golf course, Brown-headed Nuthatches twitter in the pines year-round, and the strangled honk of Fish Crows can be heard among the *caws* of American Crows. Yellow-throated Vireo and Yellow-throated Warbler are uncommon breeders in DeGray State Park, and Red-shouldered Hawk is a permanent resident. A lucky visitor might see a small flock of Wild Turkeys early in the morning. And, as this book was being completed, a pair of Bald Eagles attempted to nest on an island in the lake; they were thought to be young birds building a "practice" nest, but they could well return in the future for the real thing. (As this book was going to press, a shocking and saddening mystery was unfolding at DeGray. In the winter of 1994-95, more than two dozen Bald Eagles were found dead or dying along the northern shoreline of the lake. None had been shot, and none showed obvious signs of infectious illness or poisoning. Scientists from around the country were baffled by this occurrence, despite intensive testing of dead birds. Good numbers of apparently healthy eagles remained on other parts of the lake.)

It's in migration and winter that DeGray entices birders with an array of waterbirds. Red-throated Loon, Eared and Western Grebes, Anhinga, Least Bittern, Oldsquaw, White-winged Scoter, Willet, and Laughing Gull are among the rarities that have appeared here. Species seen regularly from fall through spring include Common Loon, Pied-billed and Horned Grebes, American White Pelican (migration), American Bittern (migration), Hooded and Red-breasted Mergansers, Osprey (migration), and Bald Eagle (common around the shoreline in winter), as well as the usual ducks. Corps of Engineers sites and the state park provide a number

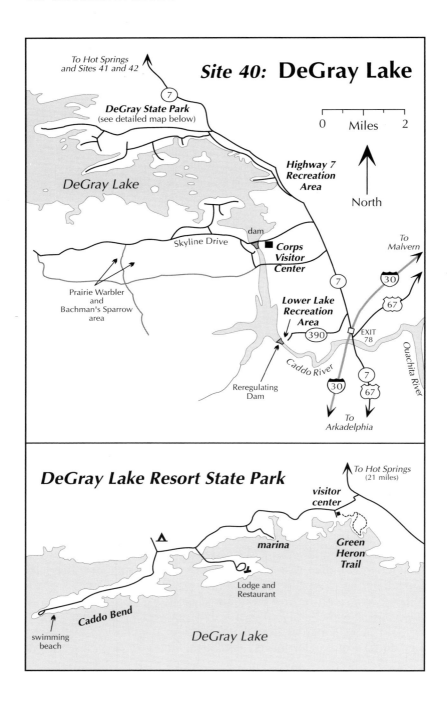

Site 40: DeGray Lake

To Hot Springs
and Sites 41 and 42

7

DeGray State Park
(see detailed map below)

0   Miles   2

DeGray Lake

**Highway 7
Recreation
Area**

North

dam

Skyline Drive

■ **Corps
Visitor
Center**

To
Malvern

7

30

Prairie Warbler
and
Bachman's Sparrow
area

**Lower Lake
Recreation
Area**

390

67

EXIT
78

Reregulating
Dam

Caddo River

30

7

67

Ouachita River

To
Arkadelphia

DeGray Lake Resort State Park

To Hot Springs
(21 miles)

**visitor
center**

marina

**Green
Heron
Trail**

Lodge and
Restaurant

Caddo Bend

swimming
beach

DeGray Lake

of places from which to view the lake; the best plan is simply to visit as many as you have time for and scan the water.

From Interstate 30, head north on State Highway 7 and immediately turn left on State Highway 390. Continue 1.8 miles to the Lower Lake recreation area, where a "reregulating" dam forms a pool below the main lake. This is a good spot for spring migrants and for Brown-headed Nuthatch and Eastern Bluebird year-round. Keep left past the restrooms to a spot where the road dead-ends at the Caddo River in an area of wet woods. Swainson's Warbler has been found here fairly often in spring.

Check the water above the dam for ducks in fall and winter. This area is closed to waterfowl hunting, so it can be especially productive during winter shooting season. Scan it from the riprap (rock) dam, or follow the dirt road that goes straight where the paved entrance drive turns left. Walking this road can also produce good migrant passerines. Incidentally, although it's a long shot, the riprap dam here is just the sort of place where Rock Wrens are occasionally found in winter.

Return to State Highway 7 and continue north 2.5 miles to the turnoff on your left toward the main dam. In 0.8 mile, the spillway parking area on the right is a good place to look for wintering waterfowl and Bald Eagle. In 0.6 mile, stop at the Corps visitor center on the left for a map of the lake, then continue over the dam; keep an eye out for Greater Roadrunner after crossing the dam. Birding skill brings results with many species, but sheer luck often seems to be the determining factor in seeing a Greater Roadrunner. You could, however, try the trick (espoused by Little Rock birder Bill Shepherd) of rattling two sticks together, imitating the roadrunner's bill-clattering, to lure one into view. If nothing else, you might discover some latent talent as a percussionist.

Watch for a pullout and dirt road on the left 2.3 miles beyond the visitor center. The adjacent scrubby area with scattered young pines has been excellent in recent years for breeding Prairie Warbler and Bachman's Sparrow. The sparrow's preferred habitat—scattered pines with grassy or weedy understory—rapidly succeeds into forest, so it can be difficult to pin down a spot where it can be found for more than a few years. Here, though, the removal of topsoil in construction work has created an environment where trees have remained small and scattered. The dirt road continues through similar habitat for several miles.

In the words of Helen Parker: "Here in south-central Arkansas, we seek this species in one- to five-year-old pine plantations.... These areas are enhanced if they happen to have a few scattered standing trees, either alive or dead.... The most important features seem to be: a well-drained site with perhaps some washes (these may become territorial boundaries);

Bald Eagle at DeGray Lake Resort State Park. *Photo courtesy of Arkansas Department of Parks and Tourism.*

plenty of low woody and herbaceous vegetation for cover, perching, and foraging (this bird feeds on or very near the ground); a sufficient growth of the *Andropogon* grass used for nest-building; and some open, bare ground mixed among the grasses." The best way to see a Bachman's Sparrow is to spend time in this kind of habitat at dawn and dusk, listening for its clear, sweet song: a whistle followed by a musical trill.

Return to State Highway 7 and turn left; drive 1.2 miles to the State Highway 7 recreation area, where the road runs down a peninsula from which it's convenient to check the water on both sides. A Red-throated Loon was seen here in March 1994. Brown-headed Nuthatches are usually easy to find in this area.

Go back to State Highway 7, turn left, drive 1.4 miles, and turn left toward DeGray State Park; make another left turn in 1.1 miles and drive 0.2 mile to the park visitor center. Stop and pick up a park map and bird list, and ask the park naturalist about any good sightings. The Green Heron Trail, a loop of less than a mile beginning behind the visitor center, is the best of the park's trails for birding; it's good for both land birds and waterbirds, and often has an interesting variety of winter sparrows. At one point it passes near an imposing riprap levee where you might look again for winter Rock Wren.

The marina, 0.9 mile farther on, provides another location for checking the lake. The turnoff to the state park lodge and restaurant (both well worth a traveler's consideration) is located 0.6 mile past the marina road. The 1994 unsuccessful Bald Eagle nest was located on an island that can be seen from the lodge, though the nest itself was not visible. In winter, continue 0.4 mile to a T intersection and turn left, following this road 1.5 miles to its dead end in the Caddo Bend picnic area. Here you'll find another narrow peninsula good for scanning the lake for loons, grebes, ducks, and eagles. For warm-weather visitors, there's an inviting swimming beach.

For information about DeGray Lake, write the Resource Manager, No. 30 IP Circle, Arkadelphia, AR 71923, or call 246-5501. For information about DeGray State Park, write Route 3, Box 490, Bismarck, AR 71929, or call 865-2801.

Birders in the DeGray area may want to visit the Arkadelphia sewage-treatment ponds, which are great for wintering ducks. To reach the site, return to Interstate 30, drive southwest 4.8 miles, and take Exit 73 at Arkadelphia. Drive east toward town on Highway 8 (Pine Street). After 2.2 miles, turn right onto 10th Street; drive one block and turn left onto Caddo Street; drive 0.1 mile and turn right onto 7th Street; drive 0.5 mile to Walnut Street and a T intersection. Turn left and continue straight ahead across the railroad tracks; drive 0.3 mile to a stop sign at 3rd Street, which may be unmarked. Turn right here and drive 1.8 miles to the sewer-pond gate on the left. *Park on the road outside the gate and walk to the ponds.* This spot has turned up a number of rarities in recent years, including Tricolored Heron, Roseate Spoonbill, Cinnamon Teal, Oldsquaw, and Surf Scoter; it's also usually good for seeing high numbers of the beautiful Hooded Merganser.

41. Hulsey State Fish Hatchery

Location: *From the intersection of U.S. Highways 70 and 270 and State Highway 7 in Hot Springs, take State Highway 7 south 7.9 miles to State Highway 290; turn left (east) on 290 and drive 2.8 miles to the hatchery entrance; turn left and drive 0.6 mile to the ponds.*

This Arkansas Game and Fish Commission operation comprises several ponds of varying sizes located near the south shore of Lake Hamilton. In winter, the ponds attract ducks, often allowing close looks at a good number of species. In migration, drained, muddy ponds provide rest and food for shorebirds.

Although some observation can be done from a car on the main road through the hatchery (and that is occasionally best, when ducks are in nearby ponds), birders should walk the levees, checking the ponds and the bordering fields, to assure complete coverage. Great Blue Herons are common all year, as are Green and Little Blue Herons in breeding season. Ospreys are regular migrants. Depending on the season and the state of the ponds, other birds can be either nonexistent or very interesting. The ducks most likely to be seen include Mallard, Northern Shoveler, Gadwall, American Wigeon, Ring-necked Duck, Lesser Scaup, and Bufflehead, although nearly any species on the Arkansas list could show up. The same could be said of shorebirds, which are most common in April and May and from late July through fall.

Among the rarities seen here have been (winter) Oldsquaw, Black and Surf Scoters, and Short-eared Owl; (fall) Glossy Ibis, White-winged Scoter, White-rumped Sandpiper, Red-necked and Red Phalaropes, Sharp-tailed Sparrow, and Yellow-headed Blackbird; and (spring) Least Bittern. It was here, too, that Max and Helen Parker found Arkansas's first, and thus far only, Mountain Bluebird.

Park near the hatchery visitor center and begin your walk eastward along a road paralleling the north boundary fence. You'll pass a grassy, marshy area good for winter sparrows and wrens, and an arm of Lake Hamilton where Pied-billed Grebes are common in winter. Belted Kingfishers rattle and dive nearby, and you'll soon scare up more than one Great Blue Heron. Keep watching the sky for a Red-shouldered Hawk or hunting falcons; a few Black Vultures usually mix with the common Turkey Vultures. Watch for birds in the grassy areas at pond edges; Common Snipe and American Pipit are seen often. Circle back and check the ponds on the west side of the entrance road before returning to your car.

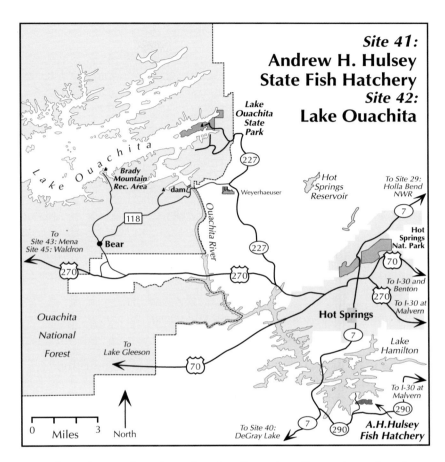

Site 41:
Andrew H. Hulsey State Fish Hatchery
Site 42:
Lake Ouachita

Follow the road to the Lake Hamilton shoreline, where there's an observation deck from which you can scan in winter for loons, grebes, and ducks. Regardless of how many ducks you've found at the hatchery, there's usually something different on the lake. Bald Eagles are fairly common winter residents.

42. Lake Ouachita

Location: *From the intersection of U.S. Highways 70 and 270 and State Highway 7 in Hot Springs, drive west on U.S. Highway 270 4.9 miles to State Highway 227. (See map on page 145.)*

Lake Ouachita (WASH-ih-taw), a Corps of Engineers reservoir covering more than 40,000 acres, is Arkansas's largest lake. The clarity of its water makes it a favorite among scuba divers; it also draws heavy use from water-skiers, houseboaters, and fishermen.

Ouachita has not been as popular with Arkansas birders. Its sheer sprawling size, its countless narrow coves, and the distances between observation points often make an expedition here seem less productive than one to, say, nearby DeGray Lake, which, although smaller, has a better list of notable sightings. This is the case despite the fact that Ouachita undeniably has great potential. Birders who have chartered boats and barges for midwinter cruises on Ouachita have found great numbers of Common Loons, Pied-billed and Horned Grebes, ducks, Bald Eagles, and gulls (mostly Ring-billed, with some Bonaparte's and Herring). Diligent searching in fall and winter no doubt would turn up occasional rarities—perhaps Red-throated Loon, Western Grebe, scoters, or even Sabine's Gull. (Probably none so spectacular, though, as the Marbled Murrelet that was photographed at Ouachita's Denby Point in November 1980.)

To check accessible areas at the lower end of the lake, drive north on State Highway 227 from U.S. Highway 270 in western Hot Springs. After 6.2 miles turn right with the highway at a huge Weyerhaeuser plant, where you can find out what happens to pine trees in southern Arkansas. Continue 5.5 miles to Lake Ouachita State Park. Camping, cabins, and picnic sites are available here, and a marina rents boats for those who'd like to explore the lake by water. (If you do this, be careful: winter winds can make Ouachita's open water rough.) You can scan from various places in and around the park, especially along the Caddo Bend trail; Bald Eagle is seen often in tall lakeside trees all winter. Brown-headed Nuthatch is a permanent resident in pines.

Return to the Weyerhaeuser plant, turn right, and drive 2.1 miles to the Blakely Mountain Dam. Just beyond is the Corps of Engineers visitor center, where you can get a free lake map. Continue a short way up the hill to the top of the dam and scan for wintering waterfowl and eagles.

Return to the bottom of the dam and turn right on a road marked Avery Recreation Area. Drive 1.8 miles and turn left, following a partly paved,

Brown-headed Nuthatch
Gail Diane Yovanovich

partly gravel road 3.9 miles to an intersection in the tiny hamlet of Bear. Turn right and drive 4.2 miles to the Brady Mountain Recreation Area, where you'll find various viewpoints over large expanses of open water. The Bald Eagle is making an encouraging comeback as a breeding species throughout Arkansas; Lake Ouachita's first eagle nest was found near here in 1992. Retrace your route, driving 6.1 miles (straight ahead through Bear) to U.S. Highway 270. Here you can turn left to return to Hot Springs or right to visit more Lake Ouachita recreation areas.

Those with limited time may wish to visit the Brady Mountain area without the earlier stops. To do so, drive west on U.S. Highway 270 7.4 miles from the 270-227 intersection and turn right toward the lake.

For information on Lake Ouachita, write Resource Manager, P.O. Box 4, Mountain Pine, AR 71956, or call 767-2101. For information on Lake Ouachita State Park, write Star Route 1, Box 1160, Mountain Pine, AR 71956, or call 767-9366.

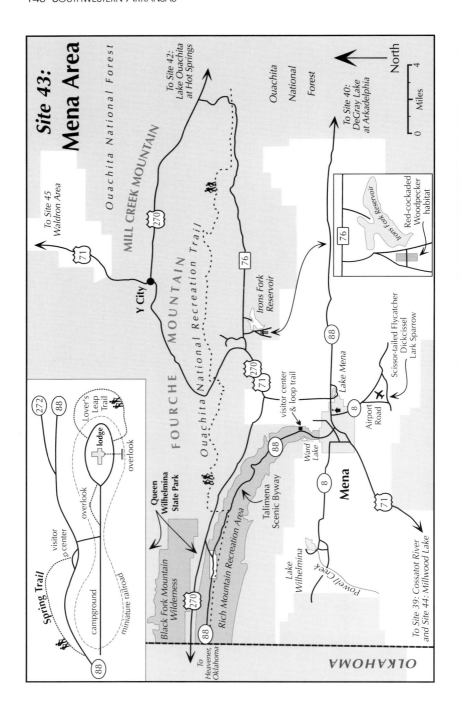

Site 43:
Mena Area

43. Mena Area

Location: *Mena is located 99 miles north of Texarkana on U.S. Highway 71.*

Several interesting birding sites are located near the town of Mena, in west-central Arkansas, including a small population of Red-cockaded Woodpeckers and reliable locations for breeding Hooded Warbler and Lark Sparrow. In addition, travelers will find great sight-seeing (and a lesson in orogeny, or mountain-building) along the Talimena Scenic Byway, which follows ridgelines through the Ouachita National Forest from Mena 54 miles west to Talihina, Oklahoma. The rocky habitat of the Ouachita Mountains is attractive to Greater Roadrunner (Mena perpetually leads the state's Christmas Bird Counts in the number of roadrunners seen), so watch for this birders' favorite along roadsides anywhere in the area.

Red-cockaded Woodpeckers are found near Irons Fork Reservoir, north of Mena. Begin at the intersection of U.S. Highway 71 and State Highway 88 north of town; drive north for 6.7 miles on U.S. Highway 71 and turn right onto a gravel road; this is County Road 76, although it may be unmarked as such. (If you're approaching from the north, this road is 12.5 miles south of the intersection of U.S. Highways 270 and 71, at Y City.) Drive 1.2 miles and turn right; where the road forks in 0.1 mile take the left fork. In 0.4 mile there is a view of the lake on the left; Bald Eagles roost here in the winter, and there usually are wintering ducks. The Red-cockaded Woodpecker habitat is just beyond this point on the right. Listen here, too, for the *squeebee* of Brown-headed Nuthatches and the trilling of Pine Warblers; in winter look for Golden-crowned Kinglets high in the pines.

Important note: *It cannot be stressed too much that the Red-cockaded Woodpecker is an endangered species, barely hanging on to existence in the face of logging practices and declining quality of habitat. No ethical birder would ever do anything to harm or harass an RCW or interfere with its nesting. This includes hitting or scratching on a roost tree to cause a bird to appear and standing too close to a cavity tree when a bird is trying to go to roost or to bring food to its young. If you spend time quietly observing, you can see an RCW without interfering with the birds' activities.*

For better views of Irons Fork Reservoir, return to County Road 76, turn right, and drive 1.1 miles to the lake entrance on the right. Turn in here and drive about 0.5 mile, watching for a left turn down a rough road toward a bluff overlooking the lake. This is the best place to find Bald

Eagles coming in to roost from mid-November to the end of February. Get here an hour before sunset and watch carefully; although it might seem easy to see such big birds, they're good at sneaking up from the lake and hiding in the pines. Bring a scope, and where you see one bird, scan the nearby trees for others. Check the lake for Common Goldeneye and Hooded Merganser. Brushy areas will have Rufous-sided Towhee and other sparrows, including Fox. The woods around the lake can be good for migrants and such typical Ouachita Mountain breeding birds as Broad-winged Hawk, Yellow-billed Cuckoo, Eastern Wood-Pewee, Red-eyed Vireo, and Summer Tanager.

Mena is more-or-less surrounded by the Ouachita National Forest, and a large-scale forest map will allow you explore an extensive network of logging roads. (Following County Road 76 eastward, for instance, will take you through the national forest, eventually depositing you on U.S. Highway 270.) As cutover areas, which change from year to year, begin to regenerate with young pines, you can find breeding Prairie Warbler, Yellow-breasted Chat, and (with luck) Bachman's Sparrow. At dawn and dusk in late winter, these areas can reward a visitor with the *bzeep* call note and twittering flight displays of American Woodcock.

Return to the intersection of U.S. Highway 71 and State Highway 88; turn back left (east) on Highway 88, and in 0.1 mile look for a large stone gateway on the right. Turn here and follow this road 1.4 mile around Lake Mena, keeping left at intersections. Much of this area is private property, but there are places from which the lake and its marshy shoreline can be viewed. Look for waterfowl in winter and waders at other times; a very unlikely White-faced Ibis showed up here in the spring of 1991.

Where the road returns to State Highway 88, turn left and drive 0.8 mile back to U.S. Highway 71, stopping, if you like, at an access point on your left to scan the lake again. Continue west on U.S. Highway 71 for 1.0 mile to State Highway 8. (There is a Forest Service office on the left side of U.S. Highway 71 where you can obtain maps and Ouachita National Forest information.) Turn left (south) on State Highway 8 and drive 2.1 miles to Airport Road on the right; turn here and drive 1.5 miles (the road changes from paved to dirt) to a T intersection; turn left here.

Along this road, which follows the boundary of the Mena airport, you can find breeding Scissor-tailed Flycatcher, Dickcissel, and Lark Sparrow. Watch for them on fence wires; you may have to pull over to the side (this is not a busy road) and look around a bit for the sparrows. In winter, White-crowned Sparrows are found here, and this is a good spot for Greater Roadrunner any time. After 1.1 miles, turn around and return to U.S. Highway 71. Turn left and drive 1.0 mile to the downtown corner

Red-cockaded Woodpecker habitat at Irons Fork Reservoir. *Photo by Mel White.*

where State Highway 88 diverges from U.S. Highway 71 to head west up Rich Mountain, toward Queen Wilhelmina State Park.

Turn right and continue 1.3 mile to the Talimena Scenic Byway visitor center. National Forest maps, trail guides, and travel information are available here. The $2 guide to the Talimena drive will increase your enjoyment and appreciation of what you're about to see. The adjoining Earthquake Ridge Trail, a 2.7-mile loop, is a good leg-stretcher, but it never gets far from the highway. Nonetheless, birding can be rewarding in the woods around the visitor center. Watch for Wild Turkey and, in winter, for Red-breasted Nuthatch.

From this point the byway climbs steeply up Rich Mountain, eventually reaching an altitude of more than 2,600 feet. At 2.7 miles from the visitor center, look on the left for exposed sedimentary rock strata of sandstone and shale, showing how these rugged mountains were once part of an ocean floor. The slight irregularities in the strata here are a hint of the enormous tectonic forces that thrust up the Ouachitas by folding and faulting. Where scenic overlooks provide a north view, look across the valley to Black Fork Mountain, with its unusual "rock glaciers" or rock slides. The origin of these "rivers" of broken sandstone is debated; they move slowly down the slope *en masse*, reminiscent of the motion of ice glaciers. All the overlooks overlook endless vistas of tree-covered mountains and rolling hills. If you're driving the byway in winter, keep an eye out for soaring Golden Eagles at overlooks and anywhere along the way; they're rare, but this is one of the best places in Arkansas to find them. Speaking of rarities, the Rich Mountain Salamander (*Plethodon ouachitae*), which lives under logs and leaf litter, is endemic to this mountain and a few spots in nearby Oklahoma.

The Ouachita Mountains, almost uniquely in North America, run east to west; the microclimates of their south- and north-facing slopes differ in noticeable ways. The most obvious difference is that the north slopes are moister and richer in vegetation. Spring wildflowers can be abundant. Along the ridgetop, notice how trees, often Post and Blackjack Oaks, are stunted by drying south winds and winter ice.

Stop at the Wilhelmina Vista overlook, 9.4 miles from the visitor center. Walk west along the road a short distance (be very careful; the shoulder is narrow) to an access point of the Ouachita National Recreation Trail on the right. This will lead you into woodland where, in spring and summer, you may find Broad-winged Hawk; Great Crested Flycatcher; Wood Thrush; Red-eyed Vireo (abundant); Black-and-white, Kentucky, and Hooded Warblers; Ovenbird; and Summer and Scarlet Tanagers. You may want to turn around before you reach the end of the trail, since it's about 120 miles away, at Little Rock.

A similar but more accessible (and better maintained) trail is found at Queen Wilhelmina State Park, 11.7 miles from the visitor center. Turn into a parking lot on the right, opposite the entrance to the park lodge and restaurant (both worth your attention). The one-third-mile Spring Trail, which begins here, crosses moist north-facing coves with White Oak, Hop Hornbeam, Ohio Buckeye, and Solomon's Seal. There are usually a few pairs of Hooded Warblers along this trail, which, unfortunately, never takes you far from the sound of traffic on the highway.

You can continue driving west along the Talimena Scenic Byway into Oklahoma and more picture-postcard scenery, or turn around here. The Robert S. Kerr Arboretum and Nature Center, across the state line 18.5 miles from Queen Wilhelmina State Park, has interpretive trails and exhibits on the natural history of the Ouachitas. The lodge at the state park is a fine place to stay, but be sure to call for reservations. For information, write HC-07, Box 53A, Mena, AR 71953, or call 394-2863.

Lake Wilhelmina, west of Mena, is a state Game and Fish Commission lake formed by a dam on Powell Creek. It's a favorite with local birders for wintering Bald Eagles and waterfowl, as well as for migrant songbirds. To reach it, begin at the south intersection of Highways 71 and 8, just southwest of downtown Mena, and drive west on Highway 8 for 7.1 miles to the lake entrance on the right. Continue 0.3 mile to the lake. A road circles the water to the left, with various access-points to scan the lake and bird the surrounding woods. A female Surf Scoter showed up here in December 1993.

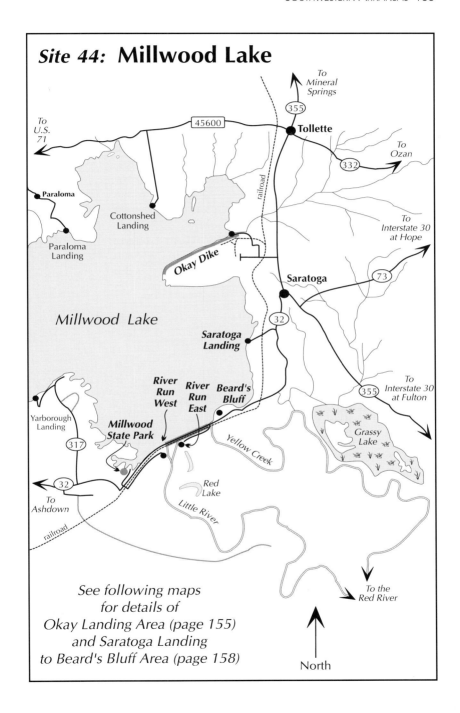

Site 44: Millwood Lake

To Mineral Springs

355

To U.S. 71

45600

Tollette

To Ozan

332

Paraloma

Cottonshed Landing

railroad

To Interstate 30 at Hope

Paraloma Landing

Okay Dike

Saratoga

73

Millwood Lake

32

Saratoga Landing

To Interstate 30 at Fulton

355

River Run West

River Run East

Beard's Bluff

Yarborough Landing

317

Millwood State Park

Yellow Creek

Grassy Lake

32

Red Lake

To Ashdown

railroad

Little River

To the Red River

*See following maps
for details of
Okay Landing Area (page 155)
and Saratoga Landing
to Beard's Bluff Area (page 158)*

North

44. Millwood Lake

Location: *For southbound travelers on Interstate 30: from the State Highway 4 exit (Exit 30) from I-30 at Hope, drive north on State Highway 4 for 1.6 miles to State Highway 73. Turn left and drive 18.6 miles west on State Highway 73 to State Highway 355. Turn right and drive 0.6 mile north to the junction of State Highways 355 and 32. For northbound travelers on Interstate 30: take the U.S. Highway 71 exit north in Texarkana 16 miles to Ashdown. In Ashdown, take State Highway 32 east 8 miles to Millwood Lake (See map on page 153.)*

Millwood Lake, a 30,000-acre Corps of Engineers reservoir in the southwestern corner of Arkansas, is one of the state's true hotspots for birders. This fact is due primarily to the diversity of habitat found in a relatively small area, and secondarily to the lake's layout. Unlike Arkansas's deep-water mountain reservoirs, which have many small coves that can be hard to cover, Millwood is a broad, shallow lake, much of which can be seen from one or two observation points. And it doesn't hurt that Millwood is in far south Arkansas, convenient for Gulf Coast wanderers. Even a summary of Millwood's highlights makes for a lengthy listing.

Of the 380 species of birds recorded in Arkansas, 311 have been seen at or within a few miles of Millwood. The first Arkansas sightings of Black-bellied Whistling-Duck, Parasitic Jaeger, Pomarine Jaeger, Long-tailed Jaeger, Little Gull, Common Black-headed Gull, Glaucous Gull, Black-legged Kittiwake, Sabine's Gull, Bridled Tern, Inca Dove, and Northern Wheatear all occurred at Millwood. Millwood is one of the best places in Arkansas for such rarities as Western Grebe, Tricolored Heron, White Ibis (may breed locally), Wood Stork, Black-bellied Whistling-Duck (almost certainly breeds locally), Greater Scaup, American Avocet, and Laughing Gull.

Bald Eagle and Great-tailed Grackle, both rare breeders in Arkansas, have nested at or near Millwood. Tree Swallow, local in the state, also nests. Among the other noteworthy Millwood sightings: Red-throated Loon, Brown Pelican, Magnificent Frigatebird (one bird carried inland by a hurricane), White-faced Ibis, Fulvous Whistling-Duck, Tundra Swan, Ross's Goose, Cinnamon Teal, Oldsquaw, Black (two sightings, both in November), Surf, and White-winged Scoters, Swainson's Hawk, Merlin, Peregrine Falcon, Hudsonian and Marbled Godwits, Red Knot, Ruff, Red-necked and Red Phalaropes, Groove-billed Ani, Burrowing Owl, "Red-shafted" Northern Flicker, Say's Phoebe, Vermilion Flycatcher,

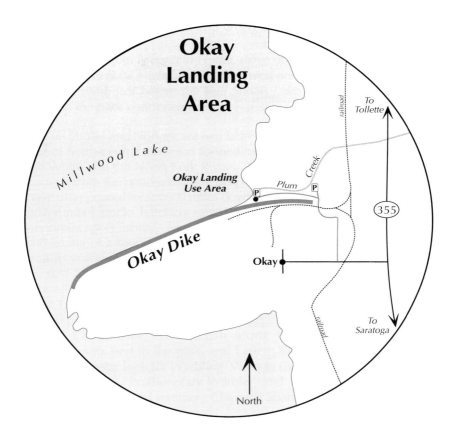

Western Kingbird, Rock Wren, Sprague's Pipit, Cape May and Black-throated Blue Warblers, Yellow-headed Blackbird, and Clay-colored, Henslow's, and Sharp-tailed Sparrows.

Of course, nothing like this cornucopia of good birds can be expected from a single visit, but there's nearly always something worth seeing at Millwood. The best time for wandering waders is late summer; for jaegers and unusual passerines, fall; and for rare gulls, fall and winter. Large mixed flocks of grebes, ducks, and coots may be present all winter.

From the State Highway 355-32 intersection in Saratoga, drive north 1.1 miles on State Highway 355 and turn left at a sign marked Okay Landing. Drive 0.5 mile and turn right onto a dirt road, where you may see Firewheel (Indian Blanket) and Purple Prairie Clover. Watch for nesting Lark Sparrow in this area, and in migration for Yellow-headed Blackbird. The roadsides can be good for migrant and wintering wrens and sparrows. Follow this road 0.8 mile, over a railroad track, to a junction. Turn right here to check out the area around a parking lot; the brush can be good for wrens, warblers, and sparrows. A Say's Phoebe was found nearby one September. Scissor-tailed Flycatcher is present from late March into November. Keep a eye on the ground as well as on the trees; do not step on one of the low dirt mounds, which are nests of the aggressive and painful fire ant.

Return to the junction, turn right, and drive 0.5 mile to a parking lot at a boat-launching area. Tricolored Heron and Wood Stork have been seen from the parking area itself, and the adjoining marsh and willow grove are worth a look. The high ground to your left is the Okay Dike (or Okay Levee), which runs westward for more than two miles. Climb to the top (be very careful on the unstable rocks) and start walking, keeping your eyes open all the while; there's really no telling what you may find. Although the levee offers a view of one arm of the lake, it isn't just for waterbirds; Beard's Bluff (described below) may have greater numbers of landbirds, especially migrant warblers, but more actual rarities have shown up here.

Most of the regularly occurring species of herons and egrets can be seen along the levee with relative ease at the proper time. The bitterns and night-herons (especially Black-crowned) are hardest to find, but even they are possible in season. Great Egret and Great Blue Heron are permanent residents. Some of the other possibilities: (spring through fall) Tricolored Heron and White Ibis; (fall) Glossy Ibis, Roseate Spoonbill, Wood Stork, Groove-billed Ani, and Clay-colored and Sharp-tailed Sparrows. A Piping Plover has been seen here in May, and an adult Laughing Gull in July. October birds have included Arkansas's one and only Northern Wheatear. Check the bushes on the inland side of the levee for Bewick's Wren (may be a rare breeder) and the cottonwoods for nesting Northern Oriole. Take time as well to look over the marshy areas on the inland side beyond the trees. Both of the Groove-billed Anis seen at Millwood were found in dense underbrush on the lake side of the levee. Anywhere in this area can be good for winter sparrows and for accipiters from fall through spring. Fish Crow is a year-round resident.

Scan the dead trees out in the lake (a scope is essential equipment at Millwood). Thousands of Double-crested Cormorants are present from fall through spring (lesser numbers have bred locally since 1988), and Anhingas are seen from March through October (rarely into mid-December); watch for Anhingas soaring overhead, too. Here, as elsewhere on Millwood, Ospreys are common spring and fall migrants, most often seen in September and October, with up to 10 birds a day present at that time. You can walk the levee as far as you have time and energy for, but the most productive area has been within a half-mile of the parking lot.

Retrace your route back to the State Highway 355-32 intersection in Saratoga. Turn right onto Highway 32, drive 1.2 miles, and turn right on State Highway 234 toward Saratoga Landing. In 0.7 mile, just before the landing area, turn left on a paved road leading up the hill. Drive 0.7 mile, make a sharp turn to the right, and follow this road a short distance to an old launching ramp. Depending on how wintering flocks of waterbirds have arrayed themselves, the birds (Common Loon, grebes, Double-crested Cormorant, ducks) seen from here can range from a few to a few thousand. Western Grebe has been seen on this part of the lake. If the heat waves from the water are distracting from this low angle, the viewing will usually be better from the higher viewpoints at Beard's Bluff Overlook and the dam later on.

Go back to State Highway 234 and turn left to the parking area at the boat ramp. Once again, scan the lake, but don't ignore the shoreline. A Rock Wren once spent part of the winter here, and Glossy Ibis has been seen in fall. Tree Swallows nest in dead trees; they are usually far out into the lake, but they can be seen from shore as well. Follow the road along the shoreline to the picnic area in 0.6 mile, where Northern Oriole breeds. Wintering Bewick's Wren and Orange-crowned Warbler are possibilities here. The old road beyond the gate leads to a grassy area where winter sparrows may be common.

Return to Highway 32, turn right, and drive 3.5 miles to the Beard's Bluff recreation area on the right. Park on the right just before the entrance booth, walk up to Beard's Bluff overlook, set up your scope, and (from fall through spring) start picking over the birds on the lake. There may be mixed flocks of literally thousands of loons, grebes, cormorants, geese, ducks, and coots in front of you. Red-throated Loon and Western Grebe have been seen here, and most of the lake's Laughing Gulls have been found in this area. Here is where you're most likely to find a jaeger or Sabine's Gull in fall, though if one is present it may be far away and hard to see. Ring-billed is by far the most common migrant and wintering gull, with a few Herrings (almost always sub-adult birds) present as well; Franklin's Gull is fairly common in spring and common in fall. Caspian, Forster's, and Black Terns are common in fall (Black is uncommon in spring); Least Tern is an uncommon fall migrant, and Common Tern is rare. American White Pelicans are common in spring and fall (the high count is 2,200 in April 1985), and a few are present in summer and winter.

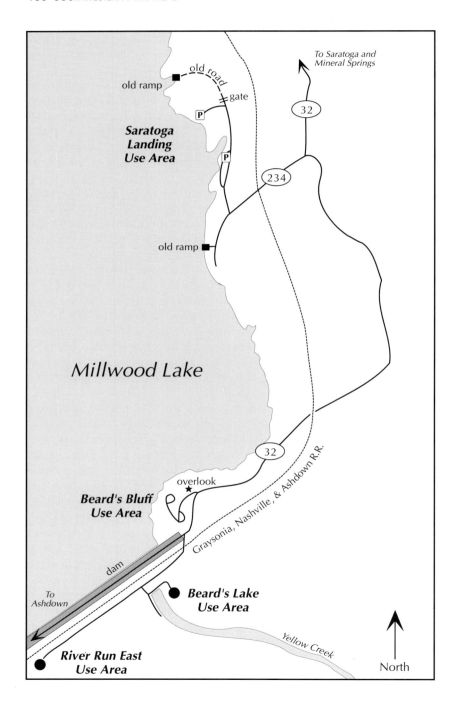

Bald Eagles have nested at Millwood; from November until spring, eagles are present in good numbers, usually perched on dead trees in the middle of the lake. By looking carefully, you can locate an eagle nest on a large cypress far out in the lake. In 1994, two young were raised here.

Sabine's Gulls tend to show up at about the same time as the first Franklin's Gulls. Sabine's have been seen at Millwood from mid-September through the third week of October, most often during the last week of September. Look for a small gull that appears dark in front, something like a first-winter Laughing Gull—which itself is a possibility. (A uniformly dark bird might be a jaeger.) Sabine's has a very active, tern-like flight. One hint to help find jaegers and gulls: look for dead fish floating on the surface; sooner or later, the birds will come. In certain light conditions, it may be better to drive down through the camping area to the shoreline, so gulls and terns will be silhouetted against the sky, to aid in finding them in the first place. You may then want to return to the overlook for a better angle to study them.

Beard's Bluff Overlook can be the prime place on the lake for migrant passerines, especially vireos and warblers. Because the overlook is at or near treetop height, birds following the ridge can be seen without that curse of the woodland birder, warbler-neck. Also check the shrubs and vines below the fence. All the warblers on the Arkansas list, save four, have been seen here over the years. If you go around the chain-link fence to the right or left to look for passerines, be careful on the steep slopes, and don't use one of the common Devil's Walking-sticks for a handhold. The picnic tables here are handy places to sit and watch the birds go by.

Return to State Highway 32, turn right, drive 0.3 mile, and turn left at the east end of the huge Millwood dam, following a road to the Beard's Lake Recreation Area. The grassy slope of the embankment to the right may have migrant Bobolinks; Yellow-headed Blackbird has been found here, too. In 0.5 mile, turn left toward a picnic area that can be very good for migrants, including vireos, warblers, tanagers, grosbeaks, orioles, buntings, and sparrows. Palm Warbler, a very uncommon bird this far west in the state, may be found here or at the Okay Dike more often than elsewhere. The grown-up grassy fields may have Sedge or Marsh Wrens in winter; Le Conte's Sparrow is also possible.

Return to the road below the embankment and turn left toward the River Run East area at the spillway, 1.2 miles farther west, where the Little River resumes its flow after being impounded in Millwood. Hundreds of gulls may gather here in winter, flying back and forth over the dam to the lake. Franklin's Gull migration peaks around early November (1,800 have been seen at one time), and Bonaparte's may number 750 or more in December. (These flocks of Bonaparte's depart the area in mid-January.) Little and Common Black-headed Gulls and Black-legged Kittiwakes have been found in flocks of Bonaparte's; bring your best lucky charm if you hope to see one. At times, shorebirds can be found along the river below the spillway.

If you haven't seen enough of the main body of the lake from Beard's Bluff, climb up the embankment, cross the highway with care, and set up your scope again. (Be sure to get well off the roadway on the lake side of the guard rail; this is a heavily traveled highway at times.) You may flush up a wintering Sprague's Pipit on the grassy lake side of the dam, or a Sharp-tailed Sparrow in autumn. Migrant shorebirds feed along the muddy edge of the lake, and at times when the Corps lowers the water level ("drawdown" periods) they can gather in large numbers. Willet, Marbled Godwit, Ruddy Turnstone, Red Knot, Dunlin, and Buff-breasted Sandpiper are among the rarer species; more common are Greater and Lesser Yellowlegs; Solitary, Spotted, Semipalmated, Western, Least, Baird's, Pectoral, and Stilt Sandpipers; Sanderling; and Common Snipe. (Least Sandpiper is a rare winter resident.) A small colony of Cliff Swallows nests under the lake side of the spillway.

At the western end of the dam, 3.4 miles from the east end, another road leads below the embankment to the other side of the spillway; depending on the afternoon light, this may be better for observation than the east road. Millwood State Park, also located at the western end of the dam, has campsites and a marina, and can be very good for passerines. Although Beard's Bluff is better overall for vireos and warblers and as a lookout for waterbirds, the woods at the state park are better for nuthatches and Eastern Bluebird, and probably for tanagers and orioles as well.

For information on Millwood Lake, write Millwood-Tri Lakes Resident Office, Route 1, Box 37A, Ashdown, AR 71822, or call 898-3343. For information on Millwood State Park, write Route 1, Box 37AB, Ashdown, AR 71822, or call 898-2800.

Least Bittern
Gail Diane Yovanovich

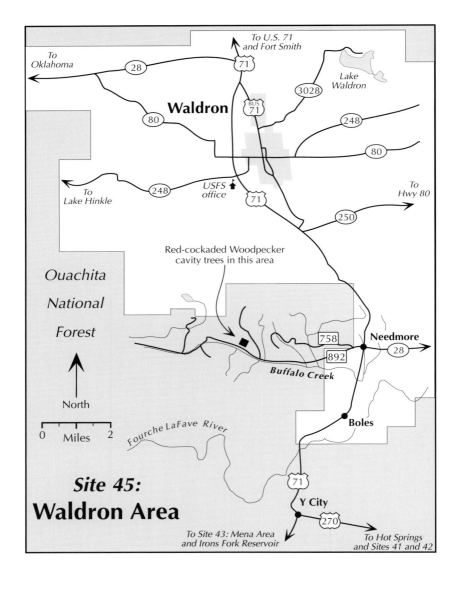

To U.S. 71 and Fort Smith

To Oklahoma

28

71

3028

Lake Waldron

Waldron

BUS 71

80

248

80

To Lake Hinkle

248

USFS office

71

To Hwy 80

250

Red-cockaded Woodpecker cavity trees in this area

Ouachita

National

Forest

North

758

892

Needmore

28

Buffalo Creek

0   Miles   2

Fourche LaFave River

Boles

Site 45:
Waldron Area

71

Y City

270

To Site 43: Mena Area and Irons Fork Reservoir

To Hot Springs and Sites 41 and 42

45. Waldron Area

Location: *Begin at the junction of U.S. Highway 71 and State Highway 248 in Waldron (at the U.S. Forest Service office).*

Three of southern Arkansas's most-wanted birds are Red-cockaded Woodpecker, Brown-headed Nuthatch, and Bachman's Sparrow. Although the nuthatch can usually be found fairly easily in stands of mature pine, the woodpecker and the sparrow are different stories. Red-cockaded Woodpecker is, of course, an endangered species, with dwindling populations found in scattered locations. Bachman's Sparrow is hard to pin down to specific sites; its preferred habitats of open pine woods (kept that way by naturally occurring fires) or young pine plantations quickly succeed to brushy undergrowth and closed woods, so the birds continually change their breeding areas.

All three of these birds, though, can be found at the U.S. Forest Service's Buffalo Road Demonstration Area south of Waldron, in the Ouachita National Forest. Here the USFS is actively managing an extensive tract of woodland to recreate an ecosystem of mature pines with an understory of grasses such as Big Bluestem, Little Bluestem, and Indian Grass. Lumbering practices and fire suppression over the past few decades have made this kind of habitat rare. By renewing it, the USFS hopes to aid in the recovery of the Red-cockaded Woodpecker, which nests in mature pines (older than 70 years) with heartwood softened by a fungal infection called red-heart disease. Management of the area includes cutting of smaller trees and regular burning, which favors larger-diameter pines by discouraging the growth of understory pine and hardwoods.

During office hours, stop at the USFS office in Waldron and buy a large, detailed map of the Ouachita National Forest—essential equipment if you'd like to explore the maze of logging roads throughout the forest. Drive south on U.S. Highway 71 for 7.3 miles to the town of Needmore. Turn right (west) onto a dirt road (County Road 892) almost directly opposite the State Highway 28 intersection on your left. After 0.4 mile, keep left where another road (Forest Road 758) turns right. Follow the main county road west, ignoring side roads on your left; watch for American Kestrel, Greater Roadrunner, Loggerhead Shrike, and Eastern Bluebird in open areas. Along the way you will ford small branches of Buffalo Creek, and the road may at times be narrow and rough.

At 3.1 miles from U.S. Highway 71 you will begin seeing parklike areas of large pines with an open understory, sometimes showing evidence of burning. There are Red-cockaded Woodpecker cavity trees close to the road on the right 4.0 miles from U.S. Highway 71; look for whitish flows of pine sap on the trunks, which give these nest and roost trees a characteristic candlestick-like appearance. Some of the cavities have had stainless-steel "restrictor plates" placed around their entrance holes to keep them from being usurped by other woodpecker species; you may also see aluminum sleeves above and below the cavities (to discourage flying squirrels) and near the base of trees (to prevent climbing by Black Rat Snakes).

Park wherever you can pull safely off the road. The best way to see the woodpeckers is to arrive an hour or so before dusk and wait for the birds to return to their roost trees from foraging. In spring and summer, you'll also hear the beautiful whistle-and-trill evening song of Bachman's Sparrow. At any time of year, listen for the twittering and peeping of Brown-headed Nuthatch and the musical trill of Pine Warbler, and in breeding season for the unmusical trill of Chipping Sparrow.

Important note: *It cannot be stressed too much that the Red-cockaded Woodpecker is an endangered species, barely hanging on to existence in the face of logging practices and declining quality of habitat. No ethical birder would ever do anything to harm or harass an RCW or interfere with its nesting. This includes hitting or scratching on a roost tree to cause a bird to appear and standing too close to a cavity tree when a bird is trying to go to roost or to bring food to its young. If you spend time quietly observing, you can see an RCW without interfering with the birds' activities.*

By traveling along the road you'll find areas of denser forest, hardwood, and brushy clearcuts; paralleling the road just downhill to the south is Buffalo Creek, which provides a streamside habitat. Among the other breeding birds of the area are Broad-winged Hawk, Yellow-billed Cuckoo, Eastern Wood-Pewee, Great Crested Flycatcher, Blue-gray Gnatcatcher, Yellow-throated and Red-eyed Vireos, Black-and-white and Kentucky Warblers, Louisiana Waterthrush (near streams), Yellow-breasted Chat (clearcuts), Summer and Scarlet (on ridges) Tanagers, and Indigo Bunting (clearcuts). Wild Turkey is a possibility year-round, and other permanent residents include Eastern Screech-Owl; Red-headed, Red-bellied, Downy, Hairy, and Pileated Woodpeckers; and White-breasted Nuthatch.

Red Crossbill, a very rare and irregular winter visitor to Arkansas (and probable sometime nester in south Arkansas), has been seen in this area.

Considering this species' strange habits, it would be worthwhile to watch for it, and listen for its *jeep-jeep* note, anytime.

If you miss Red-cockaded Woodpecker at Buffalo Road, there is another tiny cluster of cavity trees farther south near Irons Fork Reservoir. Return to U.S. Highway 71, drive south 18.8 miles (watching for Greater Roadrunner along the way), and turn left on a gravel road (this is County Road 76, although it may be unmarked as such). See the Mena Area listing (site #43) for further details.

Greater Roadrunner
Georges Dremeaux

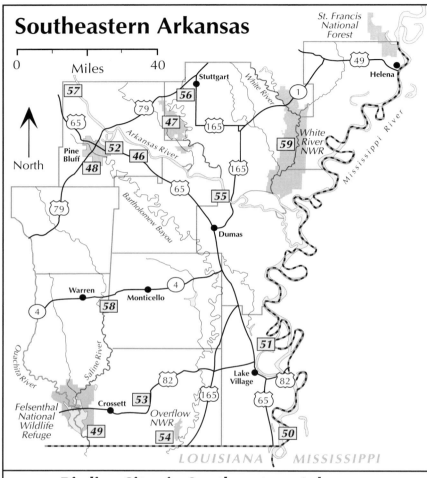

Southeastern Arkansas

St. Francis
National
Forest

0   Miles   40

North

Helena

Stuttgart

White River

Pine
Bluff

Arkansas River

Bartholomew Bayou

White
River
NWR

Dumas

Warren

Monticello

Ouachita River

Saline River

Lake
Village

Felsenthal
National
Wildlife
Refuge

Crossett

Overflow
NWR

LOUISIANA   MISSISSIPPI

Mississippi River

57 **56** **47** **59** **52** **46** **48** **55** **58** **51** **53** **49** **54** **50**

Birding Sites in Southeastern Arkansas:

46 Arkansas River Levee

47 Bayou Meto Wildlife Mgt Area

48 Byrd Lake Natural Area

49 Felsenthal Nat'l Wildlife Refuge

50 Grand Lake

51 Lake Chicot State Park

52 Lake Pine Bluff

53 Levi Wilcoxon Trail

54 Overflow Nat'l Wildlife Refuge

55 Pendleton Recreation Area

56 Roth Prairie Natural Area

57 Tar Camp Recreation Area

58 Warren Prairie Natural Area

59 White River Nat'l Wildlife Refuge

SOUTHEASTERN
ARKANSAS

Southeastern Arkansas is mostly contained within the Delta, or Mississippi Alluvial Plain, natural division. It also includes a small part of the Coastal Plain division, with its rolling hills and pines, as well as part of what's left of the Grand Prairie.

Although the Delta was once a nearly endless bottomland hardwood forest, its rich soil made it tremendously valuable for agriculture. Today it would be unrecognizable to the early explorers who fought their way through its swampy wetlands. As much as 90 per cent of the Delta has been deforested, but a significant tract of woodland remains in the White River National Wildlife Refuge and along various tributaries of the White, Arkansas, and Mississippi Rivers. This habitat is perhaps most notable for the huge numbers of wintering waterfowl (mostly Mallards) that utilize it for food and rest.

Arkansas's Grand Prairie was once an anomalous region of a half-million acres of grassland surrounded by hardwood forest. Because the impermeable clay soil underlying it made it perfect for rice farming, nearly every bit of this habitat has been lost. A few very small remnants of virgin prairie, with its tall grasses and colorfully varied wildflowers, can be seen near Stuttgart. (See also the Northeastern Arkansas section.)

The southeast is a land of Wood Ducks, Red-headed Woodpeckers, and Prothonotary Warblers. Anhinga, Black-crowned Night-Heron, Bald Eagle, and Black-necked Stilt breed here, although in scattered and sometimes inaccessible locations. Pied-billed Grebe, Least Bittern, Purple Gallinule, and Common Moorhen nest; King Rail, though drastically reduced in numbers, may hold out as a breeder somewhere in the area. Red-winged Blackbirds are ubiquitous, thanks to the artificial marshes that have been provided for them in the form of rice fields. In the fall, flocks of dozens of Mississippi Kites hawk for dragonflies along the Arkansas and Mississippi Rivers levees.

Among the best birding spots in this region is the area around Lake Chicot State Park near Lake Village, in the extreme southeastern corner of the state. The congregation of wading birds here in late summer can be spectacular, and often includes rarities like Tricolored Heron, White

167

Ibis, and Wood Stork. In agricultural fields nearby, Black-necked Stilt has been found breeding in recent years.

The pine woods near Crossett have resident Red-cockaded Woodpecker, Brown-headed Nuthatch, and Bachman's Sparrow, and there has been near-certain evidence of local breeding by Red Crossbill. What is perhaps Arkansas's healthiest population of the endangered Red-cockaded Woodpecker makes its home at Felsenthal National Wildlife Refuge.

Travel note: A new U.S. Highway 65 bypass is under construction south of Pine Bluff; directions in this section refer to the "old" 65.

46. Arkansas River Levee

Location: *From the intersection of U.S. Highways 65 and 65B in eastern Pine Bluff, drive southeast on U.S. Highway 65 for 11.2 miles to Linwood. Turn left onto a paved road toward the Rising Star Recreation Area. (See map on page 174.)*

The tall levees paralleling the lower Arkansas River can be interesting places for birders. Nearby wetlands attract wintering ducks, and spring and fall can bring herons, egrets, and other waders. One late-summer specialty of this area is Mississippi Kite, which sometimes gathers in large flocks before beginning its southward migration. This drive allows you to sample a short section of the levee, which runs all the way to the Mississsippi River, and from there south to the Gulf of Mexico.

From U.S. Highway 65 at Linwood, drive east 1.6 miles to the levee. In winter, watch the surrounding fields for hawks, Horned Lark (a few pairs stay to breed), American Pipit, Loggerhead Shrike (also breeds), and Savannah Sparrow. In early May, there may be Bobolinks in the fields of ripening winter wheat.

The road climbs the levee and turns right. (This part of the levee is paved, unlike most of the rest, which is well-maintained gravel.) After 2.0 miles, the paved road drops down the side to the Rising Star Recreation Area, a Corps of Engineers facility. Turn in here to view the Arkansas River or bird the campground (Red-headed Woodpecker, Warbling Vireo, Northern Oriole). Otherwise, continue on the gravel road atop the levee. In late summer and fall, watch the tall trees on the left for Mississippi Kites and the wet areas for waders. Dickcissels are abundant breeders.

After 4.4 miles a paved road (State Highway 11) crosses the levee. Turn left here to check out Huffs Island Park, another Corps of Engineers area; it offers little except a chance to scope wintering gulls at Lock and Dam Number 3. To return to U.S. Highway 65, turn right and drive 5.5 miles to the small town of Grady. Or, you can keep driving the levee; the road on top runs all the way to the Louisiana state line.

For other levee drives on the Arkansas and Mississippi rivers, see the Pendleton, Lake Chicot, and Grand Lake site listings (sites #55, 51, and 50 respectively).

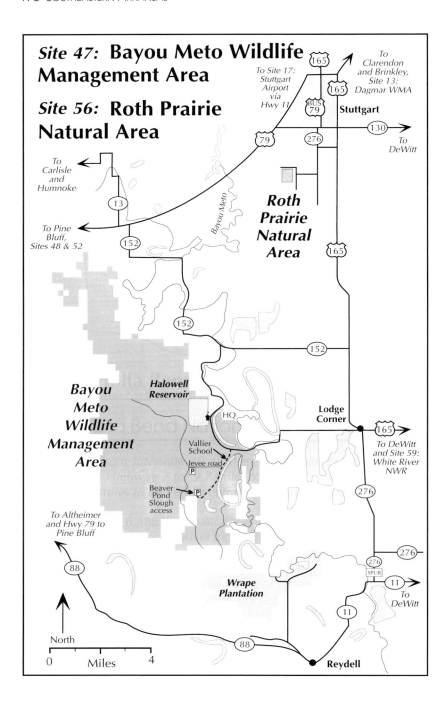

Site 47: Bayou Meto Wildlife Management Area

Site 56: Roth Prairie Natural Area

47. Bayou Meto Wildlife Management Area

Location: *From the intersection of U.S. Highways 165 and 79 in Stuttgart, drive southwest on U.S. Highway 79 for 10 miles to State Highway 152. (Alternatively, from the intersection of U.S. Highway 165 and State Highway 13 in Humnoke, drive south on State Highway 13 for about 12 miles to Highway 79; turn left onto U.S. Highway 79 for a short distance to U.S. Highway 152 and turn right.) Drive south on U.S. Highway 152 for 8.2 miles and turn right onto a paved road leading to the WMA.*

Bayou Meto is one of the most popular duck-hunting areas in Arkansas, thanks to its setting (Delta woodlands on the edge of the Grand Prairie) and to intensive management by the state Game and Fish Commission. During the winter, as much as one-third of this 33,000-acre tract of bottomland hardwoods, canals, and sloughs is flooded to provide waterfowl habitat. The birdlife here is similar to that at Dagmar WMA farther north: in other words, Acadian Flycatcher; Blue-gray Gnatcatcher; Northern Parula; Yellow-throated, Black-and-white, Prothonotary, and Kentucky Warblers; Summer Tanager; and Orchard Oriole abound in breeding season.

Halowell Reservoir, located beside the WMA office 4.2 miles from Highway 152, is a waterfowl rest area where hunting is limited. (If the WMA office is open, stop in to ask for a map.) Although the situation varies from year to year with local water levels, it can be an excellent place to observe great numbers of wintering ducks. *Walking around the levee is prohibited from 30 days before duck-hunting season through the end of the season, but most of the reservoir can be seen from the parking lot.* Mallard, Northern Pintail, Northern Shoveler, Gadwall, American Wigeon, Ring-necked Duck, and Ruddy Duck are often present, among others. Blue-winged Teal, which migrate earlier in the fall than other ducks, can be common in September. Double-crested Cormorants and American Coots may number in the hundreds, and Pied-billed Grebes are common. Careful scanning of flocks may turn up something unusual. (Morning light is best here.) Ospreys are sometimes seen in spring. Common Snipe are found around the perimeter of the reservoir in the fall. Wintering Bald Eagles roost in the trees around the perimeter, and Bonaparte's Gulls are occasional winter visitors. Black Terns hawk for insects over the reservoir in migration. Especially noteworthy, a pair of Least Bitterns has nested at Halowell in recent years. Walk along the levee and search the vegetation near the southeast corner carefully. (*WMA personnel recommend that you also keep an eye out for Cottonmouths, which can be distressingly common.*)

To look for woodland birds in spring or early summer, drive south from the headquarters 1.5 miles on the main WMA road and turn right onto a road that may be marked Vallier School Access. Park anywhere along this dead-end road and search the woods for breeding birds and migrants. Some of the side roads provide access to wetland areas where you may flush a Green Heron or other wader. By driving all the way to the Beaver Dam Slough area you'll find good mixed habitat; Pied-billed Grebe has nested nearby. Bring insect repellent.

The Wrape Plantation at the southern end of Bayou Meto can be an excellent spot for waterbirds. (*Note: this section of the WMA is closed 30 days before the start of duck-hunting season until 30 days after the end of the season to provide a waterfowl rest area.*) To reach it, begin at the intersection of the main WMA road and the Vallier School Access road and continue east 5.8 miles to U.S. Highway 165; turn right 0.1 mile to U.S. Highway 276. (Alternatively, from U.S. Highway 165 and State Highway 130 in Stuttgart, drive south 12.8 miles on U.S. Highway 165 to State Highway 276.) Go south 6.4 miles on State Highways 276 and 276 (Spur) to State Highway 11; turn right and drive 5.1 miles to State Highway 88 in the town of Reydell. Turn right (west) onto State Highway 88 and drive 0.8 mile to a sign pointing to the WMA. Turn right here and drive 0.9 mile; turn right again and drive 2.3 miles to the WMA entrance.

Continue straight past the buildings to shallow ponds on both sides of the road. In spring and summer, look for Common Moorhen in short vegetation; American Coot nests, and this is a likely-looking spot for Purple Gallinule. Least Bitterns also breed here, though they are more often heard than seen. Wood Ducks are common breeders, and American Black Duck has been seen in winter. Migrant shorebirds can often be found in areas of shallow water. Look also for such nesting birds as Yellow-billed Cuckoo, Ruby-throated Hummingbird, Wood Thrush, Prothonotary Warbler, Yellow-breasted Chat, Dickcissel, and Northern Oriole, and for such permanent residents as Red-headed Woodpecker and Loggerhead Shrike.

In late summer and fall, waders such as Great and Snowy Egrets and Little Blue Heron gather. Great Blue Heron is found all year, and Green Heron is a common breeder. Tricolored Heron and White Ibis have been seen here in fall. In winter, hundreds of dabbling ducks crowd the ponds, and Bald Eagles may perch in waterside trees. The road peters out at a parking area 1.4 miles from the entrance; turn around here and return the way you came.

48. Byrd Lake Natural Area

Location: *From the intersection of U.S. Highway 65 and State Highway 15 in Pine Bluff, drive south 4.0 miles on State Highway 15 to Main Street. Turn left and drive 0.2 mile to East 52nd Avenue. Turn right and drive 0.3 mile to a parking lot on the right. (Note: A new Highway 65 bypass is under construction south of Pine Bluff. On its completion it will be easy to reach Byrd Lake by driving north a short distance on Highway 15 from the bypass to Main Street.)* *(See map on page 174.)*

To the ear it sounds ornithological, but Byrd Lake Natural Area was in fact named for the Byrd family, which owned this 144-acre tract until the Arkansas Natural Heritage Commission bought it in 1978. Easily accessible at the southeastern edge of Pine Bluff, it's a pleasant place to see a good variety of typical wet-woodland species.

Byrd Lake itself is a half-mile-long shallow body of water covered with Duckweed and fringed by Bald Cypress and Buttonbush. The lake is an old oxbow of Bayou Bartholomew, which borders the area on the south before meandering through Arkansas to join with the Ouachita River all the way down in Louisiana. Bartholomew is known as the longest bayou in the world—though it's hard to say just what the difference is between a bayou and a small river.

As you get out of your car in the parking area, look up in spring and summer for Mississippi Kites; they're fairly common nearby, though it may be hard to see them soaring once you're in the woods. A short paved trail runs to the lake through a mixed forest of hardwood and pine. Because Byrd Lake is located at the point where the Gulf Coastal Plain meets the Delta, you'll pass some impressive specimens of Loblolly Pine, an upland tree, as well as lowland species like Overcup, Water, and Willow Oaks. Check the Loblollies for Pine Warbler, and be on the alert year-round for Wood Duck, Red-shouldered Hawk, Barred Owl, Belted Kingfisher, and Pileated Woodpecker. Both Eastern Screech- and Great Horned Owls have been seen here, too. If you walk quietly you may scare up a White-tailed Deer. You're less likely to see a Beaver; signs of them are everywhere, but they're active mostly at night.

In breeding season you'll find Green Heron, Acadian Flycatcher, and Prothonotary Warbler near the water, and you may hear the strangled *caa-aa* of a Fish Crow. Other birds nesting here include Yellow-billed Cuckoo, Ruby-throated Hummingbird, Eastern Wood-Pewee, Great Crested Flycatcher, Red-eyed Vireo, Black-and-white Warbler, Summer

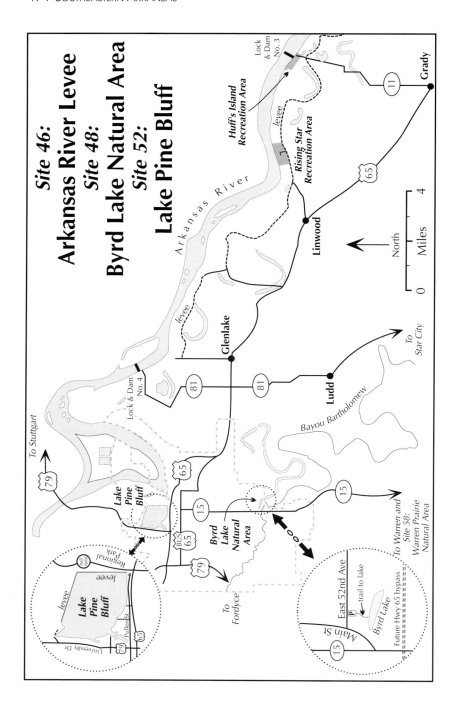

Site 46:
Arkansas River Levee
Site 48:
Byrd Lake Natural Area
Site 52:
Lake Pine Bluff

Tanager, and Rufous-sided Towhee. Yellow-crowned Night-Heron has been seen on the lake, though it's not known to breed here.

Watch for an unpaved path, marked by blue diamonds, leading to the right just as you enter the woods. This makes a short loop to a lake overlook (with a large beaver lodge just below) and continues past an old field where Northern Bobwhite, Common Yellowthroat, and Blue Grosbeak nest.

As is to be expected of such a nicely swampy woodland, Byrd Lake is good for spring warblers and other migrants.

Mississippi Kite
Louise Zemaitis

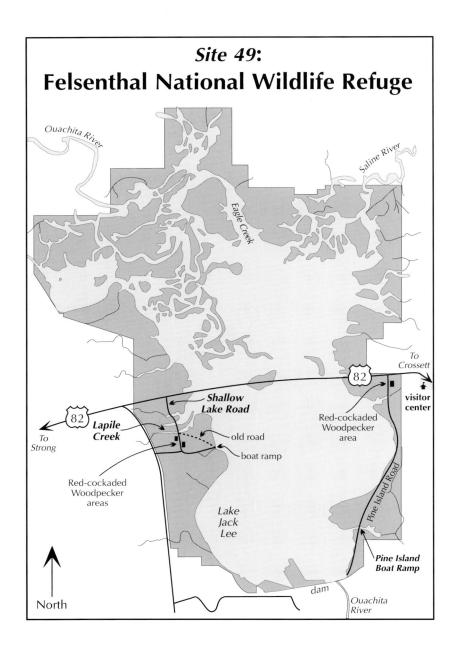

Site 49:
Felsenthal National Wildlife Refuge

Ouachita River

Saline River

Eagle Creek

*To
Crossett*

82

**Shallow
Lake Road**

visitor
center

Red-cockaded
Woodpecker
area

82

**Lapile
Creek**

*To
Strong*

old road

boat ramp

Red-cockaded
Woodpecker
areas

*Lake
Jack
Lee*

Pine Island Road

North

**Pine Island
Boat Ramp**

dam

*Ouachita
River*

49. Felsenthal National Wildlife Refuge

Location: *The refuge visitor center is on the south side of U.S. Highway 82, about 5 miles west of Crossett.*

Felsenthal National Wildlife Refuge encompasses 65,000 acres of lakes, swamps, bottomland forest, and upland pine woods surrounding the confluence of the Ouachita and Saline Rivers in south-central Arkansas. Although the refuge was established (in 1975) primarily to benefit waterfowl, the main attraction for birders is Arkansas's largest contiguous population of endangered Red-cockaded Woodpeckers. The birds are closely monitored and protected here, and most of the time they are relatively easy to see. Of course, there's more at Felsenthal than RCWs. The varied landscape provides good birding for species ranging from waders and Bald Eagles to Wild Turkeys and warblers.

Your first stop should be at the visitor center, where you can pick up a bird list and a map and talk to refuge personnel about current conditions. High water in winter and spring can sometimes cause road closings. Felsenthal is a big place, so it helps to know where you're going. This is especially true if you're interested in seeing Red-cockaded Woodpeckers. The birds abandon nesting colonies and take up new ones regularly, so a spot that's good one year may not be productive the next. The visitor center also has interesting displays on wildlife (including a cutaway nest cavity demonstrating the RCW's unfortunate preference for diseased pine trees) and archeology.

Return to U.S. Highway 82, turn left (west), and drive 1.2 miles to Pine Island Road on your left; turn here. Within 0.2 mile, you will see an open pine grove on the left. RCWs have nested here, although in a recent year they were being harassed by Pileated Woodpeckers, which enlarged their entrance holes and usurped their cavities. Red-bellied Woodpeckers also take over RCW holes, as do flying squirrels. Biologists have experimented with placing metal "restrictor plates" around holes to keep them at the size RCWs prefer; you may see these plates at nest trees. Known nest and roost trees are marked with white bands. They will also show the distinctive light-colored flows of pine sap that are thought to aid in repelling predators; the birds' habit of flaking away the outer bark will often make parts of the trees appear whitish.

The most reliable way to see RCWs is to take up a position quietly and inconspicuously within sight of a roost or nest tree, beginning about an hour before dusk, and wait for the birds to return from foraging. They will usually fly around the vicinity before going in to roost, feeding and calling. The birds may appear nearby at any time of day, though, especially during nesting season.

Important note: *It cannot be stressed too much that the Red-cockaded Woodpecker is an endangered species, barely hanging on to existence in the face of logging practices and declining quality of habitat. No ethical birder would ever do anything to harm or harass an RCW or interfere with its nesting. This includes hitting or scratching on a roost tree to cause a bird to appear and standing too close to a cavity tree when a bird is trying to go to roost or to bring food to its young. If you spend time quietly observing, you can see an RCW without interfering with the birds' activities.*

Unless the road is flooded, you can continue south for a little over six miles to the Pine Island boat ramp. Walk the levee near here for ducks in winter (most will be Mallards) and perhaps a Bald Eagle. You may find Pied-billed Grebe (they are thought to nest on the refuge), in spring an Anhinga, or in late summer wandering Wood Storks. Wood Ducks are abundant all year.

Along the way the road passes through varied habitats; stop wherever you like. Gated side roads are quieter than the main road and easy to walk; although they are closed to vehicles, you can travel on foot anywhere at any time. Among the birds you may find year round are Great Blue Heron, Turkey and Black Vultures, Red-tailed and Red-shouldered Hawks, Wild Turkey (best chance early in the morning, but sometimes seen in the middle of the day), Red-headed Woodpecker (common), Fish Crow (not as common as American), Pine Warbler, and Chipping and Field Sparrows. In breeding season: Green and Little Blue Herons; Cattle, Great, and Snowy Egrets; Black-crowned and Yellow-crowned (more likely) Night-Herons; Great Crested and Acadian Fly-catchers; Eastern Wood-Pewee; Wood Thrush; White-eyed, Yellow-throated, and Red-eyed Vireos; Northern Parula; Yellow-throated, Black-and-white, Prothonotary, Kentucky, and Hooded Warblers; American Redstart; Louisiana Waterthrush; Yellow-breasted Chat; and Summer Tanager. Cerulean Warbler has been seen at Felsenthal, although it is rare, and it wouldn't be a waste of time to listen here for Swainson's Warbler, either.

Although Bachman's Sparrow is not often seen on the refuge (it is more common on pine timberland that has been clear-cut and then grown up in grassy vegetation), it is sometimes found in open pine woods like those preferred by Red-cockaded Woodpeckers; listen for its sweet, accelerating song at dawn and dusk. The rare Henslow's Sparrow is not on the refuge bird list, but it has been seen in winter in similar habitat in this part of the state (see Warren Prairie, site # 58).

Retrace your route back to U.S. Highway 82, turn left, and drive 6.3 miles to Shallow Lake Road. Turn left and drive 1.3 miles to the bridge over Lapile Creek. Park on the left just beyond the creek. The woods road that leaves the main road here is an excellent bird walk, traversing both swampy areas and upland forest. It continues about 2 miles to a boat-launching area, but you can walk as much or as little as you like.

Continue south on Shallow Lake Road. In 0.3 mile you will pass through more open pine groves, first on the right and then on the left, where Red-cockaded Woodpeckers have nested recently. Turn right 1.3 miles from the bridge, and right again in 1.1 miles. This road goes north 2.1 miles back to Highway 82, with private property on the left and refuge land on the right.

For information about Felsenthal, write Box 1157, Crossett, AR 71635, or call 364-3167.

Green Heron
Gail Diane Yovanovich

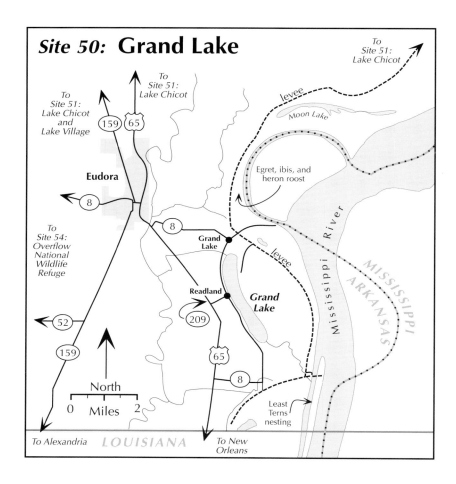

50. Grand Lake

Location: *From the intersection of U.S. Highway 65 and State Highways 8 and 159 in Eudora, drive south on U.S. Highway 65 one mile and turn left (east) on State Highway 8. When you reach Grand Lake in 2.7 miles, make a sharp left turn from the highway and drive 0.3 mile to the levee.*

This loop, which runs south to a point within two miles of Louisiana, is the best area in Arkansas to find Wood Stork and nesting Least Tern. It follows part of the extensive levee bordering the Mississippi River (see the next listing, Lake Chicot, site #51), with adjacent roadside borrow pits that attract a variety of waders, especially in late summer. The borrow (often pronounced "bar") pits, where soil was dug (or borrowed) to build the levee, are swampy wetlands of varying depth that attract these waders and ducks.

From the top of the levee, scan the borrow pits for (depending on the season) American White Pelican, egrets, herons, White Ibis, ducks, shorebirds, and Least Tern. To begin the levee drive, turn right (south). For some preliminary landbirding, drive over and down the levee and park at the base on the other side. Walk south (right) through the grass along the levee's edge toward the pits. In winter, watch for sparrows, including Henslow's (rare) and Le Conte's. Be cautious around fire-ant mounds. Return to the road and continue away from the levee to the old river channel, watching for Red-shouldered Hawk, Red-headed Woodpecker, breeding Painted Bunting, and migrant warblers. Retrace your path to the top of the levee and turn left (south).

In April and May watch for Bobolinks in the Vetch and for nesting Grasshopper Sparrows. In the first mile of borrow pits look for nesting Pied-billed Grebes, as well as migrant American White Pelicans, waders, and ducks. Most of the ibises (seen in summer and fall) will be immature White Ibis, but Glossy Ibis has been found here, and an adult White-faced was seen one August.

In the next mile of the levee the borrow pits are shallow and stumpy. During the drought of 1988 more than 200 Wood Storks were counted in these pits at one time; with them was a Roseate Spoonbill. Look for Anhinga; Great Blue, Little Blue, and Tricolored Herons; Great, Snowy, and Cattle Egrets; both night-herons; and White Ibis. (Eighty White Ibises were seen in this area in August 1994.)

Soon you will be able to see the Mississippi River. Continue down the levee to a point where the levee makes a turn to the right with a short levee spur on the left, 5.6 miles from the point at which you reached the levee. On the left just before the spur is an off-ramp that will allow you to get closer to the river. The gate is usually open except during hunting season. Drive around the levee spur and park. Walk down to the rock dike. (At certain times the river may be over this dike.) In the summer Least Terns often feed below the dike and can be seen up close. The terns nest on the large sandbar on the other end of the dike. *Please do not walk out onto the sandbar during nesting season.* In the side channel between the sandbar and the riverbank look for migrant American White Pelican, Double-crested Cormorant (fall through spring), egrets, herons, Wood Stork (late summer), and Caspian Tern (in migration).

Return to the levee and continue southwest 1.3 miles to the off-ramp to Highway 8 (which doesn't look like much of a highway here) on the right. In summer, turn left and drive the short distance to U.S. Highway 65; check rice fields nearby for nesting Black-necked Stilt. Then backtrack and follow State Highway 8 north alongside Grand Lake. In the fall scan for American White Pelican, Double-crested Cormorant, ducks, and shorebirds. On the powerlines along the road it is possible to see five species of swallows at one time during migration: Tree, Northern Rough-winged, Bank, Cliff, and Barn.

Continuing north you will come to the point at which you first reached the levee. Follow State Highway 8 as it turns left to return to Eudora. For more birding, return to the levee as you originally began this route and turn left (north) instead of right. From this point you can drive nearly 20 miles to the U.S. Highway 82 bridge over the Mississippi River, or even beyond, to the Lake Chicot Pumping Station (see the next listing, #51). On Labor Day in 1991, 713 Wood Storks were counted along the levee from the Louisiana line north to the pumping station.

At 1.3 miles north from where you reached the levee there are borrow pits surrounded by willows. In September, park on the levee an hour before sunset and watch the egrets, herons, and ibises gather in the trees to roost. Most will be Little Blue Herons and Cattle Egrets; in 1992 up to 43 Tricolored Herons accompanied the commoner species.

51. Lake Chicot State Park Area

Location: *Begin at the intersection of U.S. Highways 65, 82, and State Highway 144 in Lake Village. (Take note here of Mike's Cafe; if you're hungry, this longtime local favorite is a good place for a meal.) Drive east on State Highway 144 for 0.5 mile to Lake Chicot; turn left and follow the highway 7.3 miles to the park entrance. If you are coming from the north on U.S. Highway 65, turn east onto State Highway 257 at McMillan Corner (4 miles north of Lake Village); drive 3.9 miles to State Highway 144, turn left, and drive 4.2 miles to the park entrance. (See map on page 184.)*

Chicot (CHEE-coe—or, if you want to sound francophonic, SHEE-coe) County is the southeasternmost corner of Arkansas's Delta region, bordered by Louisiana on the south and the Mississippi River on the east. Its flat landscape of sandbars, cypress swamps, and bottomland forest was shaped by the river, as was its most distinctive natural feature, Lake Chicot. An old channel of the Mississippi, Chicot is Arkansas's largest natural lake and the largest oxbow lake in the United States, curving in a C shape almost 20 miles long and less than a mile wide. (The lake even has a footnote in aviation history: Charles Lindbergh made his first night flight over water here before he flew *The Spirit of St. Louis* across the Atlantic.) Chicot County's natural habitats, combined with man-made catfish ponds, rice fields, and pastures, make the area one of Arkansas's birding hotspots.

Lake Chicot State Park is located on the northern edge of the lake; it offers camping, cabins, and a variety of nature programs and activities. Stop at the visitor center to pick up a bird checklist and map of the area. Park Interpreter Don Simons is an avid birder; if he is in, ask him about any noteworthy recent sightings. Just across the road is a one-mile nature trail good for typical woodland birds of the area. (Rubber boots are recommended for winter and spring walks.) Eastern Screech-, Barred, and Great Horned Owls are common, and 30 species of warblers have been recorded on the trail. Mississippi Kites nest in the nearby camping area; Red-headed Woodpeckers are present but declining. Barn Owls have nested in the park water-tower.

Perhaps the most exciting local birding comes in the late summer and fall (late July through September), when thousands of waders congregate on Lake Chicot near the park. Most are Great Blue and Little Blue Herons and Great and Cattle Egrets. Less common are Double-crested Cormorant, Anhinga, Snowy Egret, Tricolored Heron, Black-crowned

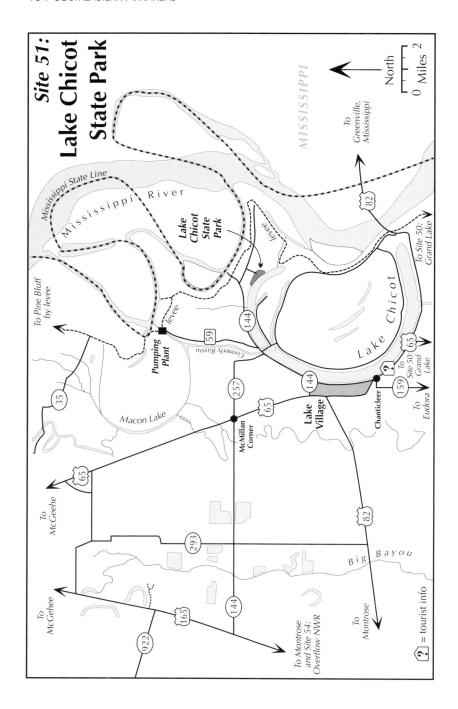

Site 51:
Lake Chicot State Park

and Yellow-crowned Night-Herons, White Ibis, Wood Stork, Osprey, and Caspian, Common, Forster's, Least, and Black Terns. To allow visitors to see these birds, most of which are in out-of-the-way locations, the park offers guided boat tours on selected evenings. For information about these tours, write Don Simons, Lake Chicot State Park, Rt. 3, Box 1555, Lake Village, AR 71653, or call 265-5480.

In winter scan the lake for loons, grebes, ducks, Bald Eagles, and gulls. Check any flocks of Bonaparte's Gulls carefully; Arkansas's second Common Black-headed Gull was seen on Lake Chicot in January 1991, and Little Gull was found in 1993. Topping even those sightings, the state's first Lesser Black-backed Gull showed up in February 1994 and stayed nearly two weeks.

A Pacific Loon was present on the lake during the early months of 1993. Two adult and two immature Black-bellied Whistling-Ducks were seen at the north end of the lake in August 1994; this species is expanding its range, and soon may be more regular in Arkansas. Oldsquaw, Black Scoter, and Black-legged Kittiwake are among the lake's other notable records.

For more information on Lake Chicot State Park, write Route 3, Box 1555, Lake Village, AR 71553, or call 265-5480.

A couple of miles south of Lake Village, on Highways 65 and 82, is an Arkansas tourist information center, with maps and other travel information. This is also a good spot from which to scan the lake.

Mississippi River Levee Tour

Driving the high levee alongside the Mississippi River bottomlands can be an exciting birding adventure. A short section of the levee near the state park offers easy access to a variety of habitats: on one side are borrow pits and dense forest; on the other is pasture and farmland. Atop the levee is a good all-weather gravel roadway.

From the park visitor center return to State Highway 144 and turn left. In the spring, watch for Black-bellied Plover, American Golden-Plover, and Horned Lark in the fields. Where the highway turns left 0.8 mile from the park entrance, make a sharp right turn, drive 0.5 mile up to the levee, turn left, and stop. Check the borrow pits for nesting Pied-billed Grebe, Wood Duck, and Hooded Merganser; you may also see Beaver, Nutria, River Otter, White-tailed Deer, or Coyote here or farther on. Dusk and dawn are the best times to see mammals. The woods a half-mile north of here are in the state of Mississippi, despite the fact that they're west of the Mississippi River. The explanation: the old channel just north of the levee was the main river bed when the state lines were set.

Continue northwest on the levee, watching for Wild Turkey, especially in August and September when hens and young of the year travel in groups of 20 to 30. In summer, a dozen or more Mississippi Kites can be seen hawking for dragonflies. Cattle Egrets are often abundant in breeding season, and other waders feed here. In August and September watch for Wood Stork. White and Glossy Ibises and Western Kingbird are other rarities that have been found along the levee.

Drive 3.1 miles after joining the levee, and watch for a levee spur with a good gravel road leading into the woods. Park here and walk the half-mile to the end of the spur. This beautiful bottomland forest offers excellent birding, particularly in spring migration. Seven species of vireos and 32 species of warblers have been found here; Barred Owls are common, and you may also see Wild Turkey. *Do not walk this road during hunting season.*

Continue driving the levee 1.3 more miles to a paved section near the Lake Chicot Pumping Station, a Corps of Engineers project that prevents siltation in the lake. Turn right in 0.2 mile to the Rowdy Bend Landing parking lot and boat-launching ramp. Check the tall grass nearby for sparrows and the waterway for waders, Belted Kingfisher, gulls (winter), and alligators (rare). Grasshopper Sparrow has been found on the levee near the pumping station.

If you've seen enough of the levee, take the paved road (unmarked here, but County Road 59) from the east end of the pumping station 4.2 miles back to Highway 144, watching for Red-headed Woodpeckers on telephone poles and Loggerhead Shrikes along the way. Turn left to return to the park or right to Lake Village and Highway 65. For more levee exploration, cross Connerly Bayou below the control structure. You can drive north on the levee nearly 100 miles alongside the Mississippi and Arkansas rivers all the way to Pine Bluff; there are exits along the way to various roads and highways. If you do this in late summer, you'll probably set a personal record for the number of Mississippi Kites seen.

Fish Farm Tour

Catfish ponds and rice fields in the western part of Chicot County attract great concentrations of waterfowl, eagles, and shorebirds. *Birders were once allowed to drive on fish-farm property here, but this is no longer the case; do your birding, carefully, from the roadside.*

Yellow Rail
David A. Sibley

From McMillan Corner on U.S. Highway 65, 4 miles north of Lake Village, drive west on State Highway 144 3.8 miles; ponds are on either side of the highway. In winter scan each pond for up to 17 species of ducks. At times hundreds of Hooded Mergansers rest here. Much to the dismay of the farm manager, there are also usually plenty of Double-crested Cormorants, Great Blue Herons, and Great Egrets, which take a share of the farm's fish. Watch for Bald Eagles in the Bald Cypress trees on the south side of the highway; Golden Eagles are rare here. Some of the ponds are drained in the spring, and the exposed mudflats attract shorebirds. (The Canada Geese in and around the ponds belong to the farm.)

At State Highway 293 (5.6 miles west of U.S. Highway 65) turn north. In 0.2 mile there will be a reservoir to the left, hidden behind a row of trees. In order to see most of it you will have to scan from both the southeast and northeast corners. (Watch for dirt roads off the highway.) The southern half is dotted with stumps; look for ducks, nesting Common Moorhen and American Coot, and shorebirds. The northern half is shallower and often becomes a mudflat in summer and fall; look here for nesting Pied-billed Grebes and seasonally for ducks and shorebirds, including Wilson's Phalarope. During the 1988 drought Tricolored Heron, White Ibis, Wood Stork, and Black-necked Stilt were seen here. In August 1992 a pair of Black-bellied Whistling-Ducks was found in the willows in the northwestern corner of the reservoir. Many Black-crowned Night-Herons and Anhingas were also present at that time.

Continue north 1.7 more miles; on the right is a narrow cattail marsh between the gravel road and a rice field. In fall and winter this is a good spot for Sora, Sedge and Marsh Wrens, and a variety of sparrows.

While birding this area in winter you are bound to see and hear wild geese; they often congregate on rice stubble. Once you have located them, stay in your vehicle and scan the flock for Ross's Geese among the thousands of Greater White-fronted, Snow, and Canada Geese.

Return to the intersection of State Highways 144 and 293. Turn right (west), drive 4.0 miles to U.S. Highway 165, and turn right again. In 1.7 miles watch for a historical marker on the right, commemorating the forced internment of 6,700 Japanese-Americans here in a "relocation camp" during World War II. (The town of Jerome has declined a little since that time; the population today is 47.) Less than a mile farther on, watch for a huge rice farm on the right, managed in cooperation with the U.S. Fish and Wildlife Service as waterfowl habitat. Scan the fields in winter for up to 14 species of ducks. At times there are thousands of geese, and Ross's has been found with Snows here. Watch for wintering Bald Eagles overhead, on the ground, or perched on irrigation equipment. Black-necked Stilts have nested in this vicinity.

In the fall, combines harvesting rice scare up rails, mostly Virginia and Sora, from the fields. Local birders who have received permission to ride with combine drivers have seen Yellow Rail with some regularity in late September and early October. Some birders prefer to walk alongside the combines, and others simply watch from the road as the farmers work. Check with Don Simons at the state park for advice if you'd like to try this technique.

Just north of the rice fields (3.7 miles from State Highway 144) is a gravel road beside a Bald Cypress slough. In winter, drive this road slowly and watch for eagles in the trees. Most will be on the far side of the water and are easily missed; up to 21 have been seen here at one time.

52. Lake Pine Bluff

Location: *Begin at the intersection of U.S. Highways 65 and 79 and State Highway 15 (U.S. Highway 65 and University Drive) in Pine Bluff. (Note: This is the old Highway 65, not the new bypass under construction at this writing.) (See map on page 174.)*

Lake Pine Bluff is a state Game and Fish Commission impoundment located just north of downtown Pine Bluff, only a few miles from the Arkansas River. The lake has had a shaky past—in the 1980s the G&FC closed it to fishing because of chemical contamination—but that problem seems to be over. Local birders visit it in fall for waders and in winter for waterfowl and Bald Eagles.

Go north on University Drive (U.S. Highway 79 and State Highway 15) from U.S. Highway 65 for 1.1 miles to a paved road on the right, just past an athletic field (the road is approximately opposite Watson Boulevard); this road was once named State Highway 935, but may not be signed now. Take this 0.1 mile to a G&FC parking lot. Cross a wooden footbridge over the small spillway to the lake's north levee. While there may be interesting birds here in summer (Green Heron, Wood Duck, Yellow-billed Cuckoo, and abundant Northern Orioles, among others), the lake is at its best from fall through spring.

Walk along the levee and scan the lake and shoreline with a scope. Post-breeding herons and egrets can show up in numbers; Merlin has been seen at this spot, as well. Shorebirds often are seen on the lake side of the levee. As winter approaches, the lake attracts all the regular duck species, and Bald Eagles sometimes visit from November into March. One year an Oldsquaw showed up. Double-crested Cormorant, Ruddy Duck, American Coot, and Bonaparte's and Ring-billed Gulls are common in winter. The grassy slopes of the levee and the brush below can be excellent for sparrows and other songbirds.

Return to University Drive and turn left, retracing your route. Drive 1.0 mile to Pullen Street (the last stoplight before Highway 65) and turn left (east). In 0.6 mile you will arrive at a park on the left from which you can scan the southern end of the lake. Fishing piers jutting out into the water provide good observation points. In 0.5 mile the road dead-ends at a circle; you can cross the fence here and walk the levee north if you want. Otherwise, return through the park 0.3 mile to a stop sign; turn left and left again immediately onto Highway 65, eastbound. Continue 0.5 mile to a stoplight and turn left into Pine Bluff Regional Park. Areas on both sides of the road may be flooded, and at times during the year they may have waders or shorebirds. Drive 0.6 mile to the softball complex, where you can turn left, park alongside the road, walk across the field, and climb the levee to scan the northeastern part of the lake. The Three Rivers Audubon Society has plans to build an observation tower near here in memory of the late Jane Stern, a well-known local birder and dedicated conservationist.

The Boyd Point Wastewater Treatment Facility (aka Pine Bluff sewer ponds) can be excellent for ducks. To reach it, return to the starting point (Highways 65 and 79) and drive north on 79 for 3.6 miles to Island Harbor Marina Road. Turn right here and drive 1.1 miles; take the right fork and drive 0.6 mile to the gate. *Call 535-6603 for permission before going to the ponds.* Most of the regular Arkansas ducks have been found here, and 32 Eared Grebes were present in a recent January—an amazing number for this scarce species.

53. Levi Wilcoxon Trail

Location: *From the intersection of U.S. Highways 82 and 425 in Hamburg, drive south 4.2 miles to a small parking area. (The site is 0.2 mile north of the intersection of U.S. Highway 82 and State Highway 52.)*

The Georgia-Pacific Corporation owns hundreds of thousands of acres of timberland in south Arkansas, and is an especially powerful presence in Ashley County. (It wouldn't be wise to walk into a cafe in Crossett wearing a Red-cockaded Woodpecker T-shirt and start loudly criticizing clear-cutting, for instance.) G-P has set up a small area along Highway 82 as a demonstration forest, with a trail system through three different habitats: a section of what is said to be virgin forest, with pines over 150 years old, as well as large oaks and other species; an area of medium-sized second-growth pine; and a tract of "superior pine seedlings" where "undesirable" species have been eliminated. Regardless of how you feel about the rhetoric (G-P points out the vigor of the pure-pine woods in "sharp contrast to the old-growth virgin forest behind you that is virtually devoid of any type natural reproduction"), a walk here is an educational experience.

The intersecting trails can be a little confusing, but it would be hard to get lost. The area isn't very big, and the sound of passing log trucks will always guide you back to the highway. There are no Red-cockadeds here (you have to go a few miles west to Felsenthal National Wildlife Refuge for them), but look for Brown-headed Nuthatches in the pines year-round; listen (when you can) for their pipping and squeaking. Pileated Woodpeckers, much easier to hear, shout from the big trees. In breeding season, listen for the *PEET-sah* of Acadian Flycatcher, the burry song of Yellow-throated Vireo, the *wee-see* of Black-and-white Warbler, and the *chi-tuck* of Summer Tanager. Where the trail passes near wet areas, you may hear the wolf whistle of the beautiful Hooded Warbler. And of course the trill of the Pine Warbler is constant, even on sunny days in winter.

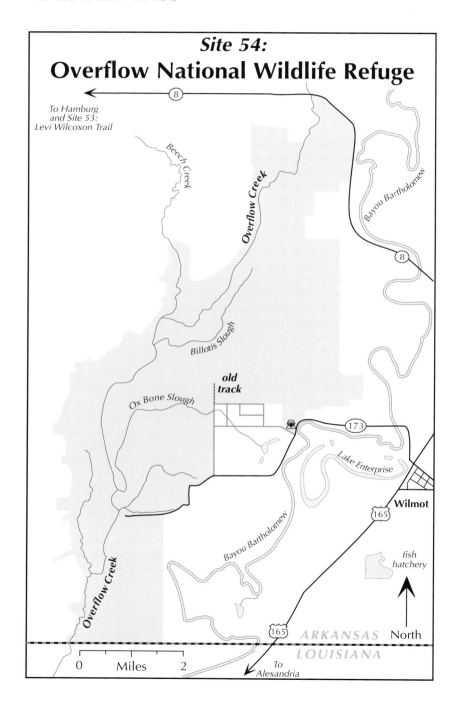

Site 54:
Overflow National Wildlife Refuge

To Hamburg
and Site 53:
Levi Wilcoxon Trail

Beech Creek

Overflow Creek

Bayou Bartholomew

Billotis Slough

old track

Ox Bone Slough

173

Lake Enterprise

Wilmot

165

Bayou Bartholomew

Overflow Creek

fish hatchery

North

165

ARKANSAS

LOUISIANA

To Alexandria

0   Miles   2

54. Overflow National Wildlife Refuge

Location: *Begin at the intersection of U.S. Highway 165 and State Highway 173, just north of the town of Wilmot in Ashley County.*

The area of southeastern Arkansas traditionally known as Overflow Bottoms (named for the bottomland around Overflow Creek) is now incorporated into a national wildlife refuge established in 1980. The 18,000-plus-acre refuge comprises mostly Delta floodplain, with extensive bottomland hardwood forests; red oaks make up more than half the trees, with lesser numbers of white oaks, hickories, Bald Cypress, Water Tupelo, and Sweetgum. The refuge also includes cropland planted and harvested in cooperation with local farmers. Overflow is managed for waterfowl, but its green-tree reservoirs and "moist-soils" areas also attract large numbers of waders and shorebirds. Painted Buntings nest in brushy areas throughout.

At this writing, the refuge has no visitor facilities, few roads, and is officially closed to the public. It is administered through the Felsenthal National Wildlife Refuge, with headquarters near Crossett (see site #49). Overflow will be more accessible in the future, though, and birders are sometimes allowed to enter one area in the central part of the refuge. Although directions are given below, you should call or write Felsenthal NWR (Box 1157, Crossett, AR 71635; 364-3167) to check on the current status before planning a visit.

Note: Check also with the Felsenthal office about access to the Oakwood unit of the refuge. This undeveloped area near Dumas is also officially closed to the public, but birders who have entered with refuge personnel have found good concentrations of shorebirds in late summer. At some time in the near future the unit may have visitor facilities.

To reach one productive area at Overflow, drive west from U.S. Highway 165 for 3.0 miles on State Highway 173. Watch for a dirt road on the right beyond a large plantation-style house. Turn and drive 0.6 mile, turn right, drive 0.5 mile, turn left, and drive 1.0 mile to an intersection. (Use caution on these roads after rains.) Park nearby, off the roadway. Where the main road makes a left (south) turn here, turn right (north) and walk along an old track (often very muddy) about a half-mile to a wetland area. In spring, late summer, and fall, shorebirds and waders are often present in large numbers. Black-necked Stilt, which has nested in recent years in rice fields east of here, has been found, along with American Avocet. Overflow has probably hosted more Glossy Ibis than any other spot in Arkansas (best chance in late summer, although

25 were seen in mid-April 1992); immature White Ibis is more likely, though. Both Yellow and King Rails have been seen here. Anytime but winter you're likely to find Great and Snowy Egrets and Little Blue Herons, as well as assorted other less-common waders, including Roseate Spoonbill.

As might be expected, huge concentrations of ducks and geese gather at Overflow in winter. As more roads, and perhaps nature trails and auto tours, are developed, few doubt that the refuge will be one of the best birding spots in Arkansas.

55. Pendleton Recreation Area

Location: *Begin at the intersection of U.S. Highway 65 and State Highway 212 in the town of Gould, in Lincoln County. (See map on page 196.)*

Pendleton is another of the many Corps of Engineers recreation areas scattered along the length of the Arkansas River. (See the Tar Camp and Arkansas River Levee site listings—#57 and #46—for other examples.) The Pendleton area is larger than most, encompassing a fairly extensive bottomland forest, as well as fields, scrub, swampy areas, and, of course, the river itself. Despite its potential and ease of access via paved roads, Pendleton is rarely visited by birders. It can be reached directly from combined Highways 165 and 1 north of Dumas, but a more scenic approach is from U.S. Highway 65 at Gould.

Take State Highway 212 east from Gould for 8.4 miles to the levee. This road runs through rice, cotton, and soybean fields of little interest except in winter, when flocks of geese (mostly Snow and Canada, with occasional Greater White-fronted and very rare Ross's) may feed. Where the highway turns right atop the levee, turn left and stop. Scan Mud Lake for (depending on the season) grebes, waders, or ducks. At times in late summer, dozens of Great Egrets decorate trees like Christmas ornaments. This is also the time to look for strays like Anhinga, Tricolored Heron, White Ibis (most will be immatures), or, if you're lucky, Roseate Spoonbill or Wood Stork. More likely are breeding-season Snowy Egret, Little Blue Heron, Cattle Egret, and Green Heron; Great Blue Heron is common all year. Bald Eagles may roost here, or anywhere near the river, in winter.

Continue left along the levee for a mile to check out Echubby Lake on the right. Mississippi Kites hawk for insects along the slopes in summer; good-sized flocks may gather in autumn. The most common breeding passerines are Mourning Dove, Indigo Bunting, and Dickcissel, with scattered pairs of Loggerhead Shrikes. The short grass along the sides of the levee is winter home for countless Savannah Sparrows; a few Le Conte's reward those willing to search taller grass.

Turn around wherever you like, return to Highway 212, and drive 3.4 miles to Highway 165-1. Highway 212 runs alongside Mud Lake; although traffic is light, this *is* a highway, so be careful where you stop. Look for levee spurs where you can pull safely off the road to scan for birds. In summer the leaves and yellow flowers of American Lotus blanket sections of the lake (actually a backwater of the Arkansas River). This "Water Lily" is also known as Water Chinquapin, Yoncapin, or

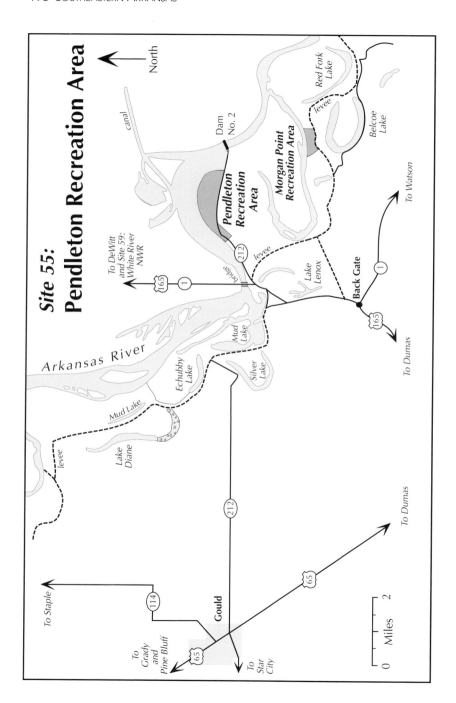

Site 55:
Pendleton Recreation Area

Yancopin; a tiny town a few miles east of here is named Yancopin, for this beautiful aquatic plant.

Turn left onto Highway 165-1, then immediately right onto State Highway 212 at the foot of the impressive bridge over the Arkansas River. Continue 1.5 miles to the Pendleton Recreation Area. Turn left just past the entrance for a good view of the river. Below this point, the heavy barge traffic on the Arkansas is shunted into an eight-mile-long canal connecting, rather amazingly, with the White River, whence it proceeds to the Mississippi. Thus has the Corps of Engineers tidied up the maze of bayous, oxbows, and chutes where these three powerful and unpredictable rivers come together.

The river is nearly deserted in summer, good in winter when waterfowl and eagles gather, and best in spring and fall, when almost anything may happen by. American White Pelican, Double-crested Cormorant, Osprey, gulls, and terns are regular. Merlin and Peregrine Falcon use the river as a migration route, but you'll need luck to spot one; your best chances are in September and October.

In spring, plan to spend an early morning in the excellent woods around the camping area. (Also plan on using your mosquito repellent.) The forest will be loud with the songs and calls of such breeding species as Yellow-billed Cuckoo; Eastern Wood-Pewee; Acadian Flycatcher; Eastern Phoebe; Great Crested Flycatcher; Fish Crow; Blue-gray Gnatcatcher; Wood Thrush; White-eyed, Yellow-throated, and Red-eyed Vireos; Northern Parula; Black-and-white, Prothonotary, and Kentucky Warblers; American Redstart; and Summer Tanager, among others. Such a fine woodland is naturally excellent for migrant thrushes, vireos, and warblers, too.

The Pendleton area has a resident population of the always-secretive Wild Turkey; stay alert (and quiet) in woods and edges at dawn for your best chance of seeing one. Red-shouldered Hawk and Barred Owl are fairly common permanent residents; listen for their two-noted scream and *who cooks for you*, respectively. All the woodpeckers except Red-cockaded can be found here (Yellow-bellied Sapsucker in winter only), and Mississippi Kites soar above the canopy in summer. Among the tall trees, notice especially the size of the Sugarberries, with their warty gray trunks.

In any season, continue down this road 3.2 miles to its end, at Dam No. 2. Along the way you'll pass scrubby fields with breeding Eastern Kingbird, Blue Grosbeak, and Orchard Oriole, as well as the ubiquitous Common Yellowthroat and Indigo Bunting. On the left beyond the fields is a section of river good for winter loons, grebes, cormorants, ducks, and

Bald Eagle, plus waders from spring through fall and American White Pelican in migration. Follow the road to the right, below the dam, to a circle turnaround. A dirt road follows the riverbank downstream. Walk it for breeding Warbling Vireo and Northern Oriole. Certain migrant passerines seem to be found more easily along the river, among them Alder Flycatcher and Yellow and Wilson's Warblers; the last-named can be rather common in fall.

For more birding in similar habitat, return toward Highway 165-1 and turn left onto the levee just before reaching the highway. Drive 5.1 miles to the Morgan Point Recreation Area, another productive location. White Ibis and Roseate Spoonbill have been seen along the levee road in July.

56. Roth Prairie Natural Area

Location: *From U.S. Highway 79B and State Highway 276 (S. Buerkle and Zion streets) in Stuttgart, drive south on Highway 276, passing the school and continuing straight for 2.0 miles to an unnamed dirt road. Turn right for 0.8 mile to the prairie. (See map on page 170.)*

Roth Prairie is of more botanical than ornithological interest: a 40-acre tract of natural virgin grassland of the type that once covered a half-million acres of Arkansas's Grand Prairie. Big Bluestem, Little Bluestem, Indian Grass, and Switch Grass are the dominant species here, sometimes creating a stand of waving stems eight feet tall or more. This small patch of prairie looks a little lonely surrounded by endless cultivated fields, but by walking to the middle and using your imagination it's still possible to get an idea of what this almost-vanished Arkansas habitat looked like in the mid-19th century.

The road borders Roth Prairie on two sides; pull off wherever it's convenient and explore it as you like. (There's a small parking area at the northwestern corner.) Wintering Short-eared Owl is probably the best bird regularly found here; you may have to traipse back and forth to flush one. Wintering Le Conte's and Swamp Sparrows hide in the grasses; American Bittern has been found in low, wet spots in migration, and during one winter a Burrowing Owl was seen after the prairie was burned to control woody vegetation.

One hopeful suggestion: A Yellow Rail was flushed in early May recently from a nearby prairie area with essentially identical habitat to Roth. It never hurts to try.

The fields nearby will have Horned Lark and Savannah Sparrow in winter, when you may also find a flock of Lapland Longspurs. Check all winter buteos in the Grand Prairie; Rough-legged Hawk has been seen here fairly regularly. The area is of little interest to birders in breeding season.

57. Tar Camp Recreation Area

Location: *Take the State Highway 46 exit (Exit 20) from U.S. Highway 65 at Redfield, 20 miles southeast of Little Rock. Drive east 1.0 mile, crossing State Highway 365, and turn left on Brodie Street. Drive 0.1 mile, turn right on River Road, and drive 5.3 miles.*

Tar Camp is a Corps of Engineers recreation area halfway between Little Rock and Pine Bluff, with campsites for both trailers and tents. The property stretches for about a mile along the south bank of the Arkansas River, offering an excellent viewpoint from which to scan in spring and fall for river-following migrants such as American White Pelican, Osprey, and gulls and terns.

Stop just beyond the entrance station to examine a map of the site mounted on a nearby sign. Continue along the main road, watching for bird activity in the riverside cottonwoods. Red-headed Woodpeckers are common here, and in spring and summer Warbling Vireos sing. In breeding season, the most obvious bird may be Northern "Baltimore" Oriole; Tar Camp sometimes seems to be the world capital for this beautiful species. Loggerhead Shrike and Indigo Bunting breed in open areas. Brown-headed Cowbird is, unfortunately, abundant. In any season but summer, pull over to look up and down the river for whatever

Foot bridge to nature trail at Tar Camp Recreation Area. *Photo by Mel White.*

Nature trail at Tar Camp. *Photo by Mel White.*

might happen along. In winter there may be ducks on the water or a Bald Eagle in a tall tree.

After 0.7 mile, watch for a right turn to a nature trail, beginning at a tall footbridge over Tar Camp Creek. The trail passes through jungle-like woodland and climbs to higher ground, making a 3,700-foot loop. These bluffs mark the edge of the Gulf Coastal Plain of south-central Arkansas, which here meets the Mississippi Alluvial Plain of the east. This is a good spot for spring migrants; among the other birds which you may see at various times of year are Barred Owl (often hoots in daylight hours), Ruby-throated Hummingbird, Pileated Woodpecker, Acadian Flycatcher, Blue-gray Gnatcatcher, Wood Thrush, White-eyed Vireo, Northern Parula, and Prothonotary and (abundant) Kentucky Warblers.

After walking the trail, check the marshy wetlands across the campground for Pied-billed Grebe in winter, Green Heron in summer, or Wood Duck (permanent resident). Any time of year, you may see or hear Red-shouldered Hawk.

Tar Camp is only a few miles from the Pine Bluff Arsenal and the National Center for Toxicological Research, where monkeys smoke marijuana and the government has experimented with all sorts of incredibly virulent nerve gasses. So if you see any strange mutants around—a pink-polka-dotted Fish Crow, say, or a Great Blue Heron as big as a construction crane—you'll know where they came from.

58. Warren Prairie

Location: *From the intersection of State Highways 4, 8, and 15 (Main and Church Streets) in Warren, drive east on combined State Highways 4 and 8 for 4.6 miles. Turn right (south) onto State Highway 8 where it diverges from State Highway 4 and drive 2.2 miles to a small parking area on the left.*

Warren Prairie is a 580-acre tract preserved by the Arkansas Natural Heritage Commission primarily to protect its unusual plant community. Saline soil inhibits tree growth on much of the area, giving it a savannah-like aspect. Palmetto (*Sabal minor*), a relatively scarce plant in Arkansas, is common in the wet oak and Loblolly Pine woods here. The uncommon Texas Sunnybell (*Schoenolirion wrightii*) and the very tiny, threatened *Geocarpon minimum* are two of the area's special plants. Although the Texas Sunnybell has noticeable white flowers in April, you're unlikely to see *Geocarpon* unless you spend considerable time on your hands and knees, and even then you'd have to know what to look for. A dwarf variety (*paludosa*) of Post Oak also grows here.

Visitors are welcome at Warren Prairie, but there are no marked trails; it's easy to get disoriented once you're away from roads. It wouldn't be a bad idea to carry a compass while wandering through the area, or at least to note your route carefully. Dropping bread crumbs may not work. *Avoid this area during the gun deer season.*

Warren Prairie is a reliable, easily accessible place to find Bachman's Sparrow, which sings its sweet song in open pine woods at dawn and dusk during the breeding season. Henslow's Sparrow, rare and hard to

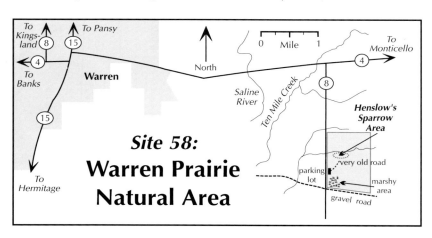

To Kingsland (8) (15) To Pansy

(4)

To Banks

Warren

(15)

North

0 Mile 1

To Monticello

(4)

Saline River

Ten Mile Creek

(8)

Henslow's Sparrow Area

very old road

parking lot

marshy area

gravel road

To Hermitage

Site 58:
Warren Prairie
Natural Area

find in Arkansas, is the area's best bird, though. It has been seen in February, late March, early April, and November, with up to four birds in close proximity. Search in the edges of open grassy areas where there are scattered small trees. Walk east and then north from the parking lot to find an extensive area of suitable habitat within 300 yards or so. Other winter and migrant sparrows will be found here as well, of course, including Field, Vesper, Savannah, Song, Swamp, and White-throated, and possibly Le Conte's and Lincoln's.

Just south of the parking area, also on the east side of State Highway 8, is a marshy area where Sedge and Marsh Wrens have been found in winter and migration. You'll need rubber boots to flush them from the wet grass. Among the other birds found here in the proper habitat and season: American Bittern, Red-shouldered Hawk, American Woodcock, Brown-headed Nuthatch, and Red Crossbill.

Continue south 0.1 mile on State Highway 8 from the parking lot and turn left (east) on a gravel road. Drive 0.3 mile to an open, "prairie" part of Warren Prairie, another good place to look for winter sparrows.

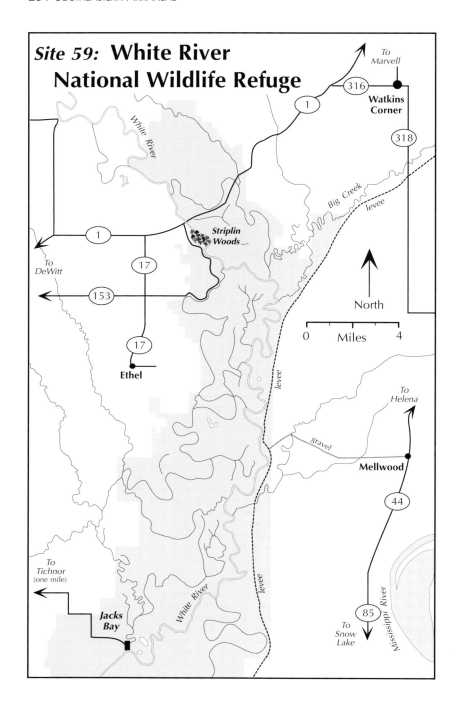

Site 59: **White River National Wildlife Refuge**

59. White River National Wildlife Refuge

Location: *The refuge office is at 321 West 7th Street in DeWitt, about 65 miles southeast of Little Rock.*

White River National Wildlife Refuge is one of Arkansas's true natural wonders, comprising 113,000 acres of bottomland forest, rivers, sloughs, bayous, lakes, and farmland stretching for 35 miles along the White River near its confluence with the Mississippi. The refuge is the largest publicly owned tract of bottomland forest in the Mississippi Delta. (The Atchafalaya Swamp in Louisiana is larger but is in many different ownerships.) Together with the Cache River National Wildlife Refuge to the north and several nearby Game and Fish Commission areas, White River refuge was named a Wetland of International Importance in 1990. The Cache/Lower White River system comprises the most important wintering area for Mallards in North America—possibly in the world—with an average of 10 per cent of the total Mississippi Flyway population wintering in the area. Up to 350,000 ducks are sometimes found on the refuge, along with 10,000 Canada Geese. When the Black Bear had been nearly extirpated from the rest of Arkansas, there was still a healthy population in the refuge. When Bald Eagles returned to nest in Arkansas after an absence of a quarter-century, White River NWR was one of their first breeding sites. (The location of eagle nests is kept secret to protect the birds from harassment, intentional and unintentional.)

Unfortunately, the very things that make White River NWR such a magnificent natural area also make access very difficult at times. Much of the refuge is under water for long periods in the winter and spring. Roads in the refuge are closed from November 1 through February, and even when they are open they can be muddy in the spring. Large areas are inaccessible to all but well-prepared boaters who know the infinite loops and meanderings of the river and countless bayous and backwaters.

Still, it is possible to experience White River without undertaking a wilderness float trip. Make your first stop at the refuge headquarters in DeWitt, where you can pick up a map and inquire about road conditions.

From the intersection of State Highway 1 and U.S. Highway 165 in DeWitt, go north on State Highway 1 (the Great River Road) 15.7 miles and take the last road on the right just before the bridge over the White River. The area on your left, known as Striplin Woods, is filled with huge old trees reminiscent of what all of eastern Arkansas must have looked like two centuries ago. There are no formal trails, but wander in wherever you can down toward the river. (Watch for Poison Ivy and, as always in warm weather, for snakes.) Swainson's Warbler has been seen here, and it's a good place to find many of the typical southern swamp birds such as Barred Owl, Pileated Woodpecker, Great Crested Flycatcher, Northern Parula, and Prothonotary Warbler. This section of road is open even when the rest of the refuge roads are closed. (Note that after 0.4 mile this area becomes private property for a short distance.)

This road continues south along the White River, but after another half-mile or so it is closed in spring until the river goes down, which may be as late as May or June. (Even if the gate is closed, you can walk in as far as conditions allow.) When it is open, it circles through an area of forest and lakes and leaves the refuge after about 5 miles. This is a great road to drive slowly, listening out an open window for anything interesting and stopping often to explore the small creeks and bayous. When you leave the refuge, continue on a dirt road 1.5 miles to State Highways 153 and 17; go west on the former or north on the latter to return to State Highway 1, depending on whether you're heading south or north.

To visit an accessible area in the southern part of the refuge, return to the intersection of State Highway 1 and U.S. Highway 165 in DeWitt and drive south on U.S. Highway 165 for 8.4 miles to State Highway 44. Turn left (east) on 44 for 6.8 miles, through the town of Tichnor, to a sharp left turn; continue straight on a gravel road for 1.4 miles to an intersection and turn right. (There may be a small sign here pointing the way to Jacks Bay.) Follow this road one mile to the refuge entrance sign, and another 3.6 miles to the Jacks Bay primitive camping area. Once you're in the refuge, stop anywhere you like to investigate the woods and side roads. The uncommon Swainson's Warbler breeds here, in areas with stands of cane, so listen carefully for its song amid the spring chorus of Yellow-billed Cuckoo; Acadian and Great Crested Flycatchers; Carolina Chickadee; Tufted Titmouse; Carolina Wren; Blue-gray Gnatcatcher; Wood Thrush; White-eyed, Yellow-throated, and Red-eyed Vireos; Northern Parula; Prothonotary, Kentucky, and Hooded Warblers; Common Yellowthroat; Summer Tanager; Indigo Bunting; and Orchard and Northern Orioles.

Mississippi Kites (breeding season) and Red-shouldered Hawks often soar above the canopy, and Red-headed Woodpeckers nest in the telephone poles near Jacks Bay. An early-morning visit might turn up a group of Wild Turkeys along the road. A few Hooded Mergansers nest in Wood Duck boxes throughout the refuge, but they're hard to find, as are Yellow-crowned Night-Herons.

A word of warning: The mosquitoes here can be absolutely horrendous in warm weather, so come prepared with the highest-power repellent you can find.

In winter, most of the refuge is off-limits to the public, but the farmland nearby can be productive for flocks of geese (Snow and Canada, with smaller numbers of Greater White-fronted), raptors, Brewer's Blackbird, and open-country birds such as Horned Lark and Lapland Longspur. A good bet is to drive State Highways 1, 17, and 153 just west of the upper refuge. Flocks of larks and longspurs often number in the hundreds in the bare fields here. Keith Sutton, compiler of the White River Christmas Bird Count, has seen as many as 5,000 Lapland Longspurs in a day's birding in this area. Red-tailed Hawks are common, and there's a slim chance of Rough-legged Hawk. Golden Eagle is rare, but is seen regularly; in fact, White River refuge may be the best place in the state for this species.

To see Bald Eagles, and possibly Goldens, in winter, drive the White River levee on the east side of the refuge (this road is open all year). To reach it, go north 9.8 miles from the Highway 1 bridge over the White River. Turn right onto State Highway 316, drive 3.5 miles, turn right onto State Highway 318, and drive 4.3 miles to the levee. Turn right onto the levee here and drive slowly, watching on both sides of the road. On the left is farmland with extensive swampy areas and borrow pits; on the right is wet forest where eagles perch in the tall trees. The levee can also be good for viewing some of the tens of thousands of ducks that winter here; large numbers of Ring-necked Ducks are a special attraction. You can drive south for quite a distance here; turn around (carefully) wherever you like and return, or continue along the levee 13 miles from State Highway 318 to a gravel road on your left that leads east to State Highway 44.

For information on White River National Wildlife Refuge, write Box 308, DeWitt, AR 72042, or call 946-1468.

NOTES ON SELECTED ARKANSAS SPECIES

On the following pages are listed a number of selected "specialty birds" that may be of interest to birders in Arkansas, be they residents of the state or visitors. Each of the species accounts will usually have some abundance and location hints included, and will often refer to places already covered in the birdfinding sections of this book. You might find it especially useful to use the specialty treatments in conjunction with the next section of the book, the bar-graphs. Please note that the following initials appear frequently in the following pages:

FH = Fish Hatchery
NA = Natural Area
NF = National Forest
NMP = National Military Park
NR = National River
NWR = National Wildlife Refuge
RA = Recreation Area
SMA = State Management Area
SP = State Park
WMA = Wildlife Management Area

Common Loon—Found from fall through early spring on the state's big reservoirs; e.g., Beaver, Bull Shoals, Greers Ferry, Maumelle, Ouachita, DeGray, and Millwood. Less common in midwinter than during migration.

Rarer loons—Scattered records for Red-throated, Pacific, and Yellow-billed Loons; possible in same locations as Common. Best bet: check the hotline (753-5853).

Pied-billed Grebe—Common on all sorts of ponds and lakes from fall through spring. Has nested recently near Lonoke (Joe Hogan FH), near Lake Chicot, and at Bayou Meto WMA.

Horned Grebe—Common fall through spring in same locations as Common Loon.

Eared Grebe—Very uncommon; less confined to large reservoirs than Horned Grebe.

American White Pelican—Easily seen during spring and fall migration along the Arkansas River (peaks mid-April and mid-October). Often congregates in large numbers at Millwood Lake; 2,200 were present on April 17, 1985. Increasingly, pelicans are being seen in both summer and winter along the Arkansas River, at Millwood, and in Chicot County.

Double-crested Cormorant—Increasingly abundant (distressingly so, for fish farmers) on rivers and lakes from fall through spring. Has begun breeding recently at Millwood Lake, where it is abundant except in summer.

Anhinga—Breeds at a few mostly inaccessible places in southern Arkansas; uncommon at other sites in southern and eastern Arkansas. From spring through fall, check the Okay Levee at Millwood Lake; try Lake Chicot in late summer.

American Bittern—Best chance is to look in marshy areas in eastern Arkansas in spring and fall (borrow pits along Arkansas and Mississippi River levees, edges of wetlands at Bayou Meto WMA, Wapanocca NWR). Suspected of nesting, but no confirmed recent records.

Least Bittern—Has been found and/or nested recently at Faulkner Lake (see Scott listing), Bayou Meto WMA (Halowell Reservoir and Wrape Plantation), and Hogan FH at Lonoke. Undoubtedly breeds at other places in eastern Arkansas; Wapanocca and Big Lake NWRs would be worth checking.

Great Blue Heron—Common permanent resident throughout the state, and easy to find at such places as Holla Bend and Wapanocca NWRs and Lake Chicot. The birds are less common in the northern mountains, but a herony has existed across the White River from the Gaston's Resort nature trail (see Bull Shoals listing) in recent years.

Great Egret—Easy to find from spring through fall at nearly any wetland in southern or eastern Arkansas; e.g., Lake Chicot, Lonoke, Bayou Meto WMA, Millwood Lake. A few winter in the southern part of the state, as at Lake Chicot and Millwood.

Snowy Egret—Same as Great Egret, except that it does not winter in the state.

Tricolored Heron—Rare post-breeding wanderer; try Millwood Lake or Lake Chicot in late summer.

Black-crowned Night-Heron—A scarce bird in Arkansas except at one inaccessible breeding colony in the southwest. Check in migration at Bayou Meto WMA, White River NWR, and along the Arkansas and Mississippi river levees. May show up at Okay Levee (Millwood Lake) or with the mixed flocks of waders at Lake Chicot in late summer.

Yellow-crowned Night-Heron—More common than Black-crowned, but not easy to find. Has nested recently in Little Rock's Boyle Park and Bayou Meto WMA. Sometimes occurs with mixed flocks of waders at Lake Chicot. Single birds, or small groups, may show up at even small, temporary, roadside wetlands almost anywhere. Check the Hulsey (Lake Hamilton) and Hogan (Lonoke) FHs.

White Ibis—Best bets for this and other ibises are Lake Chicot (levee drives) and Millwood Lake in the fall (the species may nest near Millwood). Overflow NWR may be a good spot, too. Has been seen recently in late summer at the Wrape Plantation area of Bayou Meto WMA.

Roseate Spoonbill—Post-breeding wanderer to Lake Chicot (levee drives) and Millwood Lake.

Wood Stork—Similar behavior to Roseate Spoonbill, but more common than that species.

Black-bellied Whistling-Duck—Most likely in fall at Millwood Lake, where it is suspected of breeding somewhere nearby. Has also been seen at Lake Chicot, where two adults and two young were seen in August 1993. One adult and five flightless young were seen at Ft. Chaffee WMA (near Fort Smith) in the early fall of 1994. This species is expanding its range and may soon be more common in Arkansas.

Swans—Tundra Swan is a very rare migrant and winter visitor. Trumpeter Swans have been showing up near Heber Springs in recent winters, increasing in number each year since 1991 (see the Greers Ferry Lake listing). These birds are thought to be from introductions in the upper Midwest.

Greater White-fronted Goose—Uncommon; found with other geese at places such as Holla Bend, White River, and Wapanocca NWRs and in agricultural lands near Lonoke, Lake Chicot, Stuttgart, and Black River WMA.

Snow Goose—Easily found in winter at Holla Bend and Wapanocca NWRs; large flocks wander through the agricultural lands of eastern Arkansas at that time.

Ross's Goose—Find a flock of Snow Geese and put your scope to work. No doubt more of the Snow's little cousins show up in Arkansas than are reported. Holla Bend NWR is a consistent location and a good place to start looking.

Canada Goose—Compare Snow Goose listing. The Arkansas Game and Fish Commission is attempting to introduce the "giant" race of this species, which is nonmigratory, into the state along the Arkansas River Valley; these birds are often seen at Bona Dea and the Dardanelle Dam in summer. The population seems to be doing well; numbers were estimated at 5,000 in northwestern Arkansas in January 1994.

Wood Duck—Common in wooded wetlands and bottomlands as a breeder statewide. Check Wapanocca, White River, and Felsenthal NWRs, Bayou Meto WMA, Bona Dea, Lake Fayetteville, and the levee drives in Chicot County.

Greater Scaup—Has been reported recently from Lake Atalanta, Lonoke, and Millwood Lake; possibly more regular than reports indicate.

Hooded Merganser—This beautiful duck nests at Big Lake and Wapanocca NWRs, but usually in inaccessible locations; it's not often seen at that season. Has also nested at Pinnacle Mountain SP.

Other ducks—Mallards can seem as thick as flies at times in the White River bottoms of eastern Arkansas—which, with other tributaries such as the Cache River, has been called the most important wintering area in the world for this cosmopolitan species. To study waterfowl, look for flocks at the national wildlife refuges, occasionally at the state fish hatcheries, and at Millwood Lake. As might be expected, the very uncommon American Black Duck is more likely in eastern Arkansas (check Big Lake NWR), and the rare Cinnamon Teal is more likely in the west (check the Centerton FH or Lake Fayetteville). Rarities such as scoters (all three have been seen in Arkansas) and Oldsquaw may turn up at any of the big lakes mentioned in this guide; the best place to find them may be on the hotline (753-5853).

Black Vulture—Not as common as the ubiquitous TV; look for its broader wings and faster flapping in soaring flocks in the western half of the state.

Osprey—Sit on the bank of the Arkansas River during April or October and you're bound to see one fly by. The migratory "fish hawk" is fairly easily found at those times on many lakes (common at Millwood) and smaller rivers, as well. Has nested recently at Big Lake NWR in the northeast: an encouraging sign of a comeback?

Mississippi Kite—Breeds locally in the central and southern parts of the state. One consistent nesting location for this raptor is, surprisingly enough, the residential areas of central and western Little Rock, where occasional birds can be seen flying over the hills all summer. Nests regularly in Boyle Park, and has nested in the pines near the University of Arkansas at Little Rock. Gathers in flocks in fall, when it can be seen by driving the levees along the Arkansas and Mississippi rivers in the southeast.

Bald Eagle—Found in winter at any of the big reservoirs and along the Arkansas and White rivers; Millwood Lake, Holla Bend NWR, and Dardanelle Dam are can't-miss sites. Every year since the mid-1980s seems to have brought reports of another nest or two; in 1994 it was DeGray Lake. Nests could be seen from land in 1993 at Millwood Lake and Big Lake NWR, among other places. Young birds from other states are being "hacked" at an out-of-the-way location at Holla Bend, so watch for immatures with colored wing-markers.

Red-shouldered Hawk—Can be hard to find, but check bottomland forests at sites such as Bayou Meto, Dagmar, and Harris Brake WMAs, White River and Felsenthal NWRs, Lake Conway, and Cossatot River SP. Listen for its two-part call.

Swainson's Hawk—A western wanderer, most likely to show up in the western part of the state at places like the Centerton FH and Baker Prairie NA. Nested near Fayetteville in 1986.

Rough-legged Hawk—Seldom seen, but most likely in mid-winter in agricultural areas of northeastern Arkansas and around Stuttgart.

Golden Eagle—Very rare in Arkansas (and perhaps rarer than records indicate, since many confuse this bird and the immature Bald Eagle). Often seen on the White River NWR Christmas Bird Count. Holla Bend NWR is another place to try. To be looked for in winter in the rugged mountains of the west; e.g., from the Talimena Scenic Byway west of Mena.

Peregrine Falcon—Rare migrant statewide; occasionally seen in winter. Young birds from out of state have been hacked in recent years near Newark (Independence County) and on the tallest building in downtown Little Rock. (Be on the lookout for Prairie Falcon, especially in the western third of the state in winter.)

Ruffed Grouse—Native grouse were extirpated in Arkansas by 1900. Since 1981, more than 1,200 birds have been reintroduced at several sites in the Ozark Mountains, including Ponca (the upper Buffalo National River), Magazine Mountain, near Pelsor, and near Redding RA. Males are heard giving their courtship "drumming" in spring.

Wild Turkey—Elusive; best looked for at dawn on backroads in the Ouachita Mountains. Lake Sylvia, Mena, and Waldron are all centers of healthy populations. Birders in the east should try the St. Francis NF. Avoid the turkey woods during turkey-hunting season!

Rails—These secretive birds are always hard to find. Eastern Arkansas birders have had success recently hitching rides with friendly farmers during the rice harvest, when combines may flush up several rails from one field. If you don't want to ride, park along a road and watch the harvest from a distance. For others: find a marshy spot, put on hip boots, and good luck.... Sometimes vegetation grows along the edge of a pond or ditch at the Lonoke or Centerton FHs in which a Sora or Virginia Rail may be found. There are likely-looking places at Bayou Meto WMA, Lake Chicot, and Wapanocca NWR. Yellow Rail was flushed recently from a prairie near Stuttgart very similar to Roth Prairie; it's worth a try.

Purple Gallinule—Nests at an inaccessible location in southwestern Arkansas, but otherwise rarely reported. Once was seen regularly at Faulkner Lake (see Scott listing), but not in recent years. The Wrape Plantation area of Bayou Meto WMA looks like good habitat.

Common Moorhen—Much the same situation as Purple Gallinule; birds have been seen at Bayou Meto during the nesting season. Has nested recently near Lake Chicot and at the edges of fish ponds near Lonoke.

American Coot—Common on lakes and ponds in winter and migration. Has nested near Lake Chicot and Lonoke.

Shorebirds—The most consistent shorebirding spots in Arkansas are the fish ponds at Centerton, Lonoke, and near Lake Chicot. However, temporary conditions—a "drawdown" at a reservoir exposing mudflats, or a flooded farm field—can attract flocks of various sizes in migration. Late summer is usually the best time, but spring and fall can be good, too.

Black-necked Stilt—Once considered only a rare spring visitor, this species has been found nesting in recent years near Lake Chicot, Grand Lake, and Lonoke.

Hudsonian Godwit—Scarce in Arkansas; best chance may be the Centerton FH in early May.

American Woodcock—Usually flushed by accident from wet woods in the southern half of the state in winter. Some places where the bird's early-spring courtship flight has been observed recently include Willow Beach (see Scott listing), the Lake Maumelle dam (see Pinnacle Mountain SP listing), old clearcuts in the Ouachita NF (see Mena), and consistently at Lake Fayetteville. Don't wait too long to look for woodcock; they begin their courtship flights as early as December!

Phalaropes—Wilson's is a fairly common migrant, seen with other shorebirds. Red-necked (spring and fall) and Red (fall) are "how lucky can you get" rarities. Check the hotline (753-5853).

Jaegers—Go to Millwood Lake in the fall, and take your most potent lucky charm. All three have been seen there.

Laughing Gull—Rare in fall (almost annual at Millwood Lake) in the south. Very rare in spring.

Franklin's Gull—Uncommon spring migrant; more common in fall. Charles Mills reports: Franklin's Gulls have, in recent years, utilized Millwood Lake as a minor staging area. Although a few individuals are usually present by late September, the migratory peak, which may involve up to 1800± birds, does not occur until the last week of October or the first two weeks of November." Also check the Centerton FH and Lake Fayetteville. Several dozen were seen on October 23, 1994, at Lake Maumelle.

Little Gull—Very rare winter visitor to Millwood Lake and Lake Chicot. Check out the flocks of Bonaparte's Gulls.

Bonaparte's Gull—Fairly common fall migrant and early-winter visitor; numbers decrease in mid-winter. Less common spring migrant. Easy to find at Millwood Lake and Lake Chicot in December; small flocks are often present at Lake Maumelle, Lonoke, and other bodies of water, including the tailwaters of dams.

Ring-billed Gull—The common gull in Arkansas, seen all winter around dams, along major rivers, and at fish ponds.

Herring Gull—A few are seen with Ring-bills; far less common; most are immatures.

Glaucous Gull—Accidental at Millwood Lake and at Dardanelle Lock and Dam.

Black-legged Kittiwake—Accidental at Millwood Lake, Lake Chicot, and Beaver Lake.

Sabine's Gull—All of the dozen or so records are from Millwood Lake, ranging from September 17 to October 21. All but one of the birds were in juvenile plumage.

Caspian Tern—Uncommon spring migrant (best chance in late May) and common fall migrant (peaking in September). Easy to find in fall along the Arkansas River. On September 19, 1980, 96 birds were seen on a mudflat at Millwood Lake; on September 17, 1994, several dozen passed by Murray Park in Little Rock.

Common Tern—Rare migrant, slightly more common in fall than in spring. Extreme caution must be used in separating this bird from the more common Forster's. Again, best chance might be Millwood Lake in September.

Forster's Tern—Fairly common migrant, more numerous in fall than spring (peaking in September). The Arkansas River, the Lonoke and Centerton FHs, Millwood Lake, and Lake Chicot are good bets. Small numbers now winter in south Arkansas, especially Millwood Lake and Lake Chicot.

Least Tern—Uncommon migrant, especially along the Arkansas and Mississippi Rivers. Once a fairly common breeder on river sandbars, but now threatened in Arkansas. Alterations to the natural stream flow for navigational purposes have affected the birds' nesting areas, and increasingly popular off-road vehicles sometimes disrupt colonies. See the Grand Lake listing for one Mississippi River colony. Those with a boat and a sense of adventure can see good numbers of Least Terns at the confluence of the White and Mississippi Rivers, where huge sandbars nearby provide nesting opportunities. Also nests at scattered and shifting sites along the Arkansas River between Little Rock and Fort Smith.

Black Tern—"The most numerous species of tern seen in Arkansas," according to James and Neal in *Arkansas Birds*. Most often seen from mid-April to June and (with hardly a break before fall migration) from late June through September. Found around almost any kind of water.

Black-billed Cuckoo—Very uncommon migrant throughout the state; in central Arkansas, most often seen May 5-12. A few old nesting records from extreme northern Arkansas.

Greater Roadrunner—Badly hurt by severe winters in the late 1970s, but now seemingly recovered and once again seen regularly across the state, except for the extreme east. A bird that's found where you find it, and then often only as a shape dashing into the trees along the road. See Devil's Den, Mount Nebo, and Pinnacle Mountain SPs, Holla Bend NWR, Mena, and DeGray Lake for good sites. Concentrate your efforts in areas that look like Texas: dry, rocky hillsides with open, scrubby woods.

Groove-billed Ani—Very rare wanderer to western Arkansas. Among the few records are two from the Okay Levee at Millwood Lake in early October.

Barn Owl—Found across Arkansas (less common in the mountains) but hard to see unless a nest has been located, usually in a barn or abandoned house. Has been seen recently in the water tower at Lake Chicot SP and in a hangar at the Stuttgart Airport.

Long-eared Owl—Rare winter visitor. Has been seen regularly in recent years in thick junipers along the levee at Holla Bend NWR. Conscientious cold-weather birders peer into similar stands of juniper whenever they get the opportunity.

Short-eared Owl—Winter resident, roosting in the tall grass of prairies, rice fields, and airports. A few can usually be flushed up at the Stuttgart Airport and at Roth Prairie NA, south of Stuttgart. Little Rock birder Bill Shepherd's favorite way to find them is to drive back roads of eastern Arkansas farmlands at dusk and watch for flying owls silhouetted against the sky as they begin their hunting. ("You have to get extremely close to the ground to see the owls against the sky," advises Bill.)

Whip-poor-will—Migrates through the entire state, and breeds in upland areas. A map of summer records in James and Neal's *Arkansas Birds* shows the nesting range to cover the northwestern half of the state. Always less frequently reported than its common cousin, the Chuck-will's-widow.

Red-cockaded Woodpecker—Endangered in Arkansas, as elsewhere. Early harvesting of pines eliminates the mature, "red-heart" trees that the birds need for nesting, and fire suppression works against the open, parklike woods that they prefer. The Ouachita NF, which has done an about-face in its environmental posture in the past few years, is now committed to helping the species, so the RCW's future seems slightly brighter than it has been in the recent past. The easiest place to find it is at Felsenthal NWR; birds can also be seen at the Ouachita NF's Buffalo Road Demonstration Site (see Waldron listing).

Willow Flycatcher—As the pre-split "Traill's" Flycatcher, this species was discovered by John James Audubon at Arkansas Post in 1822, though it no longer nests in the Grand Prairie area. Its only known breeding site in Arkansas is at Lake Bentonville. As of this writing, development may be threatening habitat at Lake Bentonville. The future of Willow Flycatcher (also of Bell's Vireo, Blue Grosbeak, and Painted Bunting) at Lake Bentonville is in question. Elsewhere in the state Willow Flycatcher is an uncommon migrant.

Scissor-tailed Flycatcher—Common breeder in open areas in the western part of the state, east to about Lonoke, with a few records even as far east as Big Lake NWR. A traveler on Interstate 40 from Little Rock to Fort Smith is bound to see at least a few during breeding season. Sometimes gathers in large flocks in October, prior to leaving the state for the winter.

Horned Lark—Usually easy to find through most of the winter in extensive open areas, such as fields around Lonoke and elsewhere in eastern Arkansas (where large flocks may associate with Lapland Longspurs) and at Holla Bend NWR. Nests in similar areas, including Baker Prairie NA at Harrison. Drive roads along newly plowed cropland in spring and listen for its tinkling song.

Tree Swallow—This common migrant has been found nesting at a few sites around Arkansas, usually in old woodpecker holes in dead trees in standing water. Bull Shoals (Gaston's Resort nature trail), Lake Norfork,

Lake Conway, Millwood Lake, Harris Brake WMA, and Big Lake NWR have all had breeding Tree Swallows in recent years.

Northern Rough-winged Swallow—Nests throughout the state in bluff faces, riverbanks, and gravel pits.

Bank Swallow—Once nested in Arkansas in riverbanks, but has declined; no regular colonies known. More common in migration in the eastern part of the state.

Cliff Swallow—This species has steadily expanded its breeding range in recent years, thanks to its colonization of dams and bridges. Look for it at nearly any dam on the Arkansas River (except possibly in the southeast), at the Interstate 430 bridge at Little Rock, at the Lake Maumelle pumping-station and the bridge at the western end of the lake (see Pinnacle Mountain SP listing), at the Bull Shoals, Greers Ferry, and Beaver dams, and at the Millwood Lake spillway, among many other places.

Fish Crow—Breeds near bodies of water throughout the state (possibly less common in the northwest). Winters in southern Arkansas; can always be found in winter at Millwood Lake.

Brown-headed Nuthatch—Look for this little pipsqueak in mature pines in the southwestern third of the state; DeGray Lake, around Mena, and the Buffalo Road Demonstration Site near Waldron are reliable. Visitors to Little Rock short of time can try the Lake Maumelle dam area (see Pinnacle Mountain SP listing).

Rock Wren—Very rare wanderer from the west. If you're going to find one, it will probably be on riprap (large rocks used for bank stabilization) in the western part of the state in fall and winter. Check out levees at Millwood and DeGray lakes.

Bewick's Wren—Once a fairly common breeder in western Arkansas, but now rare. James and Neal (1986) report: "In Fayetteville, where Bewick's Wren was 'fairly common' thirty years ago, the common wren of the dooryard in the 1980s is the House Wren, a species that was first observed nesting at Fayetteville only a decade ago." They speculate that the decline in the number of "neglected sheds and junky open lots" may have contributed to the decline of the Bewick's Wren—another sad victim of gentrification. Scattered pairs are still found; two birds were seen at Steel Creek on the Buffalo National River in the summer of 1993, and the species may breed at the Okay Levee at Millwood Lake. Migrants are most often seen in March and October; winters mostly in the south.

House Wren—Fairly common migrant and uncommon winter resident (mostly in the south). James and Neal: "Since 1972, when they first nested in Fayetteville, House Wrens have been reported regularly in summer in Benton and Washington counties, and have become a common summer resident in urban areas there."

Winter Wren—Look for this tiny winter resident in brushpiles in wet woods throughout the state.

Sedge Wren—Once nested in the Grand Prairie region, but no recent records. Look for it in marshy, grassy places throughout the state in migration and in south Arkansas in winter. Some likely sites include the Centerton FH, the fields below the Millwood Lake dam, the sandbar at Murray Park in Little Rock, and Roth Prairie NA at Stuttgart.

Marsh Wren—Much the same as Sedge Wren, except that it has not nested in Arkansas. Often found when it sings, even in fall migration.

American Pipit—Look for it in migration and winter in drained ponds at the Lonoke, Hulsey, and Centerton FHs, along the runways at the Stuttgart Airport, and in bare fields in cropland. Large numbers are sometimes seen along the Okay Levee at Millwood Lake.

Sprague's Pipit—Very rare in Arkansas in winter. Walk shortgrass areas such as the Stuttgart Airport runways or the Millwood Lake dam. Few recent records.

Cedar Waxwing—An erratic, sometimes common winter resident, moving in flocks to wherever food is available. Scarce and scattered nesting records over the years from the Ozark Mountains. Two confirmed nesting records from the summer of 1993: one near Cass and one north of Dover.

Bell's Vireo—A fairly uncommon breeder in Arkansas that is more common in the north, but is occasionally hard to find. Some good sites lately have been Willow Beach RA (see Scott listing), Bull Shoals SP, Holla Bend NWR, Lake Bentonville, and Lake Ashbaugh at Black River WMA. Knowing this bird's scratchy song is vital to seeing it.

Yellow-throated Vireo—Nests widely, but is most common in the west. Can be found at Devil's Den, Cossatot, Bull Shoals, and Pinnacle Mountain SPs, at Redding Campground and Page Hollow in the Ozark NF, at Lake Sylvia in the Ouachita NF, and at Buffalo NR. Again, knowing the song is important: the Scarlet Tanager is sometimes described as sounding like an American Robin with a sore throat; this bird sounds like a Red-eyed Vireo with a sore throat.

Warbling Vireo—Likes trees along rivers; most common in the eastern lowlands. Can't be missed in spring and summer at Maumelle Park (see Pinnacle Mountain SP listing), Willow Beach RA (see Scott listing), Tar Camp RA, and Holla Bend NWR.

Blue-winged Warbler—Nests in the northwestern part of the state in old fields with scattered small trees. Found at Lake Wedington RA,

Devil's Den SP, Pea Ridge NMP, near Greers Ferry Lake, Hobbs SMA, and near Page Hollow. Otherwise, a fairly common migrant.

Yellow Warbler—Common migrant, and a scarce summer resident in Arkansas. Check willow trees along the Buffalo NR, especially near Buffalo Point. The species has been suspected of nesting at a Game and Fish Commission pond near Greers Ferry Lake, as well.

Chestnut-sided Warbler—Four singing males of this common migrant species were found in mid-summer in 1993 near Pelsor in the Ozark NF; in 1994, breeding was confirmed here. See that listing for details.

Black-throated Green Warbler—Formerly considered only a common migrant, this species was found nesting in the Ozark NF in 1993, far from its nearest known breeding-grounds. See the Page Hollow listing for details of this amazing discovery. In July 1994 a female was seen atop Magazine Mountain.

Yellow-throated Warbler—Likes sycamores along streams and rivers; also likes pines, and reaches peak density in cypress swamps. Look for it at Pinnacle Mountain, Cossatot River, and Devil's Den SPs, Buffalo NR, Hobbs SMA, Lake Wedington, and around Millwood Lake.

Prairie Warbler—Can be very common in clearcuts in south Arkansas. Found at DeGray Lake, Pea Ridge NMP, Mena, and Cossatot River SP.

Cerulean Warbler—This species has declined in Arkansas as its preferred habitat of mature deciduous forest has been cut. Known to nest along the Buffalo NR, at Cossatot River SP, and at Redding Campground, Cherry Bend, and Page Hollow in the Ozark NF.

American Redstart—An uncommon nesting bird in wet woods, both bottomland and upland, throughout the state. Look for it at Buffalo NR, Devil's Den SP, Felsenthal NWR, and Hobbs SMA.

Prothonotary Warbler—Common in swampy bottomlands throughout the state. Easy to find at Wapanocca NWR, Dagmar and Harris Brake WMAs, Pinnacle Mountain and Louisiana Purchase SPs, Byrd Lake NA, and Lake Conway, among many other places.

Worm-eating Warbler—A bird that needs extensive forest, and so is found as a breeder mostly in the Ozarks and Ouachitas. Can be fairly common on moist slopes. Look for it at Page Hollow and Redding Campground in the Ozark NF, at Devil's Den SP, at Hobbs SMA, and on hillsides along the Buffalo NR.

Swainson's Warbler—Prefers bottomland forests and canebrakes. A good population lives in the White River NWR, which is probably the best place to find the bird. Other fairly reliable sites have been Village

Creek SP, St. Francis NF, Redding Campground (uncommonly) in the Ozark NF, and Buffalo NR (at Buffalo Point and Rush).

Ovenbird—Common nesting species in Ozark and Ouachita highland forests. Easy to find at Magazine Mountain, Devil's Den and Cossatot River SPs, Lake Sylvia RA, and Page Hollow.

Louisiana Waterthrush—Common nester along streams except in the eastern lowlands. Look for it at Buffalo NR, Hobbs SMA, Lorance Creek NA, and Cossatot River, Devil's Den, and Pinnacle Mountain SPs.

Kentucky Warbler—Common nester in wet woodland. Among the many places it breeds are Holla Bend NWR, Bona Dea, Dagmar WMA, Devil's Den and Pinnacle Mountain SPs, Lake Wedington RA, and the Buffalo NR.

Hooded Warbler—Likes dense thickets of vines and shrubs in wet woodland, where clearing or a blowdown has caused a small opening. Look for it on Rich Mountain (see Mena listing), along the Buffalo NR, at Page Hollow and Redding Campground in the Ozark NF, at Devil's Den SP, and at Hobbs SMA.

Scarlet Tanager—Its congener the Summer Tanager is a common breeder all across Arkansas, but the beautiful Scarlet is seen most often in the Ozark and Ouachita mountains. It nests on Magazine Mountain, near the Beaver Lake dam, at Devil's Den and Cossatot SPs, at Hobbs SMA, at Lake Sylvia RA, along the Buffalo NR, and at Page Hollow and Redding Campground in the Ozark NF.

Blue Grosbeak—Look for it in brushy areas and old fields. Has nested at Willow Beach RA (see Scott listing), Bull Shoals and Devil's Den SPs, Lake Bentonville, near Page Hollow in the Ozark NF, Pea Ridge NMP, and at Lake Wedington RA.

Painted Bunting—This little gem is often considered common in Arkansas, but many people work hard before they finally get a look at one. It helps to know the song. See the Baker Prairie NA, Grand Lake, Holla Bend NWR, Lake Bentonville, Lonoke, and Scott listings for likely locations.

Rufous-sided Towhee—The eastern form of this species is a common permanent resident throughout the state (although rare in summer in the southwest). The western race ("Spotted Towhee") is a rare winter visitor to the western two-thirds of the state. Bill Shepherd reports that habitat, as well as call note, is often a good clue to the presence of a Spotted bird, which is usually founds in thickets, not in woods. Several Spotteds have shown up at feeders, as well.

Bachman's Sparrow—The "pinewoods sparrow" likes young pines (growing back after clearcutting) and open pine woods. If you drive around in timberland in south Arkansas, looking for replanted clearcuts, you'll eventually hear its pretty song, and you may find the birds to be common locally. One researcher found seven singing birds in a 35-acre pine plantation near Malvern. As habitat succession occurs, Bachman's Sparrows move on, so it's hard to specify a site where they'll be found for more than a year or two. See the DeGray Lake and Warren Prairie NA listings for reliable locations. The Buffalo Road Demonstration Site (see Waldron listing) is under long-term management by the Forest Service to create the kind of parklike woods that these sparrows (and Red-cockaded Woodpeckers) like, so it's another good bet.

Rufous-crowned Sparrow—First found in Arkansas in 1972 on the rocky slopes of Magazine Mountain, where habitat management is currently attempting to restore preferred conditions for a dwindling number of birds. Another location was discovered in 1985 at Mount Nebo SP, where the birds have been seen reliably for several years. Here, too, vegetative succession (a 1980 fire created the open habitat) has threatened the population; management measures are under way. These sparrows were also found in 1991 in two remote sites in the Ouachita Mountains, and, in recent years, atop Pinnacle Mountain near Little Rock. At this writing, Mount Nebo is probably still the most reliable spot, followed by Magazine Mountain; it's not yet known whether or not the birds will eventually colonize Pinnacle. At any of the sites, finding the birds may be very easy, or it may take considerable patience.

Lark Sparrow—Found most often as a breeder in western and northwestern Arkansas in landscapes with bare soil, sand, or rock: e.g., along dirt roads and in cultivated fields. Check the Mena airport, Holla Bend NWR, and the road to Okay Levee at Millwood Lake.

Grasshopper Sparrow—Sparsely distributed as a breeding bird. Can be found at Pea Ridge NMP, Baker Prairie NA in Harrison, and along the levee on the Grand Lake route in Chicot County.

Henslow's Sparrow—In most parts of the state, an elusive winter visitor. However, Warren Prairie NA has proved to be a very reliable site; see that listing for details.

Le Conte's Sparrow—Can almost always be found in winter at the Stuttgart Airport and at Roth Prairie NA. Also try Baker Prairie NA, the fields below the Millwood Lake dam, and the Grand Lake route. Finding one is not as hard as getting a decent look at it.

Harris's Sparrow—Arkansas is on the eastern edge of this bird's winter range, so the western part of the state is where to look. Carefully check winter flocks of White-crowned Sparrows in fencerows in agricultural areas. One fairly reliable spot is the entrance road (off Highway 155) to

Holla Bend NWR; sort through the sparrows in the shrubs and bushes alongside the road. Check *high* in the bushes for Harris's.

Lapland Longspur—Drive backroads through flat, bare farmland around Lonoke or Stuttgart in midwinter and you'll eventually come across a flock of dozens or hundreds of these visitors from the Arctic. Can almost always be found at the Stuttgart Airport, either along the runways or in nearby fields. Another good area is the farmland along Highway 17 near Ethel, west of the White River NWR.

Smith's Longspur—See the Stuttgart Airport listing for one good location for this very scarce winter visitor. Has also been occasionally seen in recent years at the airport in Siloam Springs in northwestern Arkansas.

Bobolink—Check fields of winter wheat or tall grass anywhere during the first two weeks of May. Farmlands near Scott, Lonoke, Stuttgart, and Holla Bend will usually have at least a few migrants. Very rarely seen in fall.

Western Meadowlark—A fall and winter wanderer from the western United States; was more commonly reported when there were more cattle feedlots (a favorite habitat for this species). Listen for it anyplace where there are Eastern Meadowlarks.

Yellow-headed Blackbird—Another western bird that occasionally wanders to western Arkansas, most often during spring migration. Has been seen recently at Holla Bend NWR, Centerton FH, and along the road to Okay Levee at Millwood Lake.

Rusty Blackbird—Uncommon to fairly common winter visitor, not arriving in numbers until November. Frequents low, flooded woods, such as those at Felsenthal, Holla Bend, and Wapanocca NWRs, as well as temporary swampy spots in agricultural areas anywhere in the state. Often a few are mixed in with the huge nightly blackbird roosts that are scattered across Arkansas in the winter.

Brewer's Blackbird—Small flocks of these birds, often traveling separately from other blackbird species, can be found in winter in the farmland of eastern Arkansas. Check areas around Lake Chicot, Lonoke, and the extensive open fields around White River NWR.

Great-tailed Grackle—First nested in the state near Ashdown (west of Millwood Lake) in 1976, and since then small numbers have bred in Miller and Little River counties in the southwest and Benton and Washington counties in the northwest, sometimes in association with heronries. Good numbers have been seen lately near Farmington, just west of Fayetteville; 87 were seen on the 1991 Fayetteville Christmas Bird

Count. Check with local birders for the best current locations to find them.

House Finch—As this pretty little finch has spread across the eastern U.S., it was inevitable that Arkansas would eventually be colonized. Stragglers began showing up in the state in the 1970s, and the first known nesting occurred at Jonesboro in 1985. Today these birds gather in numbers at feeders across the state and breed in building façades in downtown Little Rock. Their enthusiastic song is heard often in cities and suburbs. Maybe they'll run off a few House Sparrows....

Red Crossbill—This species, well known for its erratic wanderings and nesting behavior, has given strong evidence that it has nested sporadically in the pine woods of Hot Spring, Cleveland, and Ashley counties in southern Arkansas. Although crossbills are unpredictable, it's well worth listening for the *jeep-jeep* calls of small flocks in winter whenever you're birding in pines. Lake Georgia-Pacific near Crossett has probably been the most consistent wintering site for crossbills.

American Goldfinch—Common across the state in winter, in brushy areas and at feeders. Breeds mostly in the hills and mountains of the northwestern half of Arkansas. In summer look for it at Cossatot and Devil's Den SPs, Hobbs SMA, and Lake Fayetteville.

BIRDS IN ARKANSAS

The bar-graphs that follow include the overwhelming majority of birds occurring in Arkansas. However, for some of these species there are only a few accepted records. Other species that are "seldom seen" or "accidental" are listed separately after the graphs.

The purpose of these bar-graphs is to indicate the *probability* of seeing a bird, rather than its *abundance*. Thus a large bird such as Great Blue Heron is shown as "hard to miss," while a shy or hard-to-identify species such as Swamp Sparrow is shown as "may see," even though it may occur in larger numbers, at some seasons.

For those not familiar with Arkansas, it is a state with diverse habitats that are not always sharply delineated. For this reason, the codes given may not always seem appropriate to the observer. A familiarity with the bird's song, habits, and habitat preference will certainly be helpful.

The bar-graphs often include some short notes on individual species and their status in the state.

Hard to Miss
Should See (3 out of 4 trips)
May See (1 out of 4 trips)
Lucky to Find (1 out of 10 trips)
How Lucky Can You Get (infrequent)
Irregular

On your first trip to a specific area, you may think that some species are harder to find than is indicated. But remember that these charts were prepared from the point of view that the observer would be in the RIGHT AREA and the RIGHT HABITAT, and at the PROPER SEASON. With these conditions met, you should be able to see the "hard to miss" birds on nearly every field trip, the "should see" birds on 3 out of 4 trips, the "may see" birds on 1 out of 4 trips, and the "lucky to find" birds on 1 out of 10 trips—or even less often. "Irregular" species are sporadic and erratic in both *occurrence* and *abundance*.

If you find a bird that you believe is unusual, take notes, and report your findings to the sub-regional editors for the *National Audubon Society Field Notes*: Max and Helen Parker, 2426 S. Main Street, Malvern, AR 72104. Sightings of rarities may also be reported to the statewide Rare Bird Alert, sponsored by the Audubon Society of Central Arkansas (753-5853).

✓

Common Loon
Large lakes

Pied-billed Grebe

Horned Grebe
Large lakes

Eared Grebe

American White Pelican
Non-breeding

Double-crested Cormorant
Nests locally; winters primarily south

Anhinga
Nests locally

American Bittern

Least Bittern
Nests locally

Great Blue Heron

Great Egret
Winters locally in south

Snowy Egret

Little Blue Heron

Tricolored Heron
Nests locally

Cattle Egret

Green Heron

Black-crowned Night-Heron

Yellow-crowned Night-Heron

White Ibis
Probably nests in south; nest not found

Roseate Spoonbill

Wood Stork
South

Black-bellied Whistling-Duck
Extremely rare nester

Greater White-fronted Goose

Snow Goose

	January	February	March	April	May	June	July	August	September	October	November	December

✓	January	February	March	April	May	June	July	August	September	October	November	December
☐ Ross's Goose												
Small numbers are expected in large concentrations of Snow Geese												
☐ Canada Goose												
Individuals present in summer result from release program												
☐ Wood Duck												
☐ Green-winged Teal												
☐ American Black Duck												
Primarily eastern lowlands												
☐ Mallard												
Nests irregularly												
☐ Northern Pintail												
☐ Blue-winged Teal												
Nests irregularly												
☐ Northern Shoveler												
☐ Gadwall												
☐ American Wigeon												
☐ Canvasback												
☐ Redhead												
☐ Ring-necked Duck												
☐ Greater Scaup												
☐ Lesser Scaup												
☐ Oldsquaw												
☐ Common Goldeneye												
☐ Bufflehead												
☐ Hooded Merganser												
Rare north in winter												
☐ Common Merganser												
☐ Red-breasted Merganser												
☐ Ruddy Duck												
Nests irregularly												
☐ Black Vulture												
☐ Turkey Vulture												

✓	January	February	March	April	May	June	July	August	September	October	November	December
☐ Osprey Nests rarely												
☐ Mississippi Kite Rare north												
☐ Bald Eagle Nests rarely; increasing												
☐ Northern Harrier												
☐ Sharp-shinned Hawk Rare breeder in Ozarks												
☐ Cooper's Hawk Nests rarely												
☐ Red-shouldered Hawk												
☐ Broad-winged Hawk												
☐ Swainson's Hawk Western half												
☐ Red-tailed Hawk												
☐ Rough-legged Hawk												
☐ Golden Eagle												
☐ American Kestrel												
☐ Merlin												
☐ Peregrine Falcon Hacked at two sites												
☐ Prairie Falcon Northwest												
☐ Wild Turkey												
☐ Northern Bobwhite												
☐ Yellow Rail												
☐ King Rail												
☐ Virginia Rail												
☐ Sora												
☐ Purple Gallinule												
☐ Common Moorhen												
☐ American Coot												

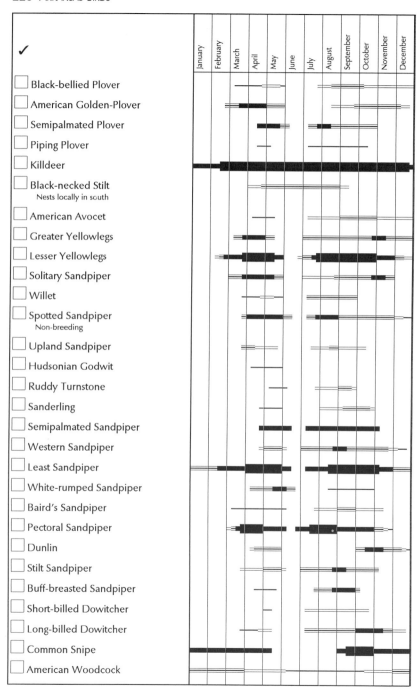

✓	January	February	March	April	May	June	July	August	September	October	November	December
☐ Black-bellied Plover												
☐ American Golden-Plover												
☐ Semipalmated Plover												
☐ Piping Plover												
☐ Killdeer												
☐ Black-necked Stilt Nests locally in south												
☐ American Avocet												
☐ Greater Yellowlegs												
☐ Lesser Yellowlegs												
☐ Solitary Sandpiper												
☐ Willet												
☐ Spotted Sandpiper Non-breeding												
☐ Upland Sandpiper												
☐ Hudsonian Godwit												
☐ Ruddy Turnstone												
☐ Sanderling												
☐ Semipalmated Sandpiper												
☐ Western Sandpiper												
☐ Least Sandpiper												
☐ White-rumped Sandpiper												
☐ Baird's Sandpiper												
☐ Pectoral Sandpiper												
☐ Dunlin												
☐ Stilt Sandpiper												
☐ Buff-breasted Sandpiper												
☐ Short-billed Dowitcher												
☐ Long-billed Dowitcher												
☐ Common Snipe												
☐ American Woodcock												

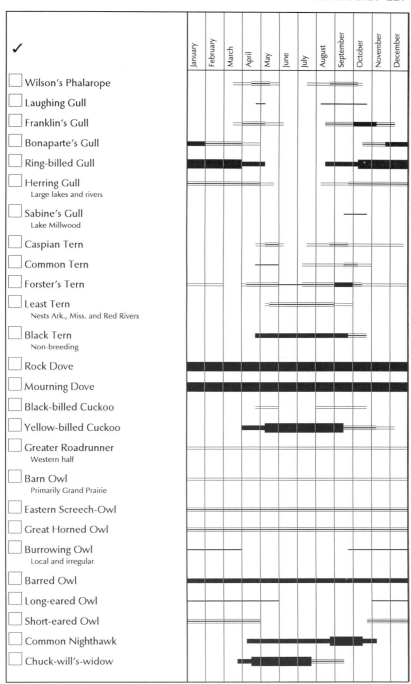

✓	January	February	March	April	May	June	July	August	September	October	November	December
☐ Wilson's Phalarope												
☐ Laughing Gull												
☐ Franklin's Gull												
☐ Bonaparte's Gull												
☐ Ring-billed Gull												
☐ Herring Gull Large lakes and rivers												
☐ Sabine's Gull Lake Millwood												
☐ Caspian Tern												
☐ Common Tern												
☐ Forster's Tern												
☐ Least Tern Nests Ark., Miss. and Red Rivers												
☐ Black Tern Non-breeding												
☐ Rock Dove												
☐ Mourning Dove												
☐ Black-billed Cuckoo												
☐ Yellow-billed Cuckoo												
☐ Greater Roadrunner Western half												
☐ Barn Owl Primarily Grand Prairie												
☐ Eastern Screech-Owl												
☐ Great Horned Owl												
☐ Burrowing Owl Local and irregular												
☐ Barred Owl												
☐ Long-eared Owl												
☐ Short-eared Owl												
☐ Common Nighthawk												
☐ Chuck-will's-widow												

✓	January	February	March	April	May	June	July	August	September	October	November	December
☐ Whip-poor-will												
☐ Chimney Swift												
☐ Ruby-throated Hummingbird												
☐ Rufous Hummingbird Irregular												
☐ Belted Kingfisher												
☐ Red-headed Woodpecker												
☐ Red-bellied Woodpecker												
☐ Yellow-bellied Sapsucker												
☐ Downy Woodpecker												
☐ Hairy Woodpecker												
☐ Red-cockaded Woodpecker Local												
☐ Northern Flicker												
☐ Pileated Woodpecker												
☐ Olive-sided Flycatcher												
☐ Eastern Wood-Pewee												
☐ Yellow-bellied Flycatcher												
☐ Acadian Flycatcher												
☐ Alder Flycatcher												
☐ Willow Flycatcher Nests locally												
☐ Least Flycatcher												
☐ Eastern Phoebe Summers north and west-cent., winters south												
☐ Great Crested Flycatcher												
☐ Western Kingbird Primarily west												
☐ Eastern Kingbird												
☐ Scissor-tailed Flycatcher												
☐ Horned Lark Uncommon SW												

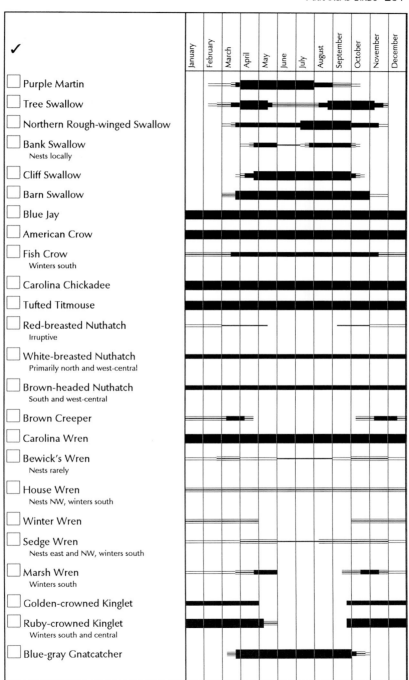

✓	January	February	March	April	May	June	July	August	September	October	November	December
☐ Purple Martin												
☐ Tree Swallow												
☐ Northern Rough-winged Swallow												
☐ Bank Swallow Nests locally												
☐ Cliff Swallow												
☐ Barn Swallow												
☐ Blue Jay												
☐ American Crow												
☐ Fish Crow Winters south												
☐ Carolina Chickadee												
☐ Tufted Titmouse												
☐ Red-breasted Nuthatch Irruptive												
☐ White-breasted Nuthatch Primarily north and west-central												
☐ Brown-headed Nuthatch South and west-central												
☐ Brown Creeper												
☐ Carolina Wren												
☐ Bewick's Wren Nests rarely												
☐ House Wren Nests NW, winters south												
☐ Winter Wren												
☐ Sedge Wren Nests east and NW, winters south												
☐ Marsh Wren Winters south												
☐ Golden-crowned Kinglet												
☐ Ruby-crowned Kinglet Winters south and central												
☐ Blue-gray Gnatcatcher												

✓	January	February	March	April	May	June	July	August	September	October	November	December
☐ Eastern Bluebird												
☐ Veery												
☐ Gray-cheeked Thrush												
☐ Swainson's Thrush												
☐ Hermit Thrush Winters central and south												
☐ Wood Thrush												
☐ American Robin												
☐ Gray Catbird Winters south												
☐ Northern Mockingbird												
☐ Brown Thrasher Winters south												
☐ American Pipit Winters south												
☐ Cedar Waxwing												
☐ Loggerhead Shrike												
☐ European Starling												
☐ White-eyed Vireo												
☐ Bell's Vireo Summers north												
☐ Solitary Vireo Winters south												
☐ Yellow-throated Vireo												
☐ Warbling Vireo												
☐ Philadelphia Vireo												
☐ Red-eyed Vireo												
☐ Blue-winged Warbler Nests north												
☐ Golden-winged Warbler												
☐ Tennessee Warbler												
☐ Orange-crowned Warbler Winters south												

✓

	January	February	March	April	May	June	July	August	September	October	November	December
☐ Nashville Warbler												
☐ Northern Parula												
☐ Yellow Warbler Nests locally north												
☐ Chestnut-sided Warbler Breeds locally in Ozarks												
☐ Magnolia Warbler												
☐ Cape May Warbler												
☐ Yellow-rumped Warbler												
☐ Black-throated Green Warbler Breeds locally in Ozarks												
☐ Blackburnian Warbler												
☐ Yellow-throated Warbler												
☐ Pine Warbler												
☐ Prairie Warbler												
☐ Palm Warbler												
☐ Bay-breasted Warbler												
☐ Blackpoll Warbler												
☐ Cerulean Warbler												
☐ Black-and-white Warbler												
☐ American Redstart												
☐ Prothonotary Warbler												
☐ Worm-eating Warbler												
☐ Swainson's Warbler												
☐ Ovenbird												
☐ Northern Waterthrush												
☐ Louisiana Waterthrush												
☐ Kentucky Warbler												
☐ Mourning Warbler												
☐ Common Yellowthroat												
☐ Hooded Warbler												

✓	January	February	March	April	May	June	July	August	September	October	November	December
☐ Wilson's Warbler												
☐ Canada Warbler												
☐ Yellow-breasted Chat												
☐ Summer Tanager												
☐ Scarlet Tanager Nests north and west-central												
☐ Northern Cardinal												
☐ Rose-breasted Grosbeak												
☐ Blue Grosbeak												
☐ Indigo Bunting												
☐ Painted Bunting												
☐ Dickcissel												
☐ Rufous-sided Towhee												
☐ Bachman's Sparrow Nests locally central and south-central												
☐ Rufous-crowned Sparrow Mt. Nebo and Magazine Mtn.												
☐ American Tree Sparrow Northwest; irruptive												
☐ Chipping Sparrow Summers north and west cent., winters south												
☐ Clay-colored Sparrow West												
☐ Field Sparrow												
☐ Vesper Sparrow Winters south												
☐ Lark Sparrow												
☐ Savannah Sparrow												
☐ Grasshopper Sparrow Local												
☐ Henslow's Sparrow												
☐ Le Conte's Sparrow Winters east-central and south												
☐ Sharp-tailed Sparrow												

✓	January	February	March	April	May	June	July	August	September	October	November	December
☐ Fox Sparrow												
☐ Song Sparrow												
☐ Lincoln's Sparrow Winters south												
☐ Swamp Sparrow												
☐ White-throated Sparrow												
☐ White-crowned Sparrow												
☐ Harris's Sparrow Winters west and central												
☐ Dark-eyed Junco												
☐ Lapland Longspur Primarily east												
☐ Smith's Longspur Stuttgart Airport												
☐ Bobolink												
☐ Red-winged Blackbird												
☐ Eastern Meadowlark												
☐ Western Meadowlark West and central												
☐ Yellow-headed Blackbird West												
☐ Rusty Blackbird												
☐ Brewer's Blackbird Winters east and southwest												
☐ Great-tailed Grackle Extreme west												
☐ Common Grackle												
☐ Brown-headed Cowbird												
☐ Orchard Oriole												
☐ Northern Oriole Summers east and south												
☐ Purple Finch Irruptive												
☐ House Finch Population increasing rapidly												

✓	January	February	March	April	May	June	July	August	September	October	November	December
☐ Red Crossbill												
Probably nests; nest not found												
☐ Pine Siskin												
Irruptive												
☐ American Goldfinch												
Summers north and west-central												
☐ Evening Grosbeak												
Irruptive												
☐ House Sparrow												

Seldom-Seen Birds

While the species in this list have been well-documented, over the most recent 10-year period acceptable reports have been received less than annually.

Red-throated Loon
Western Grebe
Brown Pelican
Glossy Ibis
White-faced Ibis
Tundra Swan
Trumpeter Swan
Cinnamon Teal
Surf Scoter
White-winged Scoter
Ruffed Grouse (re-introduced)
Sandhill Crane
Marbled Godwit
Red Knot
Ruff

Red-necked Phalarope
Red Phalarope
Parasitic Jaeger
Little Gull
Inca Dove
Common Ground-Dove
Groove-billed Ani
Northern Saw-whet Owl
Vermilion Flycatcher
Rock Wren
Sprague's Pipit
Black-throated Blue Warbler
Connecticut Warbler
Black-headed Grosbeak
Common Redpoll

Accidental Birds

Five or fewer recent records.

Pacific Loon
Yellow-billed Loon
Red-necked Grebe
Magnificent Frigatebird
Fulvous Whistling-Duck
Mute Swan
Brant
Garganey
Black Scoter
American Swallow-tailed Kite
White-tailed Kite
Northern Goshawk
Ferruginous Hawk
Black Rail
Snowy Plover
Wilson's Plover
Mountain Plover
Whimbrel
Long-billed Curlew
Purple Sandpiper
Ruff
Pomarine Jaeger
Long-tailed Jaeger
Common Black-headed Gull
Lesser Black-backed Gull
Glaucous Gull
Black-legged Kittiwake
Royal Tern
Bridled Tern

Sooty Tern
Black Skimmer
Marbled Murrelet
White-winged Dove
Eurasian Collared-Dove
Snowy Owl
White-throated Swift
Green Violet-ear
Buff-bellied Hummingbird
Magnificent Hummingbird
Black-chinned Hummingbird
Anna's Hummingbird
Lewis's Woodpecker
Say's Phoebe
Cassin's Kingbird
Fork-tailed Flycatcher
Clark's Nutcracker
Northern Wheatear
Mountain Bluebird
Townsend's Solitaire
Sage Thrasher
Bohemian Waxwing
Western Tanager
Lazuli Bunting
Green-tailed Towhee
Chestnut-collared Longspur
Snow Bunting
Pine Grosbeak
White-winged Crossbill

SOME OTHER ANIMALS IN ARKANSAS

List of Native and Naturalized Mammals of Arkansas

ORDER MARSUPIALIA
FAMILY DIDELPHIDAE—New World Opossums
Didelphis virginiana—Virginia Opossum
ORDER INSECTIVORA
FAMILY SORICIDAE—Shrews
Sorex longirostris—Southeastern Shrew
Blarina carolinensis—Southern Short-tailed Shrew
Blarina hylophaga—Elliot's Short-tailed Shrew
Cryptotis parva—Least Shrew
Notiosorex crawfordi—Desert Shrew
FAMILY TALPIDAE—Moles
Scalopus aquaticus—Eastern Mole
ORDER CHIROPTERA
FAMILY VESPERTILIONIDAE—Vespertilionid Bats
Myotis lucifugus—Little Brown Myotis
Myotis austroriparius—Southeastern Myotis
Myotis grisescens—Gray Myotis
Myotis keenii—Keen's Myotis
Myotis sodalis—Indiana Myotis
Myotis leibii—Small-footed Myotis
Lasioncyteris noctivagans—Silver-haired Bat
Pipistrellus subflavus—Eastern Pipistrelle
Eptesicus fuscus—Big Brown Bat
Lasiurus borealis—Red Bat
Lasiurus seminolus—Seminole Bat
Lasiurus cinereus—Hoary Bat
Nycticeius humeralis—Evening Bat
Plecotus townsendii—Townsend's Big-eared Bat
Plecotus rafinesquei—Rafinesque's Big-eared Bat
FAMILY MOLOSSIDAE—Molossid Bats
Tadarida brasiliensis—Brazilian Free-tailed Bat
ORDER EDENTATA
FAMILY DASYPODIDAE
Dasypus novemcinctus—Nine-banded Armadillo
ORDER LAGOMORPHA
FAMILY LEPORIDAE—Hares and Rabbits
Sylvilagus floridanus—Eastern Cottontail
Sylvilagus aquaticus—Swamp Rabbit
Lepus californicus—Black-tailed Jackrabbit
ORDER RODENTIA
FAMILY SCIURIDAE—Squirrels
Tamias striatus—Eastern Chipmunk
Marmota monax—Woodchuck
Sciurus carolinensis—Gray Squirrel
Sciurus niger—Fox Squirrel
Glaucomys volans—Southern Flying Squirrel
FAMILY GEOMYIDAE—Pocket Gophers
Geomys breviceps—Baird's Pocket Gopher
FAMILY CASTORIDAE—Beavers
Castor canadensis—Beaver
FAMILY CRICETIDAE—New World Rats, Mice, and Voles
Oryzomys palustris—Marsh Rice Rat
Reithrodontomys montanus—Plains Harvest Mouse
Reithrodontomys humulis—Eastern Harvest Mouse
Reithrodontomys megalotis—Western Harvest Mouse
Reithrodontomys fulvescens—Fulvous Harvest Mouse
Peromyscus maniculatus—Deer Mouse
Peromyscus leucopus—White-footed Mouse
Peromyscus gossypinus—Cotton Mouse
Peromyscus attwateri—Texas Mouse
Ochrotomys nuttalli—Golden Mouse
Sigmodon hispidus—Hispid Cotton Rat
Neotoma floridana—Eastern Woodrat
Microtus ochrogaster—Prairie Vole
Microtus pinetorum—Woodland Vole
Ondatra zibethicus—Muskrat
Synaptomys cooperi —Southern Bog Lemming
FAMILY MURIDAE—Old World Rats and Mice
Rattus rattus—Black Rat*
Rattus norvegicus—Norway Rat*
Mus musculus—House Mouse*
FAMILY CAPROMYIDAE—Capromyids
Myocastor coypus—Nutria*
ORDER CARNIVORA
FAMILY CANIDAE—Canids
Canis latrans—Coyote
Canis rufus—Red Wolf**
Canis familiaris—Feral Dog*
Vulpes vulpes—Red Fox
Urocyon cinereoargenteus—Gray Fox
FAMILY URSIDAE—Bears
Ursus americanus—Black Bear
FAMILY PROCYONIDAE—Procyonids
Bassariscus astutus—Ringtail
Procyon lotor—Raccoon
FAMILY MUSTELIDAE—Mustelids
Mustela frenata—Long-tailed Weasel
Mustela vison —Mink

Taxidea taxus—Badger
Spilogale putorius—Eastern Spotted Skunk
Mephitis mephitis—Striped Skunk
Lutra canadensis—River Otter
FAMILY FELIDAE—Cats
Felis concolor—Mountain Lion
Felis catus—Feral House Cat*
Felis rufus—Bobcat
ORDER ARTIODACTYLA
FAMILY SUIDAE—Pigs

Sus scrofa—Feral Pig*
FAMILY CERVIDAE—Cervids
Cervus elaphus—Wapiti or Elk*
Odocoileus virginianus—White-tailed Deer
FAMILY BOVIDAE—Bovids
Bison bison—Bison or Buffalo**

* Introduced
** Extirpated (occurs only in captivity or under domestication)

List of Amphibians in Arkansas

ORDER CAUDATA—Salamanders
FAMILY CRYPTOBRANCHIDAE— Hellbenders
Cryptobranchus alleganiensis bishopi— Ozark Hellbender
FAMILY PROTEIDAE—Mudpuppies
Necturus maculosus louisianensis—Red River Mudpuppy
FAMILY AMPHIUMIDAE—Amphiumas
Amphiuma tridactylum—Three-toed Amphiuma
FAMILY SIRENIDAE—Sirens
Siren intermedia nettingi—Western Lesser Siren
FAMILY AMBYSTOMATIDAE—Mole Salamanders
Ambystoma annulatum—Ringed Salamander
Ambystoma maculatum—Spotted Salamander
Ambystoma opacum—Marbled Salamander
Ambystoma talpoideum—Mole Salamander
Ambystoma texanum—Smallmouth Salamander
Ambystoma tigrinum tigrinum—Eastern Tiger Salamander
FAMILY SALAMAMDRIDAE—Newts
Notophthalmus viridescens louisianensis —Central Newt
FAMILY PLETHODONTIDAE—Lungless Salamanders
Desmognathus brimleyorum—Ouachita Dusky Salamander
Desmognathus fuscus conanti—Spotted Dusky Salamander
Plethodon caddoensis—Caddo Mountain Salamander
Plethodon dorsalis angusticlavius—Ozark Zigzag Salamander
Plethodon fourchensis—Fourche Mountain Salamander
Plethodon kiamichi—Kiamichi Slimy Salamander
Plethodon sequoyah—Sequoyah Slimy Salamander

Plethodon kisatchie—Louisiana Slimy Salamander
Plethodon albagula—Western Slimy Salamander
Plethodon ouachitae—Rich Mountain Salamander
Plethodon serratus—Southern Redbacked Salamander
Hemidactylium scutatum—Four-toed Salamander
Eurycea longicauda melanopleura— Dark-sided Salamander
Eurycea longicauda longicauda/melanopleura —Longtail/Dark-sided Intergrade
Eurycea lucifuga—Cave Salamander
Eurycea multiplicata multiplicata —Many-ribbed Salamander
Eurycea multiplicata griseogaster—Graybelly Salamander
Eurycea quadridigitata—Dwarf Salamander
Eurycea tynerensis—Oklahoma Salamander
Typhlotriton spelaeus—Grotto Salamander
ORDER ANURA—Toads and Frogs
FAMILY PELOBATIDAE—Spadefoot Toads
Scaphiopus holbrooki holbrooki—Eastern Spadefoot
Scaphiopus holbrooki hurteri—Hurter's Spadefoot
Scaphiopus bombifrons—Plains Spadefoot
FAMILY BUFONIDAE—True Toads
Bufo americanus charlesmithi—Dwarf American Toad
Bufo woodhousei woodhousei/fowleri —Woodhouse's/Fowler's Toad Intergrade
Bufo woodhousei fowleri—Fowler's Toad
Bufo valliceps valliceps—Gulf Coast Toad
FAMILY HYLIDAE—Tree Frogs and Their Allies
Acris crepitans crepitans—Northern Cricket Frog
Acris crepitans blanchardi—Blanchard's Cricket Frog
Hyla cinerea—Green Treefrog

Hyla versicolor—Gray Treefrog
Hyla chrysoscelis—Cope's Gray Treefrog
Hyla avivoca—Bird-voiced Treefrog
Pseudacris crucifer crucifer—Northern
  Spring Peeper
Pseudacris triseriata—Western Chorus Frog
Pseudacris feriarum feriarum—Upland
  Chorus Frog
Pseudacris streckeri streckeri—Strecker's
  Chorus Frog
Pseudacris streckeri illinoensis—Illinois
  Chorus Frog
FAMILY MICROHYLIDAE—Narrowmouth
  Toads
Gastrophryne carolinensis—Eastern
  Narrowmouth Toad
Gastrophryne olivacea—Great Plains
  Narrowmouth Toad
FAMILY RANIDAE—True Frogs
Rana catesbeiana—Bullfrog
Rana clamitans clamitans—Bronze Frog
Rana clamitans melanota—Green Frog

Rana sylvatica—Wood Frog
Rana palustris—Pickerel Frog
Rana areolata areolata—Southern Crawfish
  Frog
Rana areolata circulosa—Northern Crawfish
  Frog
Rana utricularia utricularia—Southern
  Leopard Frog

SOME RARE OR HYPOTHETICAL
AMPHIBIANS TO LOOK FOR IN
ARKANSAS:
Eurycea cirrigera—Southern Two-lined
  Salamander
Pseudotriton ruber vioscai—Southern Red
  Salamander
Eurycea longicauda longicauda—Longtail
  Salamander
Hyla squirella—Squirrel Treefrog
Rana blairi—Plains Leopard Frog

List of Reptiles in Arkansas

ORDER CROCODILIA—Crocodilians
FAMILY ALLIGATORIDAE—Alligators
Alligator mississippiensis—American
  Alligator
ORDER TESTUDINES—Turtles
FAMILY CHELYDRIDAE—Snapping Turtles
Chelydra serpentina serpentina—Common
  Snapping Turtle
Macroclemys temminckii—Alligator
  Snapping Turtle
FAMILY KINOSTERNIDAE—Mud and Musk
  Turtles
Sternotherus carinatus—Razorback Musk
  Turtle
Sternotherus odoratus—Common Musk
  Turtle
Kinosternon subrubrum hippocrepis
  —Mississippi Mud Turtle
FAMILY EMYDIDAE—Pond, Marsh, and
  Box Turtles
Terrapene carolina triunguis—Three-toed
  Box Turtle
Terrapene ornata ornata—Ornate Box Turtle
Graptemys geographica—Map Turtle
Graptemys kohnii—Mississippi Map Turtle
Graptemys pseudogeographica ouachitensis
  —Ouachita Map Turtle
Pseudemys concinna metteri—Missouri
  River Cooter
Pseudemys concinna metteri/hieroglyphica
  —Hieroglyphic/Missouri Intergrade
Chrysemys picta dorsalis—Southern Painted
  Turtle
Trachemys scripta elegans—Red-eared Slider

Deirochelys reticularia miaria—Western
  Chicken Turtle
FAMILY TRIONYCHIDAE—Softshell Turtles
Apalone mutica mutica—Midland Smooth
  Softshell
Apalone spinifera hartwegi—Western Spiny
  Softshell
Apalone spinifera pallida—Pallid Spiny
  Softshell
Apalone spinifera spinifera—Eastern Spiny
  Softshell
ORDER SQUAMATA—SUBORDER
  LACERTILIA
IGUANIAN LIZARDS
FAMILY POLYCHRIDAE—Anoles
Anolis carolinensis—Green Anole
FAMILY CROTAPHYTIDAE—Collared
  Lizards
Crotaphytus collaris collaris—Eastern
  Collared Lizard
FAMILY PHRYNOSOMATIDAE—Spiny and
  Horned Lizards
Sceloporus undulatus hyacinthinus—
  Northern Fence Lizard
Phrynosoma cornutum—Texas Horned
  Lizard
FAMILY TEIIDAE—Racerunners
Cnemidophorus sexlineatus viridis—Prairie
  Racerunner
Cnemidophorus sexlineatus sexlineatus
  —Six-lined Racerunner
FAMILY SCINCIDAE—Skinks
Eumeces anthracinus pluvialis—Southern
  Coal Skink

Eumeces fasciatus—Five-lined Skink
Eumeces laticeps—Broadhead Skink
Eumeces septentrionalis obtusirostris
—Southern Prairie Skink
Eumeces obsoletus—Great Plains Skink
Scincella lateralis—Ground Skink
FAMILY ANGUIDAE—Glass Lizards
Ophisaurus attenuatus attenuatus—Western Slender Glass Lizard
ORDER SQUAMATA—SUBORDER SERPENTES
FAMILY COLUBRIDAE—Colubrids
Nerodia cyclopion—Mississippi Green Water Snake
Nerodia erythrogaster flavigaster
—Yellowbelly Water Snake
Nerodia erythrogaster transversa—Blotched Water Snake
Nerodia fasciata confluens—Broad-banded Water Snake
Nerodia rhombifer rhombifer—Diamondback Water Snake
Nerodia sipedon pleuralis—Midland Water Snake
Nerodia sipedon sipedon/pleuralis
—Northern/Midland Intergrade
Regina grahami—Graham's Crayfish Snake
Regina rigida sinicola—Gulf Crayfish Snake
Regina septemvittata—Queen Snake
Storeria dekayi texana—Texas Brown Snake
Storeria dekayi wrightorum—Midland Brown Snake
Storeria occipitomaculata occipitomaculata
—Northern Redbelly Snake
Storeria occipitomaculata obscura—Florida Redbelly Snake
Thamnophis proximus proximus—Western Ribbon Snake
Thamnophis sirtalis parietalis—Red-sided Garter Snake
Thamnophis sirtalis sirtalis—Eastern Garter Snake
Virginia striatula—Rough Earth Snake
Virginia valeriae elegans—Western Smooth Earth Snake
Heterodon platyrhinos—Eastern Hognose Snake
Diadophis punctatus arnyi—Prairie Ringneck Snake
Diadophis punctatus stictogenys—Mississippi Ringneck Snake
Carphophis amoenus vermis—Western Worm Snake
Carphophis amoenus helenae—Midwest Worm Snake
Farancia abacura reinwardtii—Western Mud Snake
Coluber constrictor anthicus—Buttermilk Racer

Coluber constrictor flaviventris—Eastern Yellowbelly Racer
Coluber constrictor priapus—Southern Black Racer
Masticophis flagellum flagellum—Eastern Coachwhip
Opheodrys aestivus—Rough Green Snake
Elaphe guttata emoryi—Great Plains Rat Snake
Elaphe guttata guttata/emoryi—Corn/Great Plains Intergrade
Elaphe obsoleta obsoleta—Black Rat Snake
Elaphe obsoleta spiloides—Gray Rat Snake
Lampropeltis calligaster calligaster—Prairie Kingsnake
Lampropeltis getulus holbrooki—Speckled Kingsnake
Lampropeltis triangulum amaura—Louisiana Milk Snake
Lampropeltis triangulum syspila—Red Milk Snake
Cemophora coccinea copei—Northern Scarlet Snake
Tantilla gracilis—Flathead Snake
Sonora semiannulata—Ground Snake
FAMILY ELAPIDAE—Coral Snakes
Micrurus fulvius tener—Texas Coral Snake
FAMILY VIPERIDAE—Pit VIpers
Agkistrodon contortrix contortrix—Southern Copperhead
Agkistrodon contortrix contortrix/phaeogaster—Osage/Southern Intergrade
Agkistrodon piscivorus leucostoma—Western Cottonmouth
Sistrurus miliarius streckeri—Western Pigmy Rattlesnake
Crotalus atrox—Western Diamondback Rattlesnake
Crotalus horridus—Timber Rattlesnake.

SOME RARE OR HYPOTHETICAL REPTILES TO LOOK FOR IN ARKANSAS:

Kinosternon flavescens flavescens—Yellow Mud Turtle
Eumeces inexpectatus—Southeastern Five-lined Skink
Thamnophis radix haydenii—Western Plains Garter Snake
Thamnophis sauritus sauritus—Eastern Ribbon Snake
Tropidoclonion lineatum annectens—Central Lined Snake
Pituophis catenifer sayi—Bullsnake
Tantilla coronata—Southeastern Crowned Snake
Elaphe obsoleta lindheimeri—Texas Rat Snake

List of Butterflies and Skippers in Arkansas

FAMILY MEGATHYMIDAE
Megathymus yuccae—Yucca Giant-Skipper
FAMILY HESPERIIDAE
***Hesperiineae*—grass skippers**
Panoquina ocola—Ocola Skipper
Calpodes ethlius—Brazilian Skipper
Lerodea eufala—Eufala Skipper
Amblyscirtes linde—Linda's Roadside Skipper
Amblyscirtes samoset—Pepper and Salt Skipper
Amblyscirtes aesculapius—Aesculapius Skipper
Amblyscirtes nysa —Nysa Roadside Skipper
Amblyscirtes vialis—Roadside Skipper
Amblyscirtes belli—Bell's Roadside Skipper
Amblyscirtes alternata—Least Florida Skipper
Atrytonopsis hianna—Dusted Skipper
Euphyes alabamae—Alabama Skipper
Euphyes dukesi—Duke's Skipper
Euphyes ruricola—Dun Skipper
Poanes hobomok—Hobomok Skipper
Ponnes zabulon—Zabulon Skipper
Poanes yehl—Yehl Skipper
Poanes viator—Broad-winged Skipper
Poanes byssus—Byssus Skipper
Atrytone delaware delaware—Delaware Skipper
Atelopedes campestris—Sachem
Pompeius verna sequoyah—Little Glassy Wing
Wallengrenia otho—Southern Broken-Dash
Wallengrenia egeremet—Northern Broken-Dash
Polites coras—Coras Skipper
Polites themistocles—Tawny-edged Skipper
Polites origines origines—Cross-line Skipper
Polites vibex—Whirlabout
Hesperia metea licinus—Cobweb Skipper
Hesperia meskei—Meske's Skipper
Hesperia leonardus—Leonard's Skipper
Hylephila phyleus—Fiery Skipper
Copaeodes aurantica—Orange Skipperling
Copaeodes minima— Southern Skipperling
Ancyloxypha numitor—Least Skipper
Lerema accius—Clouded Skipper
Nastra lherminier—Swarthy Skipper
***Pyrginae*—spread-wing skippers**
Pholisora catullus—Common Sooty Wing
Pyrgus communis—Checkered Skipper
Pyrgus oileus—Tropical Checkered Skipper
Erynnis icelus—Dreamy Dusky Wing
Erynnis brizo—Sleepy Dusky Wing
Erynnis persius—Persius Dusky Wing

Erynnis baptisiae—Wild Indigo Dusky Wing
Erynnis zarucco—Zarucco Dusky Wing
Erynnis funeralis—Funereal Dusky Wing
Erynnis martialis—Mottled Dusky Wing
Erynnis horatius—Horace's Dusky Wing
Erynnis juvenalis—Juvenal's Dusky Wing
Achlyodes thraso—Sickle-winged Skipper
Staphylus hayhurstii—Southern Sooty Wing
Cogia outis—Outis Skipper
Thorybes bathyllus—Southern Cloudy Wing
Thorybes pylades—Northern Cloudy Wing
Thorybes confusis—Confused Cloudy Wing
Achalarus lyciades—Hoary Edge
Autochton cellus—Golden-banded Skipper
Urbanus proteus—Long-tailed Skipper
Epargyreus clarus—Silver-spotted Skipper
FAMILY PAPILIONIDAE
***Papilioninae*—swallowtails**
Battus philenor—Pipevine Swallowtail
Battus polydamas—Polydamas Swallowtail
Papilio polyxenes—Black Swallowtail
Papilio joanae—Ozark Swallowtail
Papilio cresphontes—Giant Swallowtail
Papilio glaucus—Eastern Tiger Swallowtail
Papilio troilus—Spicebush Swallowtail
Papilio palamedes—Palamedes Swallowtail
Eurytides marcellus—Zebra Swallowtail
FAMILY PIERIDAE
***Pierinae*—whites**
Appias drusilla—Florida White
Pontia protodice—Checkered White
Pontia rapae—Cabbage White
Ascia monuste—Great Southern White
***Coliadinae*—sulphurs**
Colias eurytheme—Orange Sulphur
Colias philodice—Clouded Sulphur
Colias cesonia—Southern Dogface
Phoebis sennae—Cloudless Sulphur
Phoebis philea—Orange-barred Sulphur
Phobis agarithe—Large Orange Sulphur
Eurema daira—Barred Sulphur
Eurema mexicana—Mexican Sulphur
Eurema lisa—Little Yellow
Eurema nicippe—Sleepy Orange
Nathalis iole—Dainty Sulphur
***Euchloeinae*—marbles and orangetips**
Anthocharis midea—Falcate Orangetip
Euchloe olympia—Olympia Marble
FAMILY RIODINIDAE
***Riodininae*—metalmarks**
Calephelis muticum—Swamp Metalmark
FAMILY LYCAENIDAE
***Theclinae*—hairstreaks**

Satyrium titus—Coral Hairstreak
Satyrium liparops—Striped Hairstreak
Satyrium kingi—King's Hairstreak
Satyrium calanus—Banded Hairstreak
Satyrium caryaevorum—Hickory Hairstreak
Satyrium edwardsii—Edward's Hairstreak
Calycopis cecrops—Red-banded Hairstreak
Callophrys irus—Frosted Elfin
Callophrys henrici—Henry's Elfin
Callophrys niphon—Eastern Pine Elfin
Callophrys gryneus—Junior Hairstreak
Atildes halesus—Great Purple Hairstreak
Euristrymon ontario—Northern Hairstreak
Panthiades m-album—White Hairstreak
Strymon melinus—Gray Hairstreak
Miletinae—harvesters
Feniseca tarquinius—The Harvester
Lycaeninae—coppers
Lycaena hyllus—Bronze Copper
Lycaena phlaeas—American Copper
Polyommatinae—blues
Brephidium exilis—Western Pygmy-Blue
Leptotes cassius—Cassius Blue
Leptotes marina—Marine Blue
Hemiargus isola—Reakirt's Blue
Everes comyntas—Eastern Tailed-Blue
Glaucopsyche lygdamus—Silvery Blue
Celestrina argiolus—Spring Azure
FAMILY LIBYTHEIDAE
Libytheinae—snouts
Libythieana carinenta—American Snout
NYMPHALIDAE
Charaxinae
Anaia andria—Goatweed Butterfly
Apaturinae
Asterocampa celtis—Hackberry Butterfly
Asterocampa clyton—Tawny Emperor
Eurytalinae
Mestra amymone—Amymone Butterfly
Limenitinae
Limenitis astyanax—Red-spotted Purple
Limenitis archippus—The Viceroy
Vanessinae

Vanessa atalanta—Red Admiral
Cynthia virginiensis—American Lady
Cynthia cardui—Painted Lady
Junonia coenia—Common Buckeye
Nymphalinae
Nymphalis milberti—Milbert's Tortoiseshell
Nymphalis antiopa—Mourning Cloak
Polygonia interrogationis—Question Mark
Polygonia comma—Eastern Comma
Polygonia progne—Gray Comma
Melitaeinae
Chlosyne nycteria—Silvery Checkerspot
Chlosyne gorgone—Gorgone Checkerspot
Phyciodes texana—Texas Crescent
Phyciodes tharos—Pearl Crescent
Phyciodes phaon—Phaon Crescent
Euphydryas phaeton ozarkae—Baltimore
  Checkerspot
Argynninae
Speyeria idelia—Regal Fritillary
Speyeria diana—Diana Fritillary
Speyeria cybele—Great Spangled Fritillary
Euptoieta claudia—Mexican Fritillary
Heliconiinae—heliconians
Heliconius charitonius—Zebra
Dryas julia—Julia
Agraulis vanillae—Gulf Fritillary
FAMILY DANAIDAE
Danainae—monarchs
Danaus plexippus—The Monarch
Danaus gilippus strigosus—The Queen
FAMILY SATYRIDAE
Satyrinae—satyrs
Enodia portlandia missarkae—Southern
  Pearly Eye
Enodia anthedon—Northern Pearly Eye
Enodia creole—Creole Pearly Eye
Cyllopsis gemma—Gemmed Satyr
Neonympha areolata—Georgia Satyr
Hermeuptychia sosybius—Carolina Satyr
Megisto cymela—Little Wood Satyr
Cercyonis pegala—Common Wood Nymph

References

Collins, J. T. 1990. *Standard Common and Current Scientific Names for North American Amphibians and Reptiles*. SSAR Herpetological Circular No. 19.

Conant, Roger, and Joseph T. Collins. 1991. *A Field Guide to Reptiles and Amphibians of Eastern and Central North America*. Houghton-Mifflin Co., Boston.

Hanebrink, Earl L. 1980. *Birds of Northeastern Arkansas*. Stuart Rockwell.

Hunter, Carl G. 1984. *Wildflowers of Arkansas*. Ozark Society Foundation, Little Rock.

Hunter, Carl G. 1989. *Trees, Shrubs, and Vines of Arkansas*. Ozark Society Foundation, Little Rock.

James, Douglas A., and Frances C. James. 1964. *The Seasonal Occurrences of Arkansas Birds*. Arkansas Academy of Science Proceedings.

James, Douglas A., and Joseph C. Neal. 1986. *Arkansas Birds, Their Distribution and Abundance* University of Arkansas Press, Fayetteville. [At this writing, a revised second edition is being prepared.]

Neal, Joseph C., and Michael A. Mlodinow. 1988. *Birding in the Western Arkansas Ozarks.*

Paulissen, Leo G. 1978. *Checklist of the Butterflies and Skippers of Arkansas*. Arkansas Academy of Science.

Sealander, John A., and Gary A. Heidt. 1990. *Arkansas Mammals, Their Natural History, Classification, and Distribution.* University of Arkansas Press, Fayetteville.

Smith, K. G., J. C. Neal, and M. A. Mlodinow. 1991. "Shorebird Migration at Artificial Fish Ponds in the Prairie Forest Ecotone of Northwestern Arkansas" *Southwest Naturalist* 36:107 113.

Taylor, W. Carl. 1984. *Arkansas Ferns and Fern Allies*. Milwaukee Public Museum, Milwaukee.

Turnipseed, Glyn, and Matthew E. Gallagher. 1992. *Data Base for the Herptiles of Arkansas.*

Turnipseed, Glyn, Matt Gallagher, and Bill Talbert. 1993. *Checklist of the Herptiles of Arkansas.*

Other Helpful Titles
in the
ABA/Lane Birdfinding Guide Series

New wire-O format guides:

A Birder's Guide to Southern California (1991)

A Birder's Guide to the Rio Grande Valley of Texas (1992)

A Birder's Guide to the Texas Coast (1993)

A Birder's Guide to Wyoming (1993)

A Birder's Guide to Churchill (Manitoba) (1994)

A Birder's Guide to Eastern Massachusetts (1994)

A Birder's Guide to Arkansas (1995)

"Old" format guides to be revised by 1996:

A Birder's Guide to Southeastern Arizona

A Birder's Guide to Colorado

A Birder's Guide to Florida

Forthcoming New Titles:

A Birder's Guide to New Hampshire (1996)

After the Birds: A Birder's Guide to Planning Major Birding Trips

Also Published by ABA:

Birdfinding in Forty National Forests and Grasslands (1994)

American Birding Association Sales

PO Box 6599
Colorado Springs, Colorado 80934 USA
Phone: 800-634-7736 or 719-578-0607
Fax: 800-590-2473 or 719-578-9705

Notes

American Birding Association, Inc.

Since 1969, the American Birding Association has served the North American birding community by helping birders hone their field identification skills and telling them where to find birds. This membership organization exists to promote the recreational observation and study of wild birds, to educate the public in the appreciation of birds and their vital role in the environment, to assist in the study of birds in their natural habitat, and to contribute to the development of improved bird population studies. The organization also keeps North American birders informed about bird conservation, valuable birding resources, new publications, and top-notch birding equipment.

All ABA members receive **Birding**, the official bimonthly magazine of the organization, and **Winging It,** the monthly newsletter. Both publications are chock-full of birdfinding advice, identification details, and up-to-date birding news. Student Members receive **A Bird's-Eye View**, a quarterly newsletter by and for teens. Members also receive discounts from ABA Sales on bird books, tapes, optical equipment, and accessories. ABA also publishes an invaluable Membership Directory, conducts biennial conventions and regional conferences, and sponsors bird-related tours of various durations to domestic and foreign birding hotspots.

All persons interested in these aspects of bird study are invited to join. If you bird beyond your backyard, ABA membership will help you discover a whole new world of birding adventure and expertise. A membership form is included on the following page.

American Birding Association
PO Box 6599
Colorado Springs,
Colorado 80934-6599

AMERICAN BIRDING ASSOCIATION
Membership Application

All memberships include six issues of **Birding** magazine, monthly issues of **Winging It,** ABA's newsletter, member discounts offered by ABA Sales, and full rights of participation in all ABA activities.

Membership classes and dues:

❑ Individual - US	$36.00 / yr	❑ Family - US	$43.00 / yr
❑ Individual - Canada	$38.52 / yr	❑ Family - Canada	$46.01 / yr
❑ Individual - Int'l	$45.00 / yr	❑ Family - Int'l	$52.00 / yr
❑ Century Club	$100.00 / yr	❑ Life Membership	$1,200.00

US Funds only, please. Inquire about Student rates.

Application Type

❑ New Membership   ❑ Renewal

Member Information

Name _____

Address _____

_____

_____

Phone _____

Payment Information

❑ Check or Money Order enclosed (US funds only)

❑ Charge to VISA / MasterCard (circle one)

Account Number _____

Exp Date _____

Signature _____

Sent this completed form with payment to: **ABA Membership
PO Box 6599
Colorado Springs, CO 80934**

AR 5/95

INDEX

A

Amphibians 239
Anhinga 67, 139, 156, 167, 178, 181, 183, 188, 195, 209, 225
Ani
  Groove-billed 154, 156, 215, 237
Arkadelphia 143
Arkansas River Levee 169
Arkansas River Valley 3, 5, 15
Ashdown 222
Avocet
  American 30, 95, 96, 154, 193, 228

B

Baker Prairie Natural Area - see Natural Area
Bayou Meto WMA - see Wildlife Management Area
Beach
  Nude 59
Bear 147
Bear
  Black 9, 205
Beard's Bluff 159, 160
Beaver Lake - see Lake
Bentonville 77, 95, 111
Big Lake NWR - see National Wildlife Refuge
Bittern
  American 95, 139, 199, 203, 209, 225
  Least 31, 43, 95, 139, 144, 167, 171, 172, 209, 225
Black River WMA - see Wildlife Management Area
Blackbird
  Brewer's 20, 207, 222, 235
  Red-winged 5, 20, 32, 45, 47, 167, 235
  Rusty 20, 109, 222, 235
  Yellow-headed 31, 42, 77, 95, 96, 107, 144, 155, 159, 222, 235

Abbreviated Table of Contents

Bluebird
  Eastern 19, 32, 41, 80, 91, 99, 141, 160, 163, 232
  Mountain 144, 237
Bobolink 6, 43, 80, 108, 128, 159, 169, 181, 222, 235
Bobwhite
  Northern 26, 44, 107, 114, 128, 137, 175, 227
Bona Dea Trails - see Trail
Boxley 88
Boyle Park - see Park
Brant 75, 237
Brinkley 48, 62
Buffalo National River - see National River
Buffalo Point 87, 89, 219, 220
Bufflehead 41, 49, 59, 81, 92, 110, 113, 115, 144, 226
Bull Shoals State Park - see State Park
Bunting
  Indigo 20, 23, 34, 44, 55, 57, 71, 80, 87, 102, 111, 115, 126, 137, 164, 195, 197, 200, 206, 234
  Lazuli 237
  Painted 6, 15, 32, 44, 79, 85, 94, 107, 109, 111, 181, 193, 216, 220, 234
  Snow 237
Butterflies and Skippers of Arkansas 242
Butterfly
  Broad-winged Skipper 75
Byrd Lake Natural Area - see Natural Area

C

Canvasback 45, 49, 110, 226
Cardinal
  Northern 20, 234
Carlisle 48
Cass 218
Catbird
  Gray 18, 26, 232
Centerton State Fish Hatchery - see Fish Hatchery
Chat
  Yellow-breasted 18, 26, 44, 51, 57, 75, 85, 87, 102, 111, 115, 117, 126, 128, 137, 150, 164, 172, 178, 234
Cherry Bend 130, 219
Chickadee
  Carolina 34, 57, 62, 130, 206, 231
Chuck-will's-widow 71, 87, 102, 104, 137, 216, 229
Clarksville 88
Collared-Dove
  Eurasian 237

Abbreviated Table of Contents

Abbreviated Table of Contents

Pigeon
Passenger 4
Pimple
Prairie 79, 111
Pine Bluff 168, 169, 173, 189
Pine Bluff Regional Park - *see* **Regional Park**
Pinnacle Mountain State Park - *see* **State Park**
Pintail
Northern 31, 49, 171, 226
Pipit
American 7, 31, 32, 144, 169, 218, 232
Sprague's 68, 155, 160, 218, 237
Plover
Black-bellied 30, 43, 96, 185, 228
Mountain 237
Piping 30, 95, 156, 228
Semipalmated 6, 30, 96, 228
Snowy 237
Wilson's 95, 237
Ponca 87, 212
Pruitt 87

R

Rail
Black 237
King 5, 52, 95, 167, 194, 227
Virginia 95, 188, 213, 227
Yellow 188, 194, 199, 213, 227
Recreation Area
Avery 146
Beard's Bluff 157
Beard's Lake 159
Brady Mountain 147
Cove Creek 60
Lake Atalanta 110
Lake Sylvia 220
Lake Wedington 115, 220
Lakeview 94
Lower (DeGray) Lake 141
Mill Creek 61
Morgan Point 198
Oakland 94
Ozark Isle 94
Pendleton 195, 197
Pigeon Creek 94

Quarry 94
Redding 127, 129, 212, 218, 219, 220
Rising Star 169
Rocky Branch 104
Shady Lake 138
Tar Camp 35, 200, 218
Willow Beach 15, 43, 213, 218, 220
Redding Recreation Area - *see* **Recreation Area**
Redfield 200
Redhead 49, 110, 226
Redpoll
Common 77, 237
Redstart
American 17, 87, 99, 104, 178, 197, 219, 233
References 244
Regional Park
Pine Bluff 189
Reptiles of Arkansas 240
Reydell 172
River
Arkansas 3, 15, 16, 19, 36, 39, 45, 77, 97,
106, 167, 169, 189, 195, 197, 200, 209,
211, 214, 215, 217
Bartholomew Bayou 173
Bayou De View 47
Big Maumelle 41
Black 47
Buffalo 87
Buffalo Creek 163, 164
Cache 47, 211
Caddo 141
Cossatot 135
Fourche LaFave 23
L'Anguille 47
Lapile Creek 179
Lee Creek 99
Little 159
Little Maumelle 40
Little Red 47, 58, 61
Lorance Creek 15
Mississippi 3, 47, 67, 167, 180, 181, 183,
185, 197
Mulberry 130
North Fork 91
Ohio 47
Ouachita 173, 177
Palarm Creek 24
Rock Creek 17
Saline 177
Spring 47
St. Francis 47, 52, 67
Strawberry 47
Village Creek 71
White 47, 81, 91, 167, 197, 205, 211
Roadrunner
Greater 39, 88, 98, 99, 101, 107, 121, 137,
139, 141, 149, 150, 163, 165, 215, 229
Robin
American 20, 218, 232

Abbreviated Table of Contents

Birding Sites in Arkansas

Central Arkansas:

1. Boyle Park
2. Cook's Landing
3. Harris Brake
4. Lake Conway
5. Lake Sylvia
6. Lonoke
7. Lorance Creek Natural Area
8. Murray Park
9. Pinnacle Mtn State Park Area
10. Scott and Faulkner Lake

Northeastern Arkansas:

11. Big Lake National Wildlife Refuge
12. Black River Wildlife Mgt Area
13. Dagmar Wildlife Mgt Area
14. Greers Ferry Lake
15. Louisiana Purchase State Park
16. St. Francis National Forest
17. Stuttgart Airport
18. Village Creek State Park
19. Wapanocca Nat'l Wildlife Refuge

Northwestern Arkansas:

20. Baker Prairie Natural Area
21. Beaver Lake
22. Bona Dea Trails
23. Buffalo National River
24. Bull Shoals State Park Area
25. Centerton State Fish Hatchery
26. Dardanelle Dam
27. Devil's Den State Park
28. Hobbs State Management Area
29. Holla Bend Nat'l Wildlife Refuge

Northwestern Arkansas:

30. Lake Atalanta
31. Lake Bentonville
32. Lake Fayetteville
33. Lake Wedington
34. Magazine Mountain
35. Mount Nebo State Park
36. Page Hollow
37. Pea Ridge Nat'l Military Park
38. Redding Recreation Area

Southwestern Arkansas:

39. Cossatot River State Park Natural Area
40. DeGray Lake
41. Hulsey State Fish Hatchery
42. Lake Ouachita
43. Mena Area
44. Millwood Lake
45. Waldron Area

Southeastern Arkansas:

46. Arkansas River Levee
47. Bayou Meto Wildlife Mgt Area
48. Byrd Lake Natural Area
49. Felsenthal Nat'l Wildlife Refuge
50. Grand Lake
51. Lake Chicot State Park
52. Lake Pine Bluff
53. Levi Wilcoxon Trail
54. Overflow Nat'l Wildlife Refuge
55. Pendleton Recreation Area
56. Roth Prairie Natural Area
57. Tar Camp Recreation Area
58. Warren Prairie Natural Area
59. White River Nat'l Wildlife Refuge